THE PLACE OF JUDAS ISCARIOT IN CHRISTOLOGY

I can only heartily recommend and endorse the publication of this book. Theologians, I fear, have hardened hearts and obtuse minds which keep them trapped in the age old heresy that Jesus did not have Judas in mind when he prayed from the cross, 'Father forgive them...'. Anthony Cane presents a more balanced picture.

William Klassen, Professor of Biblical Studies,
Emeritus, University of Waterloo, Canada.

Exploring the significance of Judas Iscariot for Christian theology and the difficult issues surrounding Judas, Anthony Cane shows that focusing on the tension between providential and tragic interpretations of Judas in the New Testament and in subsequent writing about Judas, is the key to understanding his significance. Building on the work of Karl Barth and Donald MacKinnon, Cane's argument sheds light not simply on the way Judas is understood, but on the way Jesus and the whole economy of salvation are understood. This book also highlights implications for the way in which issues relating to anti-Semitism and evil and suffering are most effectively explored.

To Clare
with love and thanks

and Josh, Hannah and Jeremy
with thanks and love

The Place of Judas Iscariot in Christology

ANTHONY CANE
Diocese of Chichester, UK

ASHGATE

Published by
Ashgate Publishing Limited
Gower House
Croft Road
Aldershot
Hampshire GU11 3HR
England

Ashgate Publishing Company
Suite 420
101 Cherry Street
Burlington, VT 05401-4405
USA

Ashgate website: http://www.ashgate.com

British Library Cataloguing in Publication Data
Cane, Anthony, 1961-
The place of Judas Iscariot in Christology
1. Judas Iscariot 2. Jesus Christ – Person and offices
I. Title
226'.092

Library of Congress Cataloging-in-Publication Data
Cane, Anthony, 1961-
The place of Judas Iscariot in Christology / Anthony Cane.
p. cm.
Includes bibliographical references and index.
ISBN 0-7546-5284-X (hardback : alk. paper)
1. Judas Iscariot. I. Title.

BS2460.J8C28 2004
226'.092—dc22

2005011002

ISBN-10: 0 7546 5284 X

Printed and bound in Great Britain by MPG Books Ltd, Bodmin, Cornwall

Contents

Acknowledgements *vii*

Introduction 1

1 Definitions 5
2 The 'drama' of the Incarnation 7
3 Structure of the book 9

1 Judas in the New Testament 13

1.1 'One of the Twelve' 15
1.2 Translation matters: παραδίδωμι 19
1.3 Characterizing Judas – John's Pre-Passion Material 24
1.4 Fulfilment and woe: Judas' participation in the Last Supper 31
1.5 Gethsemane – encountering Judas 39
1.6 The death of Judas 47
1.7 Issues and conclusion 54

2 Judas and the Tension between Providence and Tragedy 59

2.1 Barth's 'calm' excursus on Judas 60
2.2 MacKinnon's elusive remarks on the tragedy of Judas 70
2.3 Conclusion 86

3 Judas' Participation in the Footwashing and Last Supper 89

3.1 Origen on Judas as 'holy but changing for the worse' 90
3.2 Chrysostom on the 'incorrigibility' of Judas 96
3.3 Augustine on Judas as 'not chosen' 99
3.4 Rupert of Deutz opposes Alger and Augustine 101
3.5 Jonathan Edwards and the 'difficulty' of Judas 107
3.6 Conclusion 110

4 Judas' Place in the 'Handing Over' of the Son 113

4.1 Origen, Augustine and the Cainites on the intention of Judas 116
4.2 The Trinitarian insight of Aquinas, Augustine and Donne 122
4.3 Conclusion 126

5 Judas' Repentance and Death 127

5.1 Augustine, Jerome and Leo on the absence of hope 129
5.2 Luther on Judas' despair 133
5.3 Preaching the inadequacy of Judas' repentance 140
5.4 Exploring the 'open question' of Judas' eternal destiny 145
5.5 Conclusion 153

6 Judas and Christ's Descent into Hell 155

6.1 Emmons, Pickering and Borges on the gratitude due to Judas 156
6.2 Dante and Christ's limited descent into *Inferno* 163
6.3 Hans Urs von Balthasar and Christ in the 'Lowest Hell' 169
6.4 Conclusion 179

7 A Christology Facing the Tension between Providence and Tragedy 181

7.1 Incarnation and limitation 182

Appendix *189*
Bibliography *193*
Index *207*

Acknowledgements

Inevitably I am indebted to many people, without whom this book would never have been completed. In terms of financial support alone, during the period of research that has culminated in this book, the list includes my parents Jim and Brenda Cane, the Rt Revd Eric Kemp (the Bishop of Chichester's discretionary fund), Canon Dr David Ison (Diocese of Exeter) and Canon Andrew Mayes (Diocese of Chichester), the latter two for assistance from diocesan funds for Continuing Ministerial Education. I am grateful to the many people who have discussed interpretations of Judas Iscariot with me, whether in the context of parish communities, diocesan education programmes, or university. In different ways they have confirmed to me the interest and difficulty of the topic. My debt to my PhD supervisor, Professor Gareth Jones, is immense. Amongst the many from whom I have learnt over the years I am particularly grateful to the Revd David Moss, who may be surprised to learn that conversations in our final days at Westcott House were instrumental in setting in motion the theological journey that has resulted in this book. Without the encouragement of Professor David Ford and Professor Frances Young, however, I would never have embarked upon such a project. Professor Young also gave me access to her notes of Donald MacKinnon's lectures on 'Evil' and has allowed me to quote from them in this book. Dr Ruth Etchells has kindly given permission for me to quote her poem 'The Ballad of the Judas Tree'. I am grateful to my wife Clare for reading sections of the book and offering constructive criticism, as well as her unstinting support. Thanks are due also to Mrs Nicole Blakey for her hard work on the index. Needless to say the quality of the book has benefited immeasurably from others, whilst the inadequacies that remain are of course my own.

Introduction

One will get a deep insight into the state of Christianity in every age by seeing how it interprets Judas.[1]
Søren Kierkegaard

This book examines a key Christological problem: the place of Judas Iscariot in Christology. It can be seen as a case study within the complex set of issues and questions often summed up by the phrase 'the problem of evil'. In tackling such a topic, I have sought to take seriously the power of Donald MacKinnon's insight that Christian theologising about evil cannot avoid the multifarious voices of those who have defined what is meant by the term 'tragedy'. The whole tenor of MacKinnon's writing on the subject contends that if such theologizing does not face the challenge posed by tragedy, the resultant theology is likely to be superficial (in the sense of avoiding the depth of the problem), settling the complexity, particularity and horror of suffering into bearable, even comfortable, patterns.

It would be hard for any Christian exploration of questions relating to evil, suffering and tragedy to avoid being confronted by the role of Judas Iscariot in the key Christian narratives. This is because the Gospels describe Judas as 'better unborn' (Mark 14.21) and a 'devil' (John 6.70) for his actions in *betraying*[2] Jesus, yet also as chosen by Jesus (Mark 3.13-19 and parallels) and playing a crucial role in the handing over of the Son of man to suffering and crucifixion 'as it is written of him' (see Mark 14.21, 43-46 and parallels). Judas then suffers a cruel and unpleasant death, apparently with no hope of forgiveness (Matthew 27.3-5 and Acts 1.16-20).[3] Here important questions about freedom, providence, guilt and salvation are raised. The importance is that the Gospel texts just described witness

---

1 Søren Kierkegaard, *Journals and Papers* Volume 2, F-K. Edited and translated by Howard V. Hong and Edna H. Hong (Bloomington: Indiana University Press, 1970) p512.

2 The question of the best translation of the Greek verb παραδίδωμι, usually rendered 'betray' although arguably 'hand over' or 'deliver' would be more accurate, is referred to elsewhere in this introduction and discussed in detail in Chapter 1. Here, and subsequently (particularly in biblical quotations) I use italics to indicate a reference to a form of παραδίδωμι as the underlying Greek word.

3 The English text used here and subsequently is that of the anglicized edition of the *The Holy Bible – English Standard Version* (London: HarperCollins, 2002). The Greek text I have worked from is that of the Nestle-Aland 26th Edition and Greek New Testament 3rd Edition, as contained in *Synopsis of the Four Gospels – Greek-English Edition of the Synopsis Quattuor Evangeliorum* edited by Kurt Aland, seventh edition (Stuttgart: German Bible Society, 1984).

to particular instances of the suffering human beings can cause each other, even to the point of death – instances that have a heightened theological significance because they affect the Christian understanding of God. The texts referred to contribute to the overall sense Christians make of the 'drama'[4] of their salvation, in which everything that happens contributes to the meaning. The Christian faith affirms that the trinitarian God is truly incarnate in Jesus Christ. The way in which the *totality* of the narrative of that incarnation is to be most effectively and accurately interpreted is therefore a question of some significance.

My argument is that the place of Judas Iscariot in Christology can best be understood through an examination of the tension between providence and tragedy. That tension is exemplified in the opposing readings of Judas found in the writings of Karl Barth and Donald MacKinnon, who both witness to the importance of a theologically neglected topic. Both recognize the importance of attending to the particularity and detail of the Gospel passion narratives, central as they are for the Christian faith and Christian theology. This inevitably means attending at some point to the place and role of Judas, but not (for my purposes) in terms of speculative comments about motivation or character.

For a variety of reasons the role of Judas in the Gospels is of great interest to writers who respond to it from a dramatic or novelistic point of view. There are so many examples of this that only a few of the most well-known need citation here. Amongst them is the radio play by Dorothy L. Sayers *The Man born to be King*, the musical by Andrew Lloyd-Webber and Tim Rice *Jesus Christ Superstar*, and the novels *Christ Recrucified* by Nikos Kazantzakis and *Silence* by Shusako Endo.[5] If Auden is anywhere near the mark in asserting that, 'Drama is based on the Mistake. I think someone is my friend when he really is my enemy...',[6] his insight may help to explain fascination with the 'one of the twelve' who apparently fell from grace and was eventually replaced by Matthias (Acts of the Apostles 1.15-26). This fascination is not new, either, and many attempts have been made to give Judas a background that might help to explain his role in the Gospels. One example of this is a legendary life of Judas, in which he murders his father and marries his mother in Oedipal fashion, known (with variations) in almost every language and country of medieval Europe.[7]

---

4 The use of the word 'drama' is deliberate, and receives substantial discussion in Chapter 6. What lies behind its use here is Hans Urs von Balthasar's distinction (building on Hegel) between epic, lyric and dramatic perspectives. See for example, pp53-62 of the second volume of *Theo-Drama* (San Franciso: Ignatius Press, 1990).

5 Dorothy L. Sayers *The Man born to be King* (London: Gollancz, 1943), Andrew Lloyd-Webber and Tim Rice *Jesus Christ Superstar* (London: MCA Music Ltd, 1970), *Christ Recrucified* by Nikos Kazantzakis (London: Faber and Faber, 1962), and *Silence* by Shusako Endo (London: Penguin, 1980).

6 'Notes on Music and Opera' in *The Dyer's Hand* (London: Faber and Faber, 1948) p471.

7 See in particular 'The Medieval Legend of Judas Iscariot' by P.F. Baum *Publications of the Modern Language Association 31* (1916) pp481-632. The most well known version of this legend is found in Jacobus de Voragine's *Legenda Aurea*; in English *The Golden Legend – Readings on the Saints* Volume 1, translated by William Granger Ryan,

It needs to be emphasized that this is not the approach of this book. My argument is not novelistic but *theological*. It involves addressing the complexities of the Gospel texts concerning Judas, in the conviction that there are Christological implications that follow from attention to the fact that the New Testament (for example) records Judas as both called by Jesus and yet better unborn. Like every Gospel text relating to Judas, Jesus' choice of Judas as one of the twelve has been variously interpreted in subsequent tradition. As will be seen in Chapter 1, the New Testament seems intent on showing that Jesus knew what Judas would do from the first. Chapter 3 examines Origen's contention that Judas was originally holy, but changed for the worse. John Chrysostom, on the other hand, saw him as being chosen for a particular purpose. Each of these interpretations has implications for Christology.

For example, orthodox Chalcedonian Christology indicates that Christ's judgement in choosing the twelve was subject to human limitation (although the Gospel texts could be taken to indicate otherwise), but to what extent? A complex of questions arises, amongst them the following: Did Christ simply show bad judgement in calling Judas? Should this be seen in the context of the divine self-limitation intrinsic to the doctrine of the Trinity? Is it that the presence of Christ was tragically insufficient for the salvation of Judas (an implication of Origen's approach) or was it that Judas was part of a providential design (Chrysostom)? Responses to such questions will evidence particular understandings of Christ, God, and the economy of salvation. Through attending to the difficulties inherent in considering the place of Judas Iscariot in Christology, it is therefore possible to see which understandings are more or less adequate to the complexities involved, and what the answers to the above questions might be. The exploration has significance in terms of the theologian's search for *truth*, not only in terms of a focus on narrowly Christological concerns, but also (as indicated in the opening paragraph above) in terms of finding an idiom in which to reflect on and respond to evil and suffering in the world – a Christological idiom that seeks to face difficulty and human tragedy from within a trinitarian framework.

It is my contention that most writing in the Christian tradition tends to neglect, avoid, or even exploit the problematic issues that invariably emerge when the attempt is made to identify and interpret the place Judas has within Christological discourse. This can be seen through analysis of the kinds of argument marshalled by writers who have discussed the role of Judas, as will be shown. Two interrelated reasons for the recurrent unsatisfactoriness of writing on Judas may be identified at this point.

Firstly, there is the tendency of the human intellect, when confronted by mystery, tension and difficulty, to generate what Rowan Williams has called a

---

Chapter 45, 'St Matthias, Apostle' (Princeton, New Jersey: Princeton University Press, 1993) pp166-171.

'satisfying falsehood'.[8] Rather than accept questions as apparently unresolvable by rational, propositional argument, it is tempting to sweep difficulties under a carpet of rhetoric or generalisation. Unresolvable questions are uncomfortable, even painful, and the wish to make them more bearable is therefore understandable, even if theologically regrettable.

Secondly, this tendency to produce 'satisfying falsehood' is particularly pronounced in the Christian tradition when the figure of Jesus Christ is at issue. Any line of approach that apparently sheds unfavourable light on Christ; any insight that threatens a particular understanding of Christ, is unlikely to be followed through. To take seriously the possibility, for example, that Christ made a mistake in choosing Judas will be difficult for the writer or reader whose faith in Christ is thereby threatened and undermined. This is unsurprising given that any change to the image or understanding of Christ held individually or corporately will have ramifications for the entire edifice of faith.

These two points show why problematic issues may be neglected or avoided, but I have not yet explained my use of the word 'exploit'. This is an allusion to the long and horrifying tradition of Christian anti-Semitism built partly on the similarity between the name of Judas and that of the Jewish people.[9] Judas has been seen as representative of Judaism in rejecting Christ, and this has sometimes proved an easier position to take than one of humility before the kinds of questions indicated above. Here theological argument has spilled over into destructive political and social action, most terribly in the Holocaust.[10] It should be clear, therefore, that the nature of the issues explored in this book have implications for the expression of both orthodoxy and *orthopraxis*.

As indicated above, my contention is that the tension between providence and tragedy is the key paradigm that emerges from engagement with the scriptures and subsequent tradition. This will be shown in two subsequent chapters focusing first on the relevant biblical material, and then the work of Barth and MacKinnon. At this point some preliminary definitions will prepare the ground for the way my argument will proceed.

---

[8] Rowan Williams, *The Wound of Knowledge – Christian Spirituality from the New Testament to St John of the Cross* (London: Darton, Longman & Todd; second, revised edition, 1990) p174.

[9] See Hyam Maccoby, *Judas Iscariot and the Myth of Jewish Evil* (New York: The Free Press, 1992).

[10] 'Holocaust' is used with an awareness that the nomenclature used to refer to the variety of discrete events summed up by such a term is disputed territory. Other possibilities include *'Hurban'*, *'l'univers concentrationnaire'* and *'Shoah'* (the latter usually signifying the refusal to accept any religious interpretation). I have followed Isabel Wollaston in using 'Holocaust' both because it is the most widely used and recognized term, and that 'given the ambivalence over its use, it best illustrates the complexity inherent in remembering these events.' (Isabel Wollaston, *A War Against Memory? – the future of Holocaust Remembrance*, London: SPCK, 1996, p2).

1 Definitions

The use of the word 'tension' is intended to give a sense of being stretched between opposed and incompatible interpretations, each with their own inherent plausibility. The use of the term in physics has relevance also, whereby 'tension' refers to 'forces acting in opposite directions away from each other, thus tending to draw them apart' whilst simultaneously balanced by 'forces of cohesion holding them together'.[11] This gives the sense of tension as 'necessary conflict',[12] the exploration of which opens up the Christological ground in a more fruitful way than would be achieved if only one end of the 'spectrum' was considered. The spectrum referred to here has providence and tragedy at either end, representing polar opposites.

The doctrine of providence asserts that all things are directed and ordered by God, from their beginning to their appointed end. All things are therefore subordinate to the knowledge and will of God. Barth, characteristically, argues that this doctrine cannot be understood outside Jesus Christ. He argues that 'we must never allow this name to fade or to be blurred in favour of abstract presuppositions concerning God and man, or of the abstract consequences of such abstract presuppositions.'[13] So it is that his consideration of Judas takes place in the context of the doctrine of election, and contends that the relevant 'dominating truth' is to be found in John 6.64: that Jesus knew from the beginning who would *betray* him. This truth 'stands over the whole being and behaviour of Judas as he was chosen and called with the others', and explains what Barth describes as the 'calmness'[14] with which the New Testament speaks of Judas.

In a forty-eight page excursus[15] Barth offers a brilliant reading of the way Judas' role in the New Testament should be understood. This includes an elaborate exegesis of uses of the Greek verb παραδίδωμι, in which Judas' actions in *handing over* Jesus are seen in relation to the apostolic task of Paul in *handing on* the Gospel to the Gentiles. Here, as subsequently, I have used italics to indicate a reference in English to an action described in the Greek text of the New Testament by a form of παραδίδωμι. This is particularly important for scriptural references that translate παραδίδωμι as *betray*, as it enables the parallelism with other uses of the verb (concealed by this translation) to become visible. As will be seen in Chapter 2, the parallelism found in analysis of παραδίδωμι are significant for Barth because he considers them to be part of a providential order which unifies every

---

11 *The Shorter Oxford English Dictionary*, Volume II (Oxford: Clarendon Press, 1973) p2263.

12 I have borrowed this phrase from the subtitle of H.A. Williams' book *Tensions - Necessary Conflicts in Life and Love* (Glasgow: Collins, 1976).

13 §32.2 'The Foundation of the Doctrine' *Church Dogmatics* II.2 *The Doctrine of God* (Edinburgh: T&T Clark, 1957) p59.

14 Barth writes of the 'the remarkable calm with which the New Testament speaks of Judas Iscariot' (ibid. p459).

15 The final part of §35.4 'The Determination of the Rejected' (ibid. pp458-506).

aspect of the New Testament. In this way he is able to find overarching connections between the action of God, Judas, the Jews, Pilate, and Paul. Barth explicitly states that this 'handing-over is the eternal will of God, in what sense it has to be said that it did not happen by chance, that it has nothing whatever to do with human tragedy or the like, but that it had to happen as the will of God.'[16]

MacKinnon, however, takes the contrary view that tragic discourse can offer important insights and correctives for the theologian. Tragedy as a category, deriving as it does from a wide variety of theatrical and literary works, is more difficult to define than providence. The manifold writings or 'family of resemblances'[17] that are taken to make up the tragic tradition have been variously interpreted by writers as disparate as Friedrich Nietzsche, Raymond Williams and George Steiner.[18] Each demonstrates that it is in the nature of tragedy to resist conceptualisation, and that tragedy attends to those dark and intractable aspects of existence which expose the inadequacies of human ratiocination.

For MacKinnon such aspects are reflected in the Gospel narratives, which is why he is prepared to draw on tragedy in spite of those who argue that it is a non-Christian category. So it is that in a text broadcast in 1963 MacKinnon writes that although the light of Christ is never overcome,

> ...the darkness remains, and of the end of the traitor there is no record... . There is no solution offered in the Gospels of the riddle of Iscariot through whose agency the Son of man goes his appointed way. It were good for him that he had not been born. The problem is stated; it is left unresolved, and we are presented with the likeness of the one who bore its ultimate burden... .[19]

Here MacKinnon points to what he sees as a paradox at the heart of the passion narratives. Judas is described as a 'traitor' and as 'better unborn' despite his role in Christ's 'appointed' way – appointed, presumably, by God. The implications of Mark 14.21 and parallels ('it would have been better for that man if he had not been born') is that Judas' very existence is a crime. George Steiner, a friend and colleague of MacKinnon's, has described as 'absolute tragedy' the claim that

---

[16] Ibid. p493.

[17] This phrase is quoted in Larry Bouchard's *Tragic Method and Tragic Theology – Evil in Contemporary Drama and Religious Thought* (University Park and London: The Pennsylvania State University Press, 1989) p22. It comes from Wittgenstein's *Philosophical Investigations* part one, sections 66-7 (Oxford: Blackwell, 1976) p32.

[18] See, for example, *The Birth of Tragedy* by Friedrich Nietzsche (New York: Doubleday, 1956), *Modern Tragedy* by Raymond Williams (London: Verso, 1966/1979) and *The Death of Tragedy* by George Steiner (London: Faber, 1961) For a good general account see Morris Weitz's discussion in *The Encyclopaedia of Philosophy* Volume 8 (New York: MacMillan, 1967) 'Tragedy' pp155-161.

[19] 'Order and Evil in the Gospel', *Borderlands of Theology and other essays* Edited and introduced by George W. Roberts and Donovan E. Smucker (London: Lutterworth Press, 1968) p92.

human existence is an intrusion into a world radically inimical to it.[20] The Gospel texts relating to Judas are in this way reminiscent of the 'crime of being' whereby Jew and Gypsy were obliterated in the Holocaust simply because of their birth.

For MacKinnon the insights from tragedy show that it 'is sheer nonsense to speak of the Christian religion as offering a solution to the problem of evil'.[21] From the perspective of tragedy, theodicy is exposed as a manifestation rather than explanation of the darker aspects of human life. That is, attempts to offer religious 'explanations' of evil and suffering are a symptom of the human need to account for or resolve what is in fact inexplicable. It is apparent that although MacKinnon never engages directly with Barth's excursus on Judas, his is a theological approach stringently critical of any writing characterized by the kind of providential emphasis found in that excursus. Their respective examinations of the Judas problematic exemplify the scope of the spectrum indicated in the opening paragraph of this section.

2 The 'drama' of the Incarnation

Although influenced by Barth, particularly in his early career, latterly MacKinnon wrote admiringly of the work of Hans Urs von Balthasar. In a late essay he praised Balthasar for having 'a passionate concern to present the engagement of God with his world in a way that refuses to turn aside from the overwhelming, pervasive reality of evil',[22] and discussed his understanding of the Gospels as drama bearing ontological implications. The focus falls on the doctrine of the Trinity, which MacKinnon had come to see as able to recognize the tragic dimension where (as in Balthasar's writing) its ontological idiom is integrated with the particular details and overall action of Christ's passion.

The *raison d'etre* of the essay is a discussion of three volumes of *Theodramatik.* A central thesis is that the concept of 'mission' (literally, 'sending' as in the trinitarian missions of the Son and the Spirit) is richer and more inclusive than 'kenosis' (literally, 'self-emptying') in reflecting on the work of Christ. For MacKinnon 'kenosis' remains profoundly significant, yet it is the concept of 'mission' that enables the integration of the dramatic and the ontological. He praises Balthasar's writing on Christ's self-consciousness, which probes

> ...the paradox of duality, clearly hoping that in *Sendung* [sending, mission] he has a conceptual instrument strong enough to disclose a transcription that is in the deepest

---

20 'A Note on Absolute Tragedy' in *Literature and Theology* (Volume 4.2, July 1990) p147.

21 Op cit. p92.

22 'Some reflections on Hans Urs von Balthasar's Christology with special reference to Theodramatik II/2 and III.' MacKinnon discusses the fourth volume in an Appendix. Published in *The Analogy of Beauty – The Theology of Hans Urs von Balthasar*, edited by John Riches (Edinburgh: T&T. Clark, 1986) pp164-179.

> sense ontological in character, as if here is the *Anknüpfungspunkt* [point of contact] of the divine and human in Christ. But to grasp this our concept of the divine must be transformed by finding the very being of the Trinity bodied forth for us by, because totally present in, the agony and dereliction of Gethsemane and Calvary.[23]

MacKinnon's use of the word 'transcription' should be noted. One of his criticisms of Balthasar is that he makes insufficient use of Kantian concepts such as *limitation* in writing about Christ. In an essay on 'Incarnation and Trinity' he writes that the acceptance of the

> ...complex discipline of temporality... belongs to the very substance of Jesus' defeat. Jesus' acceptance of this part of his burden can arguably be interpreted as a painfully realized transcription into the conditions of our existence, of the receptivity, the defined, even if frontierless, receptivity that constitutes his person.[24]

All that Jesus undergoes, therefore, is a 'transcription' that can be 'read' as telling of the very nature of the trinitarian God.

MacKinnon clearly admires Balthasar's awareness that 'Crucifixion and Resurrection, to be properly understood, must be treated as part of the doctrine of God himself.' In his work there is a 'remorseless emphasis on the concrete', a wish to restore the dramatic dimension to theology, and an insistence that the economic Trinity expresses 'the ultimacy of the immanent Trinity, or it is nothing'.[25] What this means is that the crucifixion and exaltation of Christ are a real engagement by God with his creation. An engagement in which the immanent Trinity is 'transcribed', at God's initiative, into the temporal world in the life and death of Christ.

Judas Iscariot is never mentioned in the essay on *Theodramatik*, yet the above paragraph indicates why a discussion of his role in the Gospels can be far more than speculative psychological analysis or character rehabilitation.[26] For if the 'drama' of the Passion expresses something of the inner nature of God, it may be that the mysterious yet pivotal role of Judas has ontological implications. A 'drama' has more than one player, and 'it is the total action that is to supply the sense.'[27] As MacKinnon writes, metaphysical issues are raised, such as Pilate's infamous question, 'What is truth?' (John 18.38), but where the truth lies is in what the innocent but condemned Jesus makes of the weakness and guilt of Pilate and Caiaphas. It is not out of place to add Judas Iscariot to that list, as more is told in the New Testament of Judas' fate than either of the latter, and his role in the

---

23 Ibid. p172.

24 'Incarnation and Trinity', *Themes in Theology* (Edinburgh: T.& T. Clark, 1987) pp162-163.

25 'Some reflections on Hans Urs von Balthasar's Christology', op cit. p167.

26 See, for one example amongst many, *Personalities of the Passion* by Leslie Weatherhead (London: Hodder and Stoughton, 1942) in which Judas is described as 'misunderstood' (p21), and as one evidencing 'the psychology of a man in whom impatience has gone mad' (p26).

27 Op cit. p171.

final days of Jesus' life is at least as significant. What does the crucified and risen Christ make of this disciple; his (apparently) necessary but disturbing actions on Maundy Thursday and his subsequent condemnation and death? Was Judas 'beyond' the words of resurrection peace spoken to the other disciples?

In an appendix to the essay under discussion, MacKinnon emphasizes the trinitarian nature of Balthasar's writing. Christ is understood as building 'on earth an extrapolation of the Trinity; he lives a perfectly trinitarian existence, although he becomes a man amongst men.'[28] The ultimate transcendent status of the immanent Trinity is shown as, through Christ, 'engaged with the bitterness of human history'.[29] Far from being 'speculative indulgence', the traditional scheme does not need jettisoning, but renewing. Above all, MacKinnon writes, 'as Hans Urs von Balthasar most clearly sees, the tragic dimension of the Christian story in its concrete historical detail needs to be integrated with the inevitably ontological styles of traditional theology.'[30] The key point is that attention to the bitterness of Christ's engagement with history will be misunderstood if it is not seen in the light of the triune God's incarnational 'transcription' into a human life.

MacKinnon never discusses one of the most striking features of Balthasar's theology, his writing on Holy Saturday. In *Mysterium Paschale* Balthasar writes of Christ's descent into Hell as characterized not by triumphalism but by the 'obedience of a corpse' whereby Christ 'takes the existential measure of everything that is sheerly contrary to God'.[31] This experience of death, and of going to the dead, is as a trinitarian event also an act of salvation. Here Christ is portrayed as engaging with 'the bitterness of human history' to the uttermost, taking in not simply the experience of dying, but also of 'being dead'.

Here Balthasar hints at a 'space' where the tension between providence and tragedy can be worked through, even if his articulation of a dramatic perspective on Christology is not entirely convincing, as I shall show in Chapter 6. He is familiar with Barth's overarching exegetical schema, and the power of tragic discourse, but rejects both in favour of an exploration of the Easter *triduum* that can take in the farthest reaches of human experience, sinfulness and alienation, conceivably even that of the 'son of destruction' (or 'son of perdition', John 17.12) who has killed himself almost simultaneously with his former master. This theme will form an important part of the final stages of my argument.

3 Structure of the book

Given the issues outlined above, a close examination of the biblical material concerning Judas, and identification of the theological questions emerging from

---

28 Ibid. p175.

29 Ibid. p176.

30 Ibid. p177.

31 *Mysterium Paschale – the mystery of Easter*, translated with an introduction by Aidan Nichols (Edinburgh: T&T Clark, 1990) p174.

such exegesis, is necessary for my book to proceed. Such is Chapter 1. I will then show that the articulation of such questions is most helpfully accomplished by attending to the tension between providence and tragedy. Chapter 2, therefore, will explore in more detail my argument that, as exemplified in the writing of Barth and MacKinnon, this tension is the key to the interpretation of biblical texts concerning Judas, and the place of Judas in Christology.

In these two chapters four key issues are identified, as briefly described below:

1. Whether or not Judas should be seen as a defeat for Jesus;
2. The significance of the New Testament use of the verb παραδίδωμι, and the linguistic parallelism between the 'handing over' of Christ by Judas and the actions of others, including God;
3. The status of Judas' repentance and death;
4. Whether or not there is any possibility of eschatological salvation for Judas.

In relation to the first point above, some writers have argued that Judas must have been excluded from both the footwashing and last supper, as his inclusion would demonstrate a lack of efficacy in the sacramental cleansing, and an inappropriate and ineffective sharing in the body and blood of Christ. This lack of effectiveness, in failing to cleanse and heal one of Jesus' inner circle of twelve, focuses the question not only of the effectiveness of the sacraments, but of the ability of the Christ who instituted them to effect the salvation of those whom he called to be part of 'the twelve'. The issue of Judas' participation (or lack of it) in the footwashing and last supper is therefore central to Chapter 3.

The second point above implies the need to explore Judas' place within the divine 'handing over' of the Son (Romans 8.32),[32] exploring the theological implications of the New Testament usage of παραδίδωμι. This is the subject matter of Chapter 4, in which there is some discussion of intention despite the fact that I have rejected a novelistic approach to Judas' motivation as theologically unhelpful. This is because Origen, Augustine and Aquinas all distinguish Judas' 'handing over' of Christ from the divine 'handing over' by referring to the motivation for it. The relative brevity of this chapter is no reflection on the importance of the theme it examines, for failure to attend to the New Testament language in relation to Judas will affect not only the way his role is understood, but also the way Christ and providence are understood.

Many writers also refer to intention and state of mind as key to understanding the status and significance of Judas' repentance and death. In Chapter 5 it will be seen that an unscriptural emphasis on Judas' *despair* is a dominant theme in the tradition, arguably as a way of resolving the tension between the repentance of Judas as recorded in the New Testament, and the conviction that Judas was eternally damned. Particular reference will be made to

---

32 '[God] who did not spare his own Son but *gave him up* for us all, how will he not also with him graciously give us all things?'

Barth's insistence that the validity of this repentance, as with the possibility of forgiveness and salvation for Judas, must remain an 'open question.' It will be seen how writers have struggled with issues of wickedness and grace; repentance, forgiveness and condemnation; individual and corporate responsibility; tragedy and providence.

Chapter 6 will discuss the fourth issue identified above, that is whether or not there is any possibility of eschatological salvation for Judas. Of importance here is Balthasar's emphasis on the importance of the dramatic perspective for theology, and Christ's descent into hell. My final chapter will then draw together the Christological and trinitarian significance of the preceding discussion and analysis, indicating the shape of a Christology attentive to the issues raised throughout the book, and in particular for facing the tension between providence and tragedy.

In Chapters 3 to 6, I seek to show the entire 'topography' of argument and discourse found in the tradition as they relate to the key themes I have identified. I have not, however, attempted to explore or cite every single instance in which a particular view of Judas is put forward. To have done so would have necessitated a vastly extended book without adding anything of significance to the exploration of the theological questions. Chapter 4 comes closest to completeness of citation, for the writers who have noted and discussed the key theological theme at its heart are relatively few.

Throughout I am seeking to reflect theologically on the intersection of Jesus and Judas; the one upon the other. A rather different book could be written exploring the novelistic approach discussed earlier ('explaining' Judas through speculative suggestions about his life and character). Such a book would need to give much space to analysis of the large body of fictional, apocryphal and legendary writings concerning Judas,[33] and more attention to the role of money and avarice in Judas' actions, as found both in scripture and tradition. This would be an interesting piece of work, but it would not be able to address the issues of providence and tragedy so key to tackling the theological and Christological issues that arise from the treatment of Judas in the New Testament and subsequent tradition. Whilst the theme of money is discussed in Chapters 1 and 4, it is not theologically significant in the way that (to take one of the four key issues outlined above) the question of whether or not Judas represents a defeat for Jesus is.

---

33 Additional examples to those given in footnote 5 can be found in *The Apocryphal New Testament – A Collection of Apocryphal Christian literature in an English Translation* edited by J.K. Elliott (Oxford: Clarendon Press, 1993) such as a Coptic narrative relating to Judas and his 'wife' (p163). See also Chapter xxxv of *The Arabic Gospel of the Infancy*, translation by B. Harris Cowper in *The Apocryphal Gospels* (London: Williams & Norgate, 1874) pp201-2, which describes a youthful encounter between Judas and Jesus where the latter tries to bite the former. Volume Two of *The New Testament Apocrypha* edited by W. Schneemelcher (London: Lutterworth Press, 1965) tells of how Thomas heals a youth bitten by the 'great serpent' who inspired Judas to betray Jesus. See pp426f. Kim Paffenroth has traced the development of such material and the connections between different depictions in *Judas – Images of the Lost Disciple* (Louisville: Westminster John Knox Press, 2001).

A methodological contrast to this book can be found in the 1930 doctoral dissertation of Donatus Haugg,[34] a Catholic biblical scholar. He sets out to trace patterns of interpretation in Christian tradition, and identifies four main strands (one of which is that Judas is a sinner dominated by greed). This kind of general survey is useful as far as it goes,[35] but it does not tackle the Christological problem identified in the first part of this introduction; that is the place of Judas Iscariot in Christology. There are a number of primarily descriptive works of this kind, varying in scope, but not seeking to address the theological issues in a substantive or systematic way. The explanatory possibilities of such an approach are theologically limited, therefore; hence the more difficult but more theologically rewarding approach taken here.

Raymond Moloney, in the first chapter of *The Knowledge of Christ*, writes that, 'With such an elusive and difficult question before us, it cannot be a matter of presenting a neat solution and then drawing a line in the sand... large areas of the question must always remain shrouded in mystery.'[36] This comes close to the spirit of this book, but in that the topic I am exploring is more limited in scope than Moloney's, it is my contention that it *is* possible to demonstrate the most effective theological strategy in explicating the place of Judas Iscariot in Christology. I am certainly not offering a 'neat solution', but I am seeking to show that it is only through attending to the tension between providence and tragedy that the place of Judas Iscariot in Christology can be articulated in a way that does justice to the complexity and difficulty of the issues involved.

Near the beginning of this introduction to my book, its scope and its method, I offered a brief account of some of the key texts from scripture relevant to its theme. I argued that any exploration of questions relating to evil, suffering and tragedy attentive to the Christian scriptures would inevitably have to examine the role of Judas Iscariot in the Gospels. My opening chapter, therefore, consists of an examination and analysis of the biblical material concerning Judas, and identifies the theological issues that emerge from such exegesis. It is to this exploration that the book now turns.

---

[34] Donatus Haugg, *Judas Iskarioth in den neutestamentlichen Berichten* (Freiburg im Breisgau: Herder, 1930).

[35] William Klassen, for example, offers (in *Judas – Betrayer or Friend of Jesus?* London: SCM, 1996) a thorough survey of the biblical material, and then a much briefer section surveying theological treatments of Judas. Kurt Luthi, in *Judas Iskariot in der Geschichte der Auslegung von der Reformation bis in die Gegenwart* (Zurich: Zwingli Verlag, 1955) surveys interpretation of Judas in the previous four hundred years. Roman Halas, in *Judas Iscariot – a scriptural and theological study of his person, his deeds and his eternal lot* (Washington: Catholic University of America Press, 1946) offers a survey of some areas of interpretation left undeveloped by Haugg, such as the significance of the name 'Judas Iscariot' (discussed in Chapter 1 of this book also).

[36] Raymond Moloney, *The Knowledge of Christ* (London and New York: Continuum, 1999) p11.

Chapter 1

Judas in the New Testament

The handing over of Jesus in the Passion remains a mystery...[1]
Hans Urs von Balthasar

There is an irony to any examination of the biblical material concerning Judas, in that it requires attention both to the earliest Christian texts and some of the most recent, namely the work of biblical commentators. This chapter, therefore, is necessarily both a discussion of New Testament texts and the exegetical material that is a prerequisite for beginning such a discussion. It has been undertaken during a period when the academic discipline of biblical studies has been reforming and reassessing its practices, and a plethora of competing and contrasting interpretative methods and approaches are available.[2] It is no part of this chapter to make judgements on, for example, the merits of form or redaction criticism (which dominated exegesis for much of the previous century) in relation to 'newer' phenomena such as literary and social-scientific approaches. The impetus to this particular exegetical chapter is provided by the theological issues and themes identified in my introduction, and insight into these will be accepted from whichever quarter it comes.

Immediately a decision has to be made. Would it be better to examine each Gospel discretely, so respecting their particular narrative and theological emphases, or to assess parallel and related texts 'side by side'? For the purposes of this book the latter option has been taken. The Gospels will not be discussed separately; rather similar material from each gospel will be compared. Care will be taken, however, to attend to differences in treatment in the light of the overall trajectory of each gospel. Raymond Brown helpfully describes such an approach as combining both horizontal and vertical study of the gospels.[3] He points out that such an approach can bring to light nuances of approach and insights that might be missed if one gospel was examined individually before moving on to the next.

The intention here is to offer a close reading of the New Testament

---

1 *Mysterium Paschale – the mystery of Easter* Translated with an Introduction by Aidan Nichols O.P. (Edinburgh: T & T. Clark, 1990) p110.

2 See, for example, John Barton (editor), *The Cambridge Companion to Biblical Interpretation* (Cambridge: University Press, 1998) and J.M. Court, *Reading the New Testament* (London and New York: Routledge, 1997).

3 *The Death of the Messiah – From Gethsemane to the Grave. A Commentary on the Passion Narratives in the Four Gospels* (London: Geoffrey Chapman, 1994) Volume One, p26.

references to Judas, bringing to bear 'a good deal of self criticism to filter out later associations'.[4] Interpretations and translations that arise from the weight of centuries of Christian tradition about Judas rather than the texts themselves (or from exaggerating aspects of the texts) will be resisted. If this sounds like an unnecessary statement, on the basis that biblical commentators and exegetes already clearly operate within a tradition of close attention to the text, what follows in this chapter will show that there is some justification for making it. One striking example will suffice at this point. It is widely recognized that the Greek verb παραδίδωμι means 'to deliver up' or 'hand over', yet it is almost invariably translated as 'to betray'. Young's Concordance[5] lists many of the New Testament references to παραδίδωμι under 'betray', even though there is another Greek word which does have that meaning but which is rarely used in the New Testament – προδίδωμι.[6] This issue will receive further attention later in this chapter.

The aims of the chapter are twofold, therefore. First, to offer as thorough an exegesis of the New Testament texts concerning Judas as is possible within the parameters of this book. Second, to discern the theological issues and difficulties emerging from such exegesis. In pursuit of these aims, the intention will be to avoid building on arguments in the biblical commentators that are not self-critical enough in being influenced by later associations, either about Judas' 'character', or about textual matters (such as the meaning of 'Iscariot', shortly to be discussed). This will clearly be a difficult task, as the line between judicious and injudicious interpretation can be hard to draw when the weight of the tradition is as it is.

Rowan Williams has commented that any attempt to understand Arius and his followers 'so far as possible in their own terms, is beset with difficulties'.[7] Some of the difficulties he has in mind concern precisely the weight of received opinion and later associations mentioned in the previous paragraph. Arius, like Judas, has been demonized and then (by way of overcompensation) cast as theological hero. Williams judges the project of avoiding such polarities in order to better understand Arius in his own terms worthwhile, as the Arian problematic is formative of what came to be considered orthodoxy. Analagously I consider the attempt to understand the problematic place of Judas Iscariot in Christology is worth making, particularly as (as I have argued in the introduction) speculation in the direction of 'comfortable falsehoods' is perhaps the commonest and most tempting way of resolving, rather than facing, difficulties and ambiguities in

---

4 Bernard Williams, *Shame and Necessity* (Berkeley: University of California Press, 1993). Whilst Williams was writing about the ancient Greeks, his wording is apposite.

5 Robert Young, *Analytical Concordance to the Bible* (Guildford and London: Lutterworth Press, 1879) p93.

6 See F.W. Danker, *A Greek-English Lexicon of the New Testament and other early Christian literature* (Chicago, London: University of Chicago Press, 2000) pp761-3 [παραδίδωμι] and p867 [προδίδωμι].

7 Rowan Williams, *Arius – Heresy and Tradition,* (London: SCM, second edition, 2001) p24.

individual texts and the overall treatment of the role of Judas in the gospels. A truthful engagement with the central narrative of the Christian faith, moreover, surely requires that such difficulties and ambiguities are faced rather than glossed over or avoided.

1.1 'One of the Twelve'

The first mention of Judas Iscariot in the synoptic gospels occurs in relation to Jesus' nomination of 'the twelve'. The list varies, but in each case begins with Peter and ends with Judas. It is made plain that the call comes from Christ and him alone, as in Mark 3.13-14:

> And [Jesus] went up on the mountain and called to him those whom he desired, and they came to him.[14] And he appointed twelve (whom he also named apostles) so that they might be with him... .

Christ 'makes' or 'appoints' the twelve, which most commentators see as implying the creation of a 'new Israel', for the nation of Israel had originally been composed of twelve different tribes named after the sons of Jacob (Genesis 35.22-26). Mark and Luke, but not Matthew, refer to the twelve as 'apostles', which is the occasion for a number of commentators[8] to discuss whether or not this term could truly to said to have originated with Jesus as opposed to the early Church. Others debate similarly about the many references to 'the twelve'.

The synoptic writers are not content simply to list Judas' name, but immediately identify him, and him alone, with an action. Matthew 10.4 and Mark 3.19 both have: '...and Judas Iscariot, who *betrayed* him' while Luke 6.16 has, 'Judas Iscariot, who became a traitor.' The result of this identification will be that there is no real narrative surprise for the reader in relation to Judas in the way that there might be, say, in relation to the denial of Peter. The implication is that 'we knew all along', and in particular that Jesus knew all along – as is explicitly spelt out by John 6.70 ('Did I not choose you, the twelve, and one of you is a devil?'). The further implication is that if the action attributed to Jesus had not been foreseen, this would undermine the gospel in some way. This is a theme that will receive further discussion later.

For those who seek to argue for the historicity of the twelve, Judas is often invoked as evidence. Vincent Taylor, for example, writes that, 'It is a striking tribute to the historical fidelity of the gospels that the presence of a traitor is so frankly disclosed.'[9] However, many also consider that the presence of Judas in the

---

8 For example G.B. Caird considers the reference to be anachronistic. *The Gospel of St Luke* (Middlesex: Penguin, 1963) p100. See also John P. Meier's discussion of, and disagreement with, Klein, Schmithals, Vielhauer and Crossan (who all argue that 'the twelve' did not exist during Jesus' life) in Chapter 26 of the third volume of *A Marginal Jew – rethinking the historical Jesus* (New York: Doubleday, 2001).

9 *The Gospel according to St Mark* (London: MacMillan, second edition, 1966) p234.

list of disciples 'brought no doubt a timely warning that discipleship did not mean immediate perfection but left open the hard road of temptation...'.[10] It seems, on these accounts, that the gospel writers may have had good homiletic reasons for including Judas in the list of the twelve; and yet also have been tempted to leave him out. That these arguments work in different directions is unremarked in the commentaries. They illustrate also that exegetes often see references to Judas as requiring justification, which commonly takes the form of an instructional point of some kind.

The issues requiring discussion here are first Judas' name, particularly the appellation 'Iscariot' (which distinguishes him from the 'Judas son of James' of Luke 6.16), and then the identifying phrase about 'betrayal/handing over' or 'becoming a traitor'. The former can be achieved relatively briefly, whilst the latter requires more extended treatment.

That my examination of the possible meanings of Judas' name can be concise is not because of any paucity of critical literature. Much has been written about the possible meaning of 'Iscariot' and what it might reveal about the background, reputation, career or motivation of Judas.[11] No one theory, however,

---

Similarly, amongst others, D.E. Nineham, *The Gospel of St Mark* (London: A. & C. Black, 1963/1968) p118; John Martin Creed, *The Gospel According to St Luke* (London: MacMillan, 1965) p87.

10 Hugh Anderson, *The Gospel of Mark* (Grand Rapids, Michigan: Eerdmans, 1976) p119. See also Alfred Plummer, *The Gospel according to S. Luke* (Edinburgh: T & T. Clark, 1901) p175; John Charles Ryle, *Expository Thoughts on the Gospels* (Cambridge: James Clark,1969) Volume 1 pp173-4.

11 The relevant critical discussion involves understanding that in the New Testament, Judas' name takes two forms, either having a semitic ending (three times) or a Greek ending (nine times, in Matthew, Luke and John). Scholars differ as to which is the original, but the Greek ending seems to have the more convincing arguments in its favour. C.C. Torrey ('The Name "Iscariot" ' in *Harvard Theological Review* 36, 1943, p56) argues that a scribe would hardly likely to alter a good Hebrew ending for a Greek, whilst the converse move might be understood as an 'improvement'. Yoel Arbeitman ('The Suffix of Iscariot' in *Journal of Biblical Literature* 99, 1980, p123) argues that the name Iscariot was the product of authors familiar both with Aramaic and Greek putting an Aramaic actor noun for '(red) dyer' into Greek form. This suggestion, from a Jewish scholar, is striking in its prosaic plausibility, especially when compared with the wide range of other proposals. Almost all convey some kind of negative judgement on Judas, or hint at an explanation of his actions. This is even true of a widespread geographical explanation of Iscariot, as being derived from a Hebrew form meaning 'man of Kerioth'. There are serious arguments against this, however, well articulated in Torrey's seminal article already referred to. If *Is* meant 'man', why not translate it as such? Why should Hebrew be used for an epithet originating in an Aramaic context? He also points out problems connected with the proposed place name. That there was a Palestinian town of called 'Kerioth' is disputed. A possible reference is Joshua 15.25, where the cities of Judah are listed, amongst them 'Kerioth-hezron (that is, Hazor)'. Jeremiah 48.24 mentions a Moabite city named Kerioth, an unlikely origin for a disciple of Jesus. Where this explanation if favoured, it is often pointed out that it indicates that Judas was the only one of the disciples to come from

has achieved widespread acceptance, and consequently little can be deduced about Judas with any certainty. The arguments have tended to focus on the meaning of 'Iscariot', with proposals ranging from the appellation indicating that Judas was from Kerioth, or was a bandit, to that it was a nickname meaning 'liar' or 'false one'. The latter, argued in a seminal article by William Torrey, is potentially the most significant as if proven, it would be crucial evidence as to how the gospel writers understood Judas. However Torrey's argument has failed to win critical approval, on both linguistic and other grounds.[12]

Albert Ehrman, for example, points out that 'all changes of name or the addition of nicknames in the NT are always explicitly noted'[13] and therefore argues

---

outside Galilee 'and this may have helped to isolate him.' (Plummer, op cit p175. See also, for example, Floyd V. Filson *A Commentary on the Gospel according to Matthew* (London: Adam and Charles Black, 1960, p127).

The issue is complicated by references in St John's gospel which appear to make Iscariot a family name, such as 6.71 and 13.26, where 'Judas' is followed by 'son of Simon Iscariot'. 13.2 refers to 'Judas Iscariot son of Simon'). Torrey argues that in each of these cases the Aramaic form *is Judah bar Simon Iscar.* meaning 'Judas Iscariot son of Simon', and that the ambiguity is the fault of a Greek interpreter. For him it is clear that there was no Simon Iscariot. This is crucial to his argument as he adduces that no person apart from Judas bore that name, and that 'Since there is no evidence that Judas was called Iscariot during his lifetime... the probability is strong that the epithet was a reproach, an opprobrious appellation given to the man because of his deed.' (op cit. p58) Against this, however Albert Ehrman points out that 'all changes of name or the addition of nicknames in the NT are always explicitly noted' ('Judas Iscariot and the Abba Saqqara' in *Journal of Biblical Literature* 97, 1978, p572) and therefore argues that Iscariot was Judas' natural surname, an opinion followed by Arbeitman as above.

12 Torrey's argument is that a Jewish Aramaic epithet meaning 'false one, liar, hypocrite' became attached to Judas' name as the story of the *betrayal* spread through Palestine. He became Judas *Isqarya*, and writers of the gospels knew this and what the sobriquet meant. 'So instead of attempting to translate it they kept it, in a regularly formed Greek transcription, giving it an ending which not only suited the meaning but also pointed to the exact form of the Aramaic word' ('The Name "Iscariot"' in *Harvard Theological Review* 36, 1943, p61).

In addition to Ehrman's objection in footnote 11, it is not necessary to be an authority in Aramaic to perceive that there can be no certainty in such derivations. For those with such expertise differ widely, as has already been seen.

The ending of Ingholt's article is interesting in that he records the assertion 'that the strongest element in favour of the historicity of Judas was the fact that his surname had not yet been satisfactorily explained.' (Many writers, including J.M. Robertson, William Benjamin Smith and Frank Kermode have argued that Judas is a fictional creation of the early church). As for his interpretation, he considers it to speak 'for his historicity, whereas a surname "the false" preceded by a name as colourless and lacking in individuality as Judas, "the Jew", could indeed be used as an additional argument by those who, for theological or other reasons, regard him as a fictitious character, however generally improbable to my mind that speculation is.' (ibid p162. The assertion comes from Guignebert, *Jesus*, New York, 1935, p453).

13 'Judas Iscariot and the Abba Saqqara' in *Journal of Biblical Literature* 97, 1978, p572.

that Iscariot was Judas' natural surname. Harald Ingholt argues that even if Torrey's linguistic argumentation is accepted, 'one might perhaps have expected another word than *saqar* [liar] to express the particular sin of Judas.'[14] Brown agrees: '...no NT account has Judas lie about Jesus.'[15] For Ingholt the natural reading of the gospels would be that Judas had the surname Iscariot from the start. It was a common name, needing a distinguishing accompaniment. This is why there is a Judas the son of James (Luke 6.16) and a Judas Barsabbas (Acts 15.22) elsewhere in the New Testament.

William Klassen, following a review of the relevant material, is correct to write that 'Regretfully we conclude that no clear light is shed on the personality of Judas by the word Iscariot. Moreover, the theories that try to explain Iscariot diverge so widely from each other that nothing can be built on them.'[16] The verdict of Gustaf Dalman is similarly apposite: 'It is a very plausible conjecture that [Iscariot] was already unintelligible to the evangelist.'[17] Whilst the latter may seem like speculation of the kind I am seeking to avoid, Dalman's main point is that any meaning the gospel writers may have perceived in the suffix is not intelligible to the contemporary reader with any degree of certainty or usefulness.

Very few commentators comment on the name 'Judas' itself. Harald Ingholt refers to 'Judas, "the Jew"' as a name that is 'colourless and lacking in individuality'.[18] Hyam Maccoby has argued that Judas was described as 'traitor' precisely because his name is that of the Jewish people, though he argues this

---

14 'The Surname of Judas Iscariot' in *Studia Orientalia Ioanni Pedersen... dicata*, Munksgaard, 1953, p157.

15 Op cit. Volume 2 p1416.

16 *Judas – Betrayer or Friend of Jesus?* (London: SCM 1996) p34.

17 Dalman, *The Words of Jesus – considered in the light of post-biblical Jewish teachings and the Aramaic language* Authorised English Version by D.M. Kay (Edinburgh: T. & T. Clark, 1902) p52. Some of the other interpretations suggested, which together back up Dalman's conclusion, include a proposed derivation from a Greek word meaning something like 'bandit' or 'dagger man' (For example it is discussed by Filson op cit. p108; C.E.B. Cranfield *The Gospel according to St Mark*, Cambridge, 1966, p132; and Sherman E. Johnson *The Gospel according to Mark*, London: A. & C. Black, 1960, p79. However none consider it very likely). There is no supporting evidence in the New Testament that Judas ever warranted such a description. Torrey is prepared to give more credence to the derivation from the Latin *scortea* if for no other reason than John Lightfoot suggested it ('Hebrew and Talmudical Exercitations upon the Gospel of St Matthew', *The Whole Works of John Lightfoot* edited by J.R. Pitman, 1823, Volume xi p172). Lightfoot hit upon a word in the Talmud meaning a coat or apron of leather, which in Greek transcription would be written *Iskortia*. The argument is that such aprons had purses woven into them for carrying money, and that Judas had the title of 'the purse bearer' (cf John 12.6 'as he had the money box he used to take what was put into it...'; and 13.29 'because Judas had the money box...') It seems unlikely that such a purse would have been called a *scortea*, and even if it were the movement from that name to Iscariot is hardly obvious. Both of these suggestions seem to owe at least as much to ideas about the kind of person Judas might have been as to linguistic argumentation.

18 Ingholt, op cit. p162.

mainly with reference to particular interpretations of the New Testament material in the subsequent tradition, rather than from the New Testament texts themselves.[19]

1.2 Translation matters: παραδίδωμι

J. Morin[20] has tried to prove that Mark 3.19 (see above) could mean 'Judas Iscariot, that means, the one who handed him over.' Brown points out Mark has written a 'that means' clause just two verses before (James the son of Zebedee and John the brother of James, whom he surnamed Boanerges, that is, sons of thunder). This indicates the usual way to write such a clause and that the common translation of 3.19 is correct: 'Judas Iscariot, who *betrayed* him'.[21] Where this conventional translation is inaccurate, however, is that the form of παραδίδωμι used is closer in meaning to the 'hand over' of Morin's suggestion than to 'betray'.

Here, then, the discussion moves from the first part of Judas' identification in the synoptic lists (his name) to the second (his action). The standard lexicon for classical Greek by Liddell and Scott defines παραδίδωμι as having the primary meaning of to 'give, hand over to another, transmit', to 'give into another's hands' or 'deliver up, surrender'.[22] They note that it sometimes has the connotation of treachery or betrayal, citing instances in Xenophon and Pausanius, although William Klassen has shown that the references they cite do not back this up, even as a 'collational notion'.[23] The word προδίδωμι also means 'to deliver up', but has far greater connotations of betrayal (moreover the word for 'traitor' is derived

---

19 Hyam Maccoby, Judas Iscariot and the Myth of Jewish Evil (New York: The Free Press, 1992). 'Judas' is certainly etymologically related to 'Jew', and the idea of seeing him as representative of the Jewish people goes back at least to Augustine, who, for example, in his *Expositions on the Book of Psalms*, wrote that '...Judas doth represent those Jews who were enemies of Christ...' (Psalm CIX. 1, Volume VIII from 'A Select Library of the Nicene and Post-Nicene Fathers', Edinburgh and Michigan: T&T Clark/Wm. B. Eerdmans 1888, reprinted 1989, p536). It is far from clear that such an understanding is intrinsic to the New Testament, where at least some of the gospel writers may rather have in mind the specific story of Joseph 'handed over' by his brothers at the instigation of Judah (Genesis 37. 26-27). Maccoby does demonstrate, however, that there is a case to be answered.

20 'Les deux derniers des Douze: Simon le Zelote et Judas Iskarioth', in *Revue Biblique* 80 (1973) pp332-358, particularly pp349-358.

21 Brown, op cit. p1415.

22 Henry George Liddell and Robert Scott *A Greek-English Lexicon* (Oxford: Oxford University Press, Ninth edition of 1940 with a 1968 supplement, 1977) p1308.

23 See his discussion in pp47-59 of *Judas – Betrayer or Friend of Jesus?* (London: SCM, 1996). Here Klassen discusses not only Liddell and Scott, but also the use of παραδίδωμι in the Septuagint and Josephus, Walter Bauer's standard lexicon of New Testament Greek, and the theological lexicon of Ceslas Spicq. Throughout he shows 'that there is no linguistic basis – in classical Greek, in the Greek translation of the Hebrew Bible, in Josephus or patristic sources – for a translation of "betray" to describe what Jesus did' (ibid. p57).

from it). Liddell and Scott define προδίδωμι as 'give up to the enemy, betray', 'play false', 'prove traitor' and 'to be false to'.[24] Consulting Arndt and Gingrich's *Greek-English Lexicon of the New Testament*[25] indicates that such definitions hold good for the New Testament period. Amongst the range of meaning they give for παραδίδωμι, the closest the word comes to having a negative sense is 'hand over, turn over, give up a person (as in hand over into the custody of...)', and yet in the examples given they refer to the 'betrayal' of Jesus. Once again this is witness to the difficulty of 'objectivity', even in textual matters, as nowhere in Arndt and Gingrich's four different sections on παραδίδωμι is its explicit meaning given as 'betray'. Klassen writes that in some cases one 'can only say that theology here determines lexicography, not the other way around'.[26]

The entry for προδίδωμι indicates that this word is the appropriate one to be used to describe 'betrayal'. Only three times in the New Testament is προδίδωμι used in this sense, however, and just once in relation to Judas – in the Lukan apostolic listing already discussed ('who became a traitor').[27] In contrast, παραδίδωμι is used 94 times. Forty of these occurrences are usually translated 'betray' and grouped as such in Young's *Concordance*,[28] the only occasion outside the Gospels being 1 Corinthians 11. 23: '...on the night when he was *betrayed* he took bread...'. The remaining number are listed in section 36 of 'Deliver' with the meaning 'To give over to, or alongside of '.[29]

This division obscures the possible relation between different aspects of 'handing over'. As Brown puts it, the tendency to translate παραδίδωμι as 'betray' blurs the 'parallelism to the agency of others expressed by this word'.[30] Wiard Popkes, for example, has classified uses of the verb in the passion narratives according to whether Jesus is given over by God, himself, or others.[31] He argues that amongst its various uses, παραδίδωμι was sometimes used as a technical legal

---

24 Ibid. pp1474-5.

25 William F. Arndt and R. Wilbur Gingrich *A Greek-English Lexicon of the New Testament and other early Christian literature* (Chicago: University of Chicago Press, 1957/1979). See also F.W.Danker's revised and edited Arndt and Gingrich, *A Greek-English lexicon of the New Testament and other early Christian literature* (Chicago, London: University of Chicago Press, 2000) pp761-3 and p867.

26 Klassen is commenting on the work of Ceslas Spicq in classifying usages of παραδίδωμι. His comments also apply to Walter Bauer, author of the standard lexicon of the Greek New Testament, later translated by Arndt and Gingrich (op cit. p50).

27 The other two occasions are in Stephen's sermon before the high priest in Acts 7, in which he refers to 'the Righteous One, whom you have now *betrayed* and murdered'. (7.52); and 2 Timothy 3.4 where precisely the same form is found in a list of the kind of people who will live in the last days – 'treacherous, reckless, swollen with conceit...'.

28 Robert Young, *Analytical Concordance to the Holy Bible*, Eighth edition, revised (Guildford and London: Lutterworth Press, 1939) p93.

29 Ibid. p243.

30 Op cit. p211.

31 W. Popkes, *Christus Traditus: Eine Untersuchung zum Begriff der Hingabe im NT*, Abhandlungen zur Theologie des Alten und Neuen Testaments no. 49 (Zurich: Zwingli Verlag 1967) pp152-169.

term in Greek for the handing over of criminals to be judged or executed; a term given a new twist in the Gospels where it is Christ who is innocent, and the human agents implicated in guilt. This 'legal' connotation will be more fully discussed shortly in relation to Derrett's arguments about παραδίδωμι in relation to its Hebrew equivalents.

Popkes' classifications illustrate how easy it is to narrow the possible meanings of a text through translation. In the verse from 1 Corinthians just quoted, for example, an ambiguity is missed by the translation 'betrayed' as it is not clear from the Greek if this is meant to be a reference to Judas, or whether Pilate, the high priests, or even God is the agent referred to. Romans 8.32, for example, records that God 'did not spare his own Son but *gave him up* for us all...'. Even where God is not explicitly mentioned, divine agency is suggested by the use of the passive voice, such as in Mark 14.41: '...the Son of man *is betrayed* into the hands of sinners'.

Friedrich Büchsel's article on δίδωμι in Kittel's *Theological Dictionary of the New Testament* [32] only briefly considers παραδίδωμι and concentrates on human agency. He points out the parallelism between Judas' 'betrayal' of Jesus; the handing over of Jesus to Pilate by the Sanhedrin (Mark 15.1 and parallels); the delivering up of Jesus to the people by Pilate (Luke 23.25); as well as texts such as the prediction in Matthew 10.17 that the disciples will be *delivered up* to councils, or Herod's *delivering* of Peter to be guarded by four squads of soldiers in Acts 12.4. Büchsel does not note the parallelism with the action of God, an omission that may partly explain his insistence, in a footnote, that the reference in 1 Corinthians 11.23 'is undoubtedly to Judas' treachery. For Jesus was betrayed *in the night* only by Judas.'[33] The matter is not so clear, with the choice in understanding 1 Corinthians 11.23 being between the action of various human agents of which Judas is one, or of God; or even of the latter working through the former.

It has been seen that there are two main reasons why 'betray' is not an adequate translation for παραδίδωμι. Firstly, it is not the primary or arguably even a secondary meaning of the word. If it was to be asserted that the overall content of the Gospels and their portrayal of Judas enable a case to be made for translating 'betray', this would be almost impossible to justify textually, although the use of 'traitor' in Luke 6.16 indicates that for that Gospel at least the possibility cannot be completely dismissed. Secondly, it may hinder understanding and interpretation not only of texts in which forms of παραδίδωμι appear, but also the relation of such texts to other usages of the verb. Both of these affect not only understandings of Judas, but also the way the providence of God is apprehended.

---

32 Grand Rapids, Michigan: Eerdmans, 1964. Volume II Δ – H.

33 Ibid. p169. He does concede that others (he cites Bauer) differ from this view. Büchsel is correct, however, in pointing out that only Judas 'delivers up' at night, for the handing over to Pilate occurs following daybreak (after Peter's threefold denial before the cock crows; John 18.25-27 and parallels).

At this point it is worth noting that it is usually *verbs* under discussion. It has already been noted that the noun 'traitor' is used only once. Westcott concluded from this that Judas' 'act is regarded in relation to the Lord's Passion, and not to his sin.'[34] He means that the way παραδίδωμι is used places the emphasis not so much on labelling Judas, but in describing the significance of what he did in relation to the overall 'drama'. This is an important insight, but the question remains as to why the Gospel writers chose to use παραδίδωμι when writing about Judas, in preference for the most part to a verb with more obviously negative connotations. Why this should be remains an issue even if it is argued that to hand some one over against their will amounts to the same thing as betrayal.

One possible suggestion has been made both by David Daube[35] and in J. Duncan Derrett. According to the latter, much of the answer lies in the fact that παραδίδωμι has 'a quite special sense in the New Testament'[36]. He explains what he means by reference to Hebrew equivalents, *natan* ('give') and the later *masar*. The *masor* (or *maser*) 'hands over (property or) a person from the "inside" to the "outside".'[37] This was often, though not necessarily (for example if the one handed over was an enemy), a treacherous act. Amongst the Jewish people, so often subjugated by foreign rulers, the *masor* was usually understood as one who handed over a fellow Jew to a foreign power at risk to himself from his compatriots. Informing the Jewish authorities of crimes against Jewish law was a different matter, and the community as a whole might hand over someone for the death penalty they themselves could not execute.

This was doing *m^{e}sira* (the word also described the crime of an individual Jew betraying his people to aliens) in respect of those worthy of death. Justification for this was partly based on 2 Samuel 20 and the story of the Benjaminite Sheba. The people of the city of Abel, besieged by Joab because they sheltered Sheba, a rival to David, decided to behead the Benjaminite on the advice of a wise woman. The point was that 'handing over' could be acceptable if done with due cause and proper authority. Indeed God had often done this with the Jewish people, and moreover promised to do so again (for example Psalm 106.40-41: 'Then the anger of the LORD was kindled against his people... he gave them into the hand of the nations', and Ezekiel 21.31: 'And I will pour out my indignation upon you... I will deliver you into the hands of brutish men').[38]

---

34 B.F. Westcott, *The Gospel According to St John – The authorized version with introduction and notes* (London: John Murray, 1903) p110.

35 D. Daube, *Collaboration with Tyranny in Rabbinic Law* (London: Oxford University Press, 1965). See in particular the first two chapters.

36 J. Duncan Derrett, 'The Iscariot, M^{e}sira and the Redemption' *Journal for the Study of the New Testament* 8 (1980) pp2-23.

37 Ibid. p3.

38 In Jewish tradition the meaning of *masor* and *masur* (hander over *and* the one who is handed over) was exemplified by Joseph. Right at the beginning of the narrative concerning him the reader learns that he 'brought an ill report of [his brothers] to their father' (Genesis 37.2) who in any event favoured him above the others (37.4). His

This proposal of Daube and Derrett's is 'intellectually defensible',[39] although it can remain only a suggestion. For Klassen, in the absence of other

---

brothers hated him and plotted to kill him. Having stripped him and cast him into an empty pit, 'they sat down to eat' (37.25). It is Judah who suggests they sell him to a passing caravan saying 'Come, let us sell him to the Ishmaelites, and let not our hand be upon him...' (37.27). The agreed price is 'twenty shekels of silver' (37.28). Later it is only because of this 'sale' that the brothers have anything to eat at all and are saved from starvation. An abominable act, perpetrated by 'twelve' (sons of Jacob – Genesis 35.23) apparently plays an essential part in the history of the Jewish people. Joseph explicitly affirms his brother's treachery as part of God's purposes at 45.5, 7: 'And now do not be distressed, or angry with yourselves, because you sold me here; for God sent me before you to preserve life... . And God sent me before you to preserve for you a remnant on earth...'.

The resonances of this narrative with that of Judas Iscariot are clear, for he was 'one of the twelve' who handed over a close associate. Derrett comments on Iscariot as follows: 'What he did made it clear that he was appropriately called "Judah", for that is what "Judas" is.' (ibid. p9).

In terms of *m^e^sira*, just who is 'inside' and who 'outside' is complicated, but presumably the chief priests were 'outside' relative to the disciples, and the Romans 'outside' relative to both. Both Judas and the chief priests would therefore be sinful in that there was no grounds for their 'handing over'; Jesus was not worthy of death in God's eyes. Derrett comments that in spite 'of Jesus' knowledge of what would happen and his despatching him on his errand (John 13.27), Judas bears the sin. Without the Old Testament pattern and precedent this would be monstrously unfair...' (ibid. p12). Derrett means that God willed that redemption should occur by such means, and that this puts Judas' actions in a wider context. He suggests that Matthew may have had the view that because of Judas' repentance he would share in the life to come (ibid. p14). This is far from clear, as will be seen later, and is any event a narrative not shared by the other evangelists. John is clear that 'not one of them has been lost but the son of destruction, that the Scripture might be fulfilled.' (17.12)

It may be that the Hebrew Bible sheds light on 'handing over' and the way παραδίδωμι should be understood in the New Testament. God, it appears, works through such acts. It is true, however, as Klassen points out, that the figure of Joseph seems of little interest to the New Testament writers and is never explicitly mentioned (Klassen, op cit. p66). In any event there are vital distinctions to be made between the Judah of Genesis and the Judas of the gospels. Judah (with the agreement of his brothers) was not acting 'according to scripture' even though it becomes clear later that Joseph saw God's purposes being played out through those actions. In the Gospels Judas' actions are predicted, 'placed' in terms of Scripture, and then he is 'lost'. Crucially, Judah is not. He receives forgiveness, as is apparent from Genesis 45.15: 'And [Joseph] kissed all his brothers and wept upon them; and after that his brothers talked with him.' Judas, although acting in accordance with Scripture and in some measure according to an Old Testament pattern (albeit one to do with an undoubtedly sinful handing over by an 'insider'), nevertheless is the recipient of an infinitely worse fate than Judah. As MacKinnon comments, the 'surd element remains' (*Explorations in Theology 5*, London: SCM, 1976, p194).

39 Klassen, op cit. p63. Some critics, such as J. Walter Holleran, have accepted the argument. He describes παραδίδωμι as a 'technical Jewish legal term [which] is used as

theories it remains the most credible explanation of the New Testament use of παραδίδωμι rather than προδίδωμι. It helps to clarify that Judas handed Jesus over to the temple authorities, not the Romans, and gives some plausibility to his proposal that Judas be understood as an 'informer' rather than a 'betrayer'.[40] This suggestion remains speculative, nevertheless, and a simpler possibility commends itself. It is clear from this section that the New Testament writers chose a verb with the primary meaning of 'hand over' when they could have used one meaning 'betray'. In doing so, they set up linguistic parallelism between the actions of Judas, other human agents, and God. There is therefore the implicit connotation, from within the New Testament itself, that these actions are to be understood as linked within the providence of God.

The linguistic parallelism is not accidental, therefore, but part of an implicit theological schema for making sense of the whole drama of the passion. This providential connotation will receive much discussion in Chapter 2, particularly in relation to the writing of Karl Barth on this issue. The basis for such examination, moreover, is not simply the parallelism discussed here, as the following section and much else in this chapter will illustrate the importance of the theme of providence.

1.3 Characterizing Judas – John's Pre-Passion Material

Following their lists of 'the twelve' the synoptic Gospels do not explicitly mention Judas again until their passion narratives. In John there is no such list, but the first reference to Judas does occur in the context of a conversation between Jesus and 'the twelve', and he has additional material before the passion narrative proper begins. It is noteworthy that the disciples are only referred to as 'the twelve' in one other place in John's Gospel, on that occasion with reference to Thomas ('Now Thomas, one of the twelve...' at 20.24). That John shares the synoptic emphasis on identifying Judas in this way is therefore all the more striking.

That first reference to Judas occurs in a passage beginning at John 6.64, where the evangelist writes that 'Jesus knew from the first who those were that did not believe, and who it was that should *betray* him'. The context is the discourse on Jesus as 'the bread of life' (6.34), an ascription many cannot accept, ending with Peter's affirmation that Jesus is 'the Holy One of God' (6.69) and Jesus' answer at 6.70-71: ' "Did I not choose you, the twelve, and one of you is a devil?" He spoke of Judas the son of Simon Iscariot, for he, one of the twelve, was to *betray* him.'

Here a refusal to accept Jesus as 'living bread' is implicitly related to the sin of Judas, and the first explicit references in John to the coming Passion are concurrent with these first allusions to Judas. The phrase 'from the first' may refer

---

such throughout the passion account.' *The Synoptic Gethsemane – a critical study* (Roma: Universita Gregoriana Editrice, 1973) p63.

40 See Chapter Four of *Judas – Betrayer or Friend of Jesus?* Op cit. pp62-76.

either to the beginning of Jesus' earthly ministry (1.39ff) or to the 'In the beginning...' that opens the Gospel. Schnackenburg comments that Jesus' foreknowledge is not emphasized here purely on apologetic grounds (to answer the question as to how one of the twelve specifically called by Jesus could have *betrayed* him), because, as the evangelist realizes, 'it gives rise to the further problem of how Jesus could have chosen [Judas].'[41] Such a criticism could have been raised by members of the Johannine community itself, or by incredulous outsiders. The implication is that for Jesus, in common with the rest of humanity, to be bound by limited perception of both present and future, and imperfect judgement in his relations with others, would undermine the credibility of the Gospel. When the Gospel writer is faced by the different problems that arise when Jesus is either described as having, or not having, foreknowledge, he opts for the former. Schnackenburg argues that for John, Jesus' prior knowledge (whatever form it took) would best take 'the sting from the reproach'.[42]

Certainly it seemed to the evangelist that God had already announced in scripture that Jesus was to be *betrayed* (for example 13.18 reads: '...I know whom I have chosen; it is that the scripture may be fulfilled, "He who ate my bread has lifted his heel against me..." '). Here it can be seen that it is not simply a question of whether or not Jesus 'foreknew', but also that the Gospel writer goes to great lengths to ensure that Judas' actions are understood as firmly within the providence of God. Yet the description of Judas as a 'devil' emphasizes that even if his actions were 'predestined' or 'predicted' the 'dark fact' of the *betrayal* still 'belongs to the mystery of evil'.[43] In 13.27 John writes that 'Satan entered him' (Luke writes similarly at 22.3), thus leaving an ambiguity about Judas' 'diabolic' status. Is he to be understood as a 'devil' from the start, or only from a later point in the narrative?

What is clear from New Testament usage is that the Greek word usually translated 'devil', and from which the English word 'diabolic' is derived, usually refers to Satan.[44] Werner Foerster shows that this correlation derives from the Septuagint (the Greek translation of the Hebrew Scriptures), which is innovative in using 'devil' in this way. In the Septuagint it comes to have the sense of 'adversary', always implying 'an attempt on the part of the [devil] to separate God and man'.[45] In John, Satan is the 'prince of this world'[46] and so the unredeemed live in Satan's sphere. This means that there are ample opportunities for serving

41 Rudolf Schnackenburg, *The Gospel According to St John* Volume Two (London: Burns & Oates, 1980) p74.

42 Ibid. p77.

43 Ibid. p74.

44 There is the occasional use in a less extreme sense, for example II Timothy 3.3 where it means 'slanderous'.

45 *Theological Dictionary of the New Testament*, op cit. p73. A good example of New Testament usage is John 8.44 where Jesus describes those who will not accept him as being 'of your father the devil'. In the same verse this devil is described as a 'murderer' who is 'a liar and the father of lies' and in whom 'there is no truth'.

46 John 12.31. See also 14.30 and 16.11.

evil rather than good. Taking account of this Johannine emphasis alerts the reader to such ambiguities as John 19.11, where Jesus responds to Pilate as follows: 'therefore he who *delivered* me to you has the greater sin'. This may refer to Caiaphas, or to the prince of this world, or indeed the latter working through the former.[47]

It is possible that John's description of Judas in Chapter 6 should be understood in terms of 13.2: 'And during supper, when the devil had already put it into the heart of Judas... to *betray* him...'. But the Greek, literally 'now having put', implies, along with 13.27, that Satan was acting in a new way at this place in the narrative. This would indicate that at 6.64 Jesus can foresee what Judas will do, or what Satan will do through him, in the future. There is no suggestion that Judas dissents from Peter's 'you are the Holy One of God' at 6.69.[48]

The ambiguities in John's portrayal of Judas are reflected in many commentaries, for example where Barrett writes of the twelve as, 'being (with the exception of Judas) men who God himself has drawn to Jesus...'.[49] There is no scriptural justification for that assertion about Judas, and yet Barrett feels he cannot allow God to have played a part in his call. It is a remark that can justly be characterized as theodicy, an attempt to justify the ways of God in the face of difficulty. Westcott is perhaps closer to the mark when he says that 'the Lord shews that even His own choice... left room for a traitor among those whom He has chosen.'[50] The implication is that Jesus' choice was not 'perfect' but limited by human, and therefore partial, perception.

---

[47] Interestingly, neither John nor Luke record Jesus giving the disciples power over demons. Both Mark (3.14-15) and Matthew (10.1) do so in relation to the call of the twelve, which perhaps goes together with the fact that neither of them describe Judas as possessed by Satan. It would read oddly for John to record the disciples receiving powers of exorcism, and then almost immediately identify one of them as a 'devil'!

[48] Prior to the passion narrative proper, John's gospel has very little material in common with the synoptic gospels. However, the Petrine affirmation of Christ (6.69) can certainly be related to Mark 8.27-33, Peter's confession of faith at Caesarea Philippi. In the latter Peter follows his confession by rebuking Jesus for predicting his suffering and death and is in turn rebuked by Jesus in diabolic terms: 'Get behind me, Satan!' (8.33), presumably for attempting to divert Jesus from his destined path. R.H. Lightfoot comments that in the Johannine passage under discussion 'the Lord speaks of Judas as a devil; and it seems probable that St John thus shows, not Peter, but Judas to be that member of the body who truly and in deed allied himself with evil.' (*St John's Gospel – A Commentary*, Oxford: Clarendon Press, 1956, p170). It may be that this is a conscious correction on the part of the evangelist. Certainly in comparing the two passages the identification of Judas as 'diabolic' has a stronger edge than the rebuke to Peter, which comes in response to a particular statement, rather than as description of who Peter is.

[49] C.K. Barrett *The Gospel According to St John – An introduction with commentary and notes on the Greek text* (London: SPCK, second edition. 1978) p301.

[50] Op cit. p111.

Sanders and Mastin raise a radically different question: could it be 'that Jesus chose Judas in order that he might betray him?'[51] Yet it has been seen that John does not portray Judas in terms of exercising 'free will', nor of simple instrumentality in the divine purpose. Rather he struggles with a series of factors that are not all compatible with one another – that Judas was one of the chosen twelve, that Judas betrayed/delivered up the one who chose him, that this 'handing over' was of the devil, that this genuinely evil act could not at any point have been hidden from Christ, nor could he have made a 'mistake' in his choosing, and indeed perhaps Judas was chosen for this purpose. As Westcott sees, this is the stuff of 'tragic pathos'[52] and does not make for a neatly rounded narrative. In John's Gospel is seen an understanding of providence in tension with a variety of difficult questions that pull in the direction of tragedy.

John's narrative leaves the reader in no doubt as to whom Judas is, however. The three verses under discussion have yielded no less than four identifying characteristics. Twice Judas is described as the one who hands over or betrays Jesus. Twice he is included in 'the twelve'. Once it is apparent that he bears the name Iscariot, and once that he is a 'devil'. The synoptic Gospels, as has been seen, concur in emphasizing membership of the twelve, the name Iscariot, and the 'handing over'. The one exception is in the latter, where Luke uses the noun 'traitor' rather than παραδίδωμι, and in that sense is most akin to John, who alone uses the term 'devil'. It is clear, therefore, that the first references to Judas in each of the four Gospels serve to 'label' Judas in no uncertain terms. At this point he has not done anything worthy of the remark, but the ground has been well and truly laid (albeit briefly) for the role he will play in the passion narratives. Indeed the synoptics do not mention him again until that point.

John does include one reference to Judas before the passion; a rare attempt to give insight into the character of the one up to now simply identified in the ways just delineated (three of which are immediately repeated). This reference comes in the opening section of Chapter 12 where, six days before the Passover, Mary (the sister of Martha) anoints Jesus with costly ointment. As in the parallel passage in Luke (but unlike Matthew and Mark), this occurs before the triumphal entry into Jerusalem. The narrative proceeds as follows (vv. 4-6):

> But Judas Iscariot, one of his disciples (he who was to *betray* him), said, [5]'Why was this ointment not sold for three hundred denarii and given to the poor?' [6]This he said, not that he cared for the poor but because he was a thief, and as he had the money box he used to take what was put into it.

---

[51] *A Commentary on the Gospel according to St John*, J.N Sanders, edited and completed by B.A Mastin (London: Adam and Charles Black, 1968) p200.

[52] Op cit. p111. Leon Morris writes that 'the tragedy of Judas... must have made a big impression on John, for he mentions it so often.' *The Gospel according to John, revised edition* (Grand Rapids, Michigan: Eerdmans, 1995) p552.

As just indicated, this passage is paralleled in each of the synoptics (though in a rather different form in Luke), but only in John is Judas singled out. In Mark 14.4 'some' object to the extravagance, while in Matthew 26.8 it is 'the disciples'. In Luke 7.39 it is a Pharisee who wonders why Jesus allows himself to be anointed by a sinner. Here John interprets the objections recorded in the other Gospels in terms of a dishonest intention on the part of Judas. Mark and Matthew mention no other motive other than helping the poor. Nowhere else but in John is Judas described as a thief or the keeper of money. That Judas kept the disciples' 'money box' is referred to again at 13.29 just before he goes out into the night, to be seen next with the arresting party. These are the only references to a 'money box' in the New Testament.[53] Following the earlier discussion of Judas as 'devil', K. Luthi has argued that Judas' demonic role as representative of the Antichrist is implied in the money theme.[54] Even if this is accepted, however, it only hardens the questions relating to the original choice of such a person as 'one of the twelve'.

It may be, as Barrett writes, that John has access to 'an independent tradition, but more probably he represents the traditional and progressive blackening of Judas' character.'[55] It may be that if Judas did indeed have access to a common fund, inevitably some accusation would be made 'to account for an almost inexplicable treachery'.[56] These are plausible conjectures, but nevertheless remain uncertain. It is the case, however, that avarice as a motive is implicit in Matthew 26.15, when Judas asks the high priests what they will give him 'if I *deliver* him to you?' Mark 14.11 and Luke 22.5-6 are less explicit in terms of avarice, but an exchange of money is nevertheless part of the agreement between Judas and the high priests. None of this provides a complete explanation for Judas' actions at the end of Jesus' life; but John particularly seems to wish to paint a picture of Judas that makes those actions accord at least partially with what has been said earlier.

This picture finds part of its resonance in the contrast with Mary. Commentators agree that her actions are meant to indicate a costly devotion to Jesus, with the implication that his body is being symbolically anointed in preparation for the burial that is to come (and to which he refers at 12.7-8). At 11.27 Mary has affirmed her faith in Jesus as the 'resurrection and the life', and she now indicates by her actions that she has fully understood the implications of that phrase. By contrast, therefore, Judas' response about waste exhibits more than the stated avarice. It also shows a lack of devotion and indeed a lack of insight.

---

53 'Money box' is used in the Septuagint for a chest for offerings of money (2 Chronicles 24.8,10). In Rabbinic literature the Greek was transliterated into Hebrew to mean a box for preserving something valuable, for example the Torah when travelling, or even a coffin carrying a corpse.

54 'Das Problem das Judas Iskarioth – neu untersucht', *Evangelische Theologie* 16 (1956) pp98-114.

55 Op cit. p413.

56 Sanders and Mastin, op cit. p285.

Perhaps 'the evident intention of the fourth evangelist is to exhibit the spiritual blindness behind [Judas'] remark as tantamount to unfaithfulness.'[57]

In terms of what John has written earlier about Jesus' foresight, the reader might well wonder why a disciple with a tendency to avarice should have been put in charge of the common purse. But that kind of question appears to have less importance to the evangelist than attempting to place the 'betrayal' that is to follow within the foreknowledge of both God the incarnate Son, and God the Father who sent Him into the world. In doing so John has added a fifth identifying 'label' to Judas, this one unique to his Gospel: thief. This tag points the reader of the Gospel to an explanation of Judas' actions in terms of his character. It does nothing, however, to answer the difficult questions relating to providence arising from John's pre-passion material; such as how Jesus, characterized by foreknowledge, could have chosen a 'devil' as 'one of the twelve'.

In Mark and Matthew, the parallel to John's account of the anointing forms an intercalation between the announcement of the chief priests' hostile intentions towards Jesus and their contact with Judas. In Luke 22.1-6 the two are linked straightforwardly. It is clear from all these accounts that the religious authorities were resolved upon the death of Jesus, and were able to utilise Judas in achieving this end. It will also be seen that, as in the Johannine material just discussed, there is a sense of the need to place the problematic actions of Judas within a scriptural and providential framework:

> **Matthew 26.14-16**
> Then one of the twelve, whose name was Judas Iscariot, went to the chief priests
> [15]and said, 'What will you give me if I *deliver* him over to you?' And they paid him thirty pieces of silver. [16]And from that moment he sought an opportunity to *betray* him.
> **Mark 14.10-11**
> Then Judas Iscariot, who was one of the twelve, went to the chief priests in order to *betray* him to them. [11]And when they heard it, they were glad and promised to give him money. And he sought an opportunity to *betray* him.
> **Luke 22.3-6**
> Then Satan entered into Judas called Iscariot, who was of the number of the twelve.
> [4]He went away and conferred with the chief priests and officers how he might *betray* him to them. [5]And they were glad, and agreed to give him money. [6]So he consented and sought an opportunity to *betray* him to them in the absence of a crowd.

In Mark 14.10-11 Judas approaches the chief priests in order that he might betray/hand over Jesus.[58] Nothing is said of his motivation. All that can inferred from the placing of the incident is that Judas may have shared the indignation of

---

57 John Marsh, *The Gospel of St John* (Middlesex: Penguin, 1968) p454.

58 The designation (literally 'the one of the twelve') is unusual. It may be there to indicate a reference to the list of disciples, to distinguish him from another Judas, to imply that he was the 'first' of the disciples; or it may simply be that the 'the' has lost its force in New Testament Greek.

those who objected to the waste of expensive ointment (14.4-5), though this is not explicitly stated. Neither is money obviously a motive, in that the chief priests (who were glad at his approach) do not offer a reward until after Judas has made his offer. From that time Judas seeks a suitable time or opportunity to hand Jesus over.

Matthew stays close to Mark, with the exception that Judas immediately receives payment of thirty pieces of silver. This is the amount of reparation required when an ox has gored a slave (Exodus 21.32), and the wages paid to the shepherd of a flock doomed to be slain (Zechariah 12b). The latter text and verses following are of particular importance to Matthew, as will be seen when discussing his account of the death of Judas (27.3ff). Here is seen the beginning of his apologetic use of Zechariah, given that being sold for money is not obviously the mark of a Messiah. Part of the significance of the use of such texts is to indicate that what happens to Jesus was anticipated in scripture, and that the actions of Judas, despite appearances, are indeed within the providence of God. Many commentators remark that the amount seems hardly sufficient of itself to explain Judas' actions; the point of the figure seems rather to be as a fulfilment of prophecy.[59] As to what was betrayed/handed over, it could hardly be the 'Messianic secret', as Judas from then on looks for an opportunity – presumably to divulge a place where Jesus could be arrested with minimum fuss.

Only in Luke is the plotting of the chief priests part of a unified account with the approach of Judas to them. Luke 'explains' Judas actions with fearsome simplicity: 'and Satan entered into Judas called Iscariot' (cf. John 13.2, 27). No explanation is made as to how this happened, however, or in what lay the particular susceptibility of Judas. Here for the first time Jesus contends with satanic possession amongst his immediate followers. According to Marshall this 'shows how more than human decisions were involved in the passion of Jesus; the early church could see no other explanation of what had happened.'[60] This is a strategy related to seeing Judas' actions as fulfilling scripture. What Judas does is difficult to account for within the Gospel framework, and potentially undermining to its purposes, and so the role of Satan is seen as an explanatory device. A device, however, which raises questions about the possibility of Satan defeating God's purposes. Portraying what Judas does as 'fulfilment' serves to negate this possibility, as will be seen in the next section.

---

[59] For example Filson argues that the amount 'hardly suggests greed for money' and 'fulfilment of prophecy held more interest for Matthew than financial profit' (op cit. p272). H. Benedict Green comments that the passage 'offers no clue to Judas' motive', (*The Gospel according to Matthew*, New Clarendon Bible, Oxford: Clarendon, 1975, p210).

[60] Howard Marshall, *The Gospel of Luke – A commentary on the Greek text* (Exeter: The Paternoster Press, 1978) p788.

1.4 Fulfilment and woe: Judas' participation in the Last Supper

The issue of providence has already arisen a number of times in examining Gospel texts relating to Judas. None, however, raise the issue as starkly as the synoptic 'better unborn' saying delivered in the context of the last supper. To put this in context, reading Mark's Gospel shows that the writer is not concerned so much with providing any motivation for Judas, but that here scripture is beginning to be fulfilled. At 9.31 and 10.33 (cf. Matthew 17.22 and 20.18) he has predicted that the Son of Man will be delivered/betrayed without any reference to Judas. To Schweizer this suggests the 'interplay of human action and divine predestination' and that Judas' guilt must not 'be measured according to moral standards alone'.[61] To illustrate these points he offers the analogy of a wild horse whose wildness is able to serve an experienced rider without being removed or excused. This is once again an assertion that the unexpected or 'wild' action of Judas can be contained within God's providential purposes. It is at variance with Mark's narrative, however, in that Mark gives the impression that Judas is not so much 'wild', as acting as he must do if scripture is to be fulfilled. Despite this, Judas does seem to be judged in moral terms at 14.21 ('...woe to that man...' as below).[62]

D.A. Carson has shown that the 'interplay' that Schweizer describes, between predestination and action, or between divine sovereignty and human responsibility, is a juxtaposition more easily stated than explained. He uses the same word to describe the way in which this interplay manifests itself in biblical texts, as I have done in relation to providence and tragedy: tension. He argues that 'a fair treatment of the biblical data leaves the sovereignty-responsibility tension restless in our hands', and that the temptation is always to reductionism, which never solves the tension, 'only changes its shape'.[63] This tension or interplay comes to the fore again in Mark 14.17-21 and parallels, when Jesus meets with his disciples to eat the Passover meal:

Matthew 26.20-25

When it was evening, he reclined at table with the twelve. [21]And as they were eating, he said, 'Truly, I say to you, one of you will *betray* me.' [22]And they were

61 Eduard Schweizer, *The Good News according to Mark* (John Knox, 1970) p293.

62 The difficulties pointed to in understanding the interplay between Jesus' predictions and Judas's actions unfortunately often receive less attention in commentaries than speculation about Judas' motivation. Rawlinson is a good example in that he correctly states that 'Nothing is said in Mark as to the motives of the betrayer' and then immediately spends fourteen lines discussing what these motives might be and just what Judas betrayed. (A.E.J. Rawlinson, *St Mark*, Westminster Commentary, Methuen, fourth edition, 1936, p199).

63 D.A. Carson *Divine Sovereignty and Human Responsibility – Biblical perspectives in tension* (London: Marshall Pickering, 1994) p220. Thomas L. Brodie also senses the difficulties involved, writing 'the mystery of the interaction between [Judas'] freedom and the plan of salvation is as complex ultimately as the similar mystery surrounding the fate of Judaism as a whole...'. (*The Gospel According to John – A Literary and Theological Commentary*, New York: Oxford University Press, 1993, p454).

> very sorrowful and began to say to him one after another, 'Is it I, Lord?' [23]He answered, 'He who has dipped his hand in the dish with me will *betray* me. [24]The Son of Man goes as it is written of him, but woe to that man by whom the Son of Man is *betrayed*! It would have been better for that man if he had not been born.' [25]Judas, who would betray him, answered, 'Is it I, Rabbi?' He said to him, 'You have said so.'
>
> **Mark 14.17-21**
>
> And when it was evening, he came with the twelve. [18]And as they were reclining at table and eating, Jesus said, 'Truly, I say to you, one of you will *betray* me, one who is eating with me.' [19]They began to be sorrowful and to say to him one after another, 'Is it I?' [20]He said to them, 'It is one of the twelve, one who is dipping bread into the dish with me. [21]For the Son of Man goes as it is written of him, but woe to that man by whom the Son of Man is *betrayed*! It would have been better for that man if he had not been born.'
>
> **Luke 22.19-22**
>
> And he took bread, and when he had given thanks, he broke it and gave it to them, saying, 'This is my body, which is given for you. Do this in remembrance of me.' [20]And likewise the cup after they had eaten, saying, 'This cup that is poured out for you is the new covenant in my blood. [21]But behold, the hand of him who *betrays* me is with me on the table. [22]For the Son of Man goes as it has been determined, but woe to that man by whom he is *betrayed*!'

The first words Jesus speaks at table are a prediction of betrayal/handing over by one of those at table with him. Rawlinson argues convincingly that

> ...the interest of the earliest Church in our Lord's anticipation of betrayal, as in the predictions ascribed to Him in general, was largely apologetic and doctrinal. It was part of the preaching of the Gospel to maintain that Jesus had not been taken by surprise, as also that all things had happened in accordance with the *determinate counsel and foreknowledge of God* (Acts 2.23).[64]

Jesus' discernment is contrasted with the lack of it in the disciples, each wondering if he might be the one (though the form of the question is such that the answer 'no' would be expected). Clarification is offered by Jesus in a way by now familiar to the reader – it is 'one of the twelve', moreover (and this is new), 'one who is eating with me... one who is dipping bread in the same dish as me.' (Mark 14.18, 20; cf. Matthew 26.23) The implication is that the disciples were indeed 'surprised' by the actions of Judas, and that the constant attempts to place these actions within the foreknowledge of God witnesses to their problematic nature.

Commentators usually relate Mark 14.18-20 to Psalm 41.9: 'Even my bosom friend in whom I trusted, who ate of my bread, has lifted his heel against me.' It is new to the disciples, not that Jesus is to be handed over, but that it is one of their number who will do it. It is precisely that he is 'one of the twelve' that heightens the discordant note Judas brings to the narrative. What follows next in verse 21 is one of the key, and most difficult, texts about Judas in relation to Jesus:

---

[64] Ibid. p202.

> 'For the Son of Man goes as it is written of him, but woe to that man by whom the Son of Man is *betrayed!* It would have been better for that man if he had not been born'.

This text is harder to place in terms of a specific Old Testament reference. This is despite the fact that it deals with the Son of Man going 'as it is written of him'. What is clear is the statement that the Son of Man will follow a path that has a definite purpose in the will of God, as has been foretold. The saying indicates Jesus' foreknowledge and stature, setting in stark contrast the words of rejection that end it. What is not clear is the role of the one who is to hand over/betray. He is apparently bound up with the fulfilment of God's purposes, yet woe is upon him, and he would have been better unborn. The difficulty inherent in the saying is its paradoxicality – if Judas had not been born, the Son of Man would apparently no longer go 'as it is written of him'. Here is highlighted the problematic aspect of interpreting Judas' actions as prophesied in the Old Testament, and so showing them to be part of God's plan. The consequence of this apologetic approach is that Judas' actions come to be seen as necessary and unavoidable, yet leading to condemnation. Asserting the providence of God involves an uncomfortable tension with injustice or even tragedy. As John Drury observes, the two parts of Mark 14.21 offer 'the two opposing insights which together grip our minds in the face of tragedy: that fate is irresistible and that nevertheless we are culpable.'[65]

The standard line taken by many commentaries is that 'the plan and working of God do not exclude freedom and responsibility.'[66] The opening paragraphs of this section indicate such general statements are unlikely to do justice to the tension between divine sovereignty and human freedom found in such passages as Mark 14.21 and parallels. Derrett is a rare exception when he writes of 'the intellectual and moral difficulties' aroused by 'an apparently implausible paradox'.[67] To spell it out, the paradox lies in that the hander over/betrayer seems to be an essential part of the economy of salvation, and also on the receiving end of words of extreme harshness. It may be that 'that man' can be read as representative of humanity generally.[68] However, this in no way reduces the severity of the words which clearly refer to Judas in the first instance.

While the 'better unborn' sayings are found only in the synoptics, there is a text in John that is its theological equivalent (although commentators tend to overlook this fact). It occurs in Jesus' farewell discourse in Chapter 17, where,

---

65 Essay on Luke in *The Literary Guide to the Bible*, edited by Robert Alter and Frank Kermode (London: Fontana Press, 1989) p437.

66 Filson op cit. p274. See also H. Benedict Green, op cit. p212 and the comments of Schweizer at the beginning of this section on 'the interplay of human action and divine predestination.'

67 Derrett, op cit. p2.

68 Cf. earlier 'Son of Man' sayings which describe the conflict between him and sinful people. A good example is Mark 9.31, 'The Son of Man is going to be *delivered* into the hands of men, and they will kill him.'

speaking of the people his Father has given him 'out of the world' (verse 6) Jesus prays as follows (17.12):

> While I was with them, I kept them in your name, which you have given me. I have guarded them, and not one of them has been lost except the son of destruction, that the Scripture might be fulfilled.

The claim here is that Jesus has 'guarded' or 'kept' those entrusted to him safe (cf. 12.25 'whoever hates life in this world will keep it for eternal life'). There is, however, an exception – the one described here as the 'son of destruction.' As used in the New Testament, this means damnation or eschatological perdition. Other examples of the Greek word here translated 'destruction' include Acts 8.20 where Peter, travelling in Samaria, says to the magician Simon, 'Your silver *perish* with you, because you thought you could obtain the gift of God with money!' and Matthew 7.13, which speaks of the wide gate and easy way 'that leads to *destruction*'.

'Son of destruction' (or 'perdition') is a Semitic expression that also occurs at 2 Thessalonians 2.3. The chapter is concerned with 'the coming of our Lord Jesus Christ and our assembling to meet him' (2.1). A sign that the day has come will be the revealing of the 'man of lawlessness... the son of destruction... [who] takes his seat in the temple of God, proclaiming to be God' (2.3-4). John's language is low-key compared to 2 Thessalonians, however, as the latter proclaims that the Lord Jesus will 'slay him with the breath of his mouth and destroy him by his appearing' (2.8). John simply says that he is 'lost... that the Scripture might be fulfilled.' The effect, however, is similar. Jesus' first coming means being lost and destroyed for Judas. That this is so strengthens the possibility that John understood Judas as in some sense an incarnation of the evil powers opposed to him.

As with the synoptics 'better unborn' sayings, we do not learn of any particular text of scripture that John may or may not have in mind. It could be something like Psalm 41.9, a text which will shortly be discussed in relation to the last supper, but alighting upon a particular text is not as significant as appreciating that John's appeal to the fulfilment of scripture indicates his apologetic concern to show that, in the words of Lindars, 'Jesus' "mistake" in choosing Judas was not due to ignorance of his real character, but was intentional, so that "scripture might be fulfilled." '[69] The poignancy of the situation is brought out by referring to John

---

[69] Barnabas Lindars, *New Testament Apologetic* (London: SCM, 1961) p109. Hoskyns relates John 17.12 to 1 John 2.19: 'They went out from us, but they were not of us; for if they had been of us, they would have continued with us.' He argues that because many in the early church 'apostasized' and returned to the world, Judas was somehow 'typical' and the source of encouragement because his actions had not occurred through lack of vigilance by Jesus, and so nor were remaining church members to blame for the actions of former Christians (*The Fourth Gospel*, edited by Francis Noel Davey, London: Faber, 1940/revised 1947, p501). Even if some did find encouragement in such a text as John 17.12, this is hardly an adequate reading of it, or of John's overall

6.39 (which commentators usually fail to do) where, in his discourse on the 'bread of life', Jesus proclaims that 'this is the will of him who sent me, that I should lose nothing of all that he has given me, but raise it up on the last day.' There are no exceptions mentioned here. No one is to be lost in order to fulfil scripture. And yet by 6.70 Jesus already speaks of one of his disciples as a 'devil' and then at 17.12 the apparent failure to fulfil God's will as perceived in 6.39 is spelt out, for 'none of them is lost except the son of destruction...'. John's language emphasises the gravity of Judas' fate, which indicates that he is damned. John 17.12 indicates that this is within the providence of God, but this is in tension with John 6.39.

A double question remains, revolving around both the justice of someone 'lost' in order to fulfil scripture, and the internal dissonance within John's Gospel indicated by a comparison of the two verses just identified. There is no question that the 'son of destruction' refers to Judas, just as it is clear that the 'better unborn' sayings refer to Judas, although only Matthew explicitly names him at that point. In Matthew's account of the last supper, Judas calls Jesus 'Rabbi', so distinguishing himself from the rest of the disciples who have called him 'Lord'.[70] The force of Jesus' reply, 'You have said so', is not entirely clear in the Greek, though his use of the phrase three times in the passion narrative helps to some extent (here at 26.25, and subsequently at 26.54 and 27.11). The second two references are in relation to questions put by Caiaphas and Pilate respectively concerning his status as 'Son of God' and 'King of the Jews.' In both cases the answer could have been 'yes' but for the particular context . Quite why Jesus does not say 'yes' in response to Judas' 'Is it I, Rabbi?' has inevitably been the source of speculation amongst commentators. One interesting example comes from H. Benedict Green who argues that

> ...the effect of an affirmative answer would have been to exonerate Judas, since his betrayal of Jesus would then only be adherence to a course of action infallibly predicted by the Lord himself. The prediction is correct, but it is the voluntary action of Judas that will make it so.[71]

Presumably Green means that Judas' question should be taken at face value (i.e. it is a genuine question) and that a 'yes' would be saying to Judas, 'this is what you are to do.' Against this, however, can be cited John 13.27, where Jesus in fact says something like this to Judas ('What you are going to do, do quickly') without there being any sense of exoneration.

The Johannine narrative of the last supper contains much that is different to the synoptics, although it does agree that such a meal took place the night before

---

portrayal of Judas within the Gospel narrative. There is nothing typical about one apparently chosen to play a crucial yet personally disastrous role in Christ's mission.

70 Jesus has spoken against the use of 'Rabbi' at 23.8 in the midst of strong criticism of the scribes and pharisees; it may be that Judas' use of it here implicitly links him with the Jewish religious leaders.

71 Op cit. p212.

the crucifixion, during which Jesus predicted his betrayal/handing over – and, importantly, on the fulfilment of scripture with reference to Judas. Amongst the differences are the lack of an institution of the Eucharist, the narrative of the footwashing, and the fact that the supper takes place on the day before the Passover rather than the Passover itself. As far as Judas is concerned, John builds on the characterisation found earlier in his Gospel, particularly with regard to the satanic influence on a member of Jesus' disciples. Chapter 13 begins with Jesus' recognition that his 'hour had come' and that 'the devil had already put it into the heart of Judas Iscariot, Simon's son to *betray* him' (vv 1 and 2 respectively):

> Now before the Feast of the Passover, when Jesus knew that his hour had come to depart out of this world to the Father, having loved his own who were in the world, he loved them to the end. [2]During supper, when the devil had already put it into the heart of Judas Iscariot, Simon's son, to *betray* him… .

Jesus' words of love for his disciples in general contrasts sharply with what is then said of one of them, a disparity that runs through the chapter. Judas is referred to or named in verses 2, 11, 18, and 21-30. He is there for the footwashing, and as with the last supper in the synoptics, there is no suggestion that he is excluded in any way.[72] He then leaves before the new commandment to 'love one another' (13.34) is given. Verse 2 is reminiscent of 6.70, where Jesus stated that 'one of you is a devil.'[73] Verse 10 records Jesus' response to Peter's saying about having not just his feet washed, but his head and hands also: 'he who has bathed does not need to wash... he is clean all over; and you are clean, but not all of you'. Clearly this is a reference to Judas, and yet John apparently needs to emphasize the point in verse 11: 'For he knew who was to *betray* him; that was why he said, "Not all of you are clean." '

The washing has evidently made no significant difference to Judas. Satan's influence remains. Given John's emphasis on Jesus' stature and power, this seems significant, and yet John offers no comment. The importance of the issue is indicated by its discussion in subsequent tradition, as will be highlighted in Chapter 3. Barrett senses something of this in commenting that 'Judas has been washed with the other disciples; all possibility therefore of a merely mechanical operation of salvation, whether by baptism or otherwise, is excluded.' This gloss, however, cannot be said to deal with the question of how it is that Satan is apparently able to influence Judas in a way undisturbed by Jesus' powerful act of footwashing. For such is the implication given the way John has chosen to characterize Judas. All Barrett can say is that 'Judas' feet were washed, but he did

---

72 The reason for noting this is that the Christian tradition came to dispute this inclusion at some points, with associated arguments relevant to this book – as will be seen in Chapter 3.

73 Barrett argues that it should be translated, 'The devil had already made up his mind that Judas should betray him [Jesus]', on the grounds that understanding the name of Judas as a genitive is a 'simplifying gloss' op cit. p439.

not enter into the meaning of Jesus' act of humility and love'.[74] Brodie comments that, 'just as the washing failed to cleanse him, so did the food fail, and [Judas] turned it instead, as one can turn almost anything good, into an occasion of evil.'[75]

The nature of both the incarnation and the sacrament is at issue in the text. Should Jesus be understood as knowing all things, and cleansing all things, or is this a form of docetism shown up when Jesus' relationship with Judas is focused on? The significance of Judas remaining unclean is only strengthened in significance by agreement amongst most commentators that 'the washing of the disciples' feet rests upon and interprets the death of the Lord, and is not a detached action containing in itself a merely ethical lesson.'[76] This foreshadowing of the cross indicates what turns out to be the case, that Judas will be the sole disciple to be excluded from salvation, the only one to be 'lost' (17.12). Given his role in the passion in enabling Jesus to go 'as it is written' (as will shortly be seen, John articulates this in his own way) this exclusion is problematic. Judas, it seems, is either treated unjustly or is evidence of a salvific failure.

In John 13.14 Jesus says that his disciples should do as he, their Lord and Teacher, has done (similarly in verse 17: 'If you know these things, blessed are you if you do them'). At 13.18 John portrays Jesus as knowing clearly the situation with regard to Judas. He has not been speaking of all his disciples, for, 'I am not speaking of all of you; I know whom I have chosen. But the Scripture will be fulfilled, "He who ate my bread has lifted his heel against me." '

Taken by itself, this text has a startling aspect. It sounds as if Jesus, in his foreknowledge, has chosen Judas precisely in order to fulfil a scripture describing opposition by a compatriot. Barrett finds this hard to countenance, and offers two possible meanings. First, that Jesus knows whom he has chosen and Judas is not one of them. This is far-fetched in this context and a contradiction of 6.70 ('Did I not choose you, the twelve, and one of you is a devil?'). Barrett accepts that this is less likely than his second possibility: 'I know (the characters of) those whom I have chosen, and therefore know that Judas, though I have chosen him, will betray me'[77] But the latter avoids the full import of the text, which does not suggest that Judas will betray *despite* Jesus' choice, but rather that Judas has been chosen for what he will do, as this will fulfil scripture.

John is clearly seeking to stress Jesus' foreknowledge, and so ensure faith in him, as is emphasized by the next verse, 'I tell you this now, before it takes place, that when it does take place you may truly believe that I am he' (verse 19). This can only be done, however, by making the betrayal/handing over an

---

74 Ibid. p442.

75 Thomas L. Brodie, *The Gospel According to John – A Literary and Theological Commentary* (New York: Oxford University Press, 1993) p454.

76 Edwyn Hoskyns, *The Fourth Gospel*, op cit. p437. See also, as further examples, Barrett: '...the washing of the disciple's feet, which prefigures the crucifixion itself... points the way to the interpretation of the crucifixion' (op cit. p436) and Leon Morris *The Gospel according to St John*, revised (Grand Rapids, Michigan: Eerdmans, 1995) pp544-5.

77 Op cit. p444.

apparently necessary act for which Judas has been chosen. The scripture quoted is, as in the synoptics, Psalm 41.9, seemingly rewritten as its Johannine form is identical neither to the Hebrew or the Septuagint.[78]

In verse 21 the handing over/betrayal is referred to explicitly, as it was in verse 3. This time, however, the tone is different:

> After saying these things, Jesus was troubled in his spirit, and testified, "Truly, truly, I say to you, one of you will *betray* me."

The emotional language is similar to that used to describe Jesus' reaction to the news of the death of Lazarus (11.33). Jesus is clearly making an important statement here as he does not simply speak but testifies or witnesses, introducing his words with the solemn 'Truly, truly'. Jesus' words here are almost identical with Mark 14.18 and Matthew 26.21, and on hearing them the disciples look at one another, 'uncertain of whom he spoke' (13.22). Simon Peter requests the 'beloved disciple' to ask Jesus who is being referred to, which he does: 'Lord, who is it?' Jesus answers as follows in verse 26 and 27:

> 'It is he to whom I will give this morsel of bread when I have dipped it.' So when he had dipped the morsel, he gave it to Judas, the son of Simon Iscariot. [27] Then after he had taken the morsel, Satan entered into him. Jesus said to him, 'What you are going to do, do quickly.'

'Morsel' may or may not refer to bread; according to Barrett it would refer most naturally to the dipping of bitter herbs at a Passover meal, but as it is not yet the Passover the most that can be said is that John might be reflecting the earlier synoptic tradition. He comments further that it is 'plain from the narrative that the beloved disciple must have understood that Judas was the traitor. To say that he failed to grasp the meaning of the sign is to make him an imbecile. His subsequent inactivity is incomprehensible...'.[79] It is not clear what Barrett thinks the disciple might have done; in any event John does not refer to him again in this scene. That Satan should now enter into Judas is not entirely consistent either with 13.2 or 6.70, though perhaps it is significant that in those places he has used 'devil' rather than 'Satan' as here. The implication is an intensifying of evil.

Finally Jesus says to Judas, 'What you are going to do, do quickly.' The Greek could as well be rendered, 'Do what you are about to do' or 'do it more quickly' (than you are at the moment). It might seem strange that Christ does nothing to prevent Judas, indeed rather the reverse. But in the light of what has been said concerning Christ's choice of Judas at 13.18 it is perhaps not surprising that Judas is encouraged to fulfil the reason for his being chosen. This seems to be the overall tenor of Chapter 13. The only note against such a reading is the way

---

78 On the use of the Psalm, Hoskyns writes, 'The metaphor of lifting the heel is that of the sudden kick of a horse' (op cit. p441). Barrett prefers 'the action of one who shakes off the dust off his feet against another' (op cit. p445).

79 Ibid. p447.

Jesus is 'troubled in spirit' in verse 21. This can be read either as a hint that perhaps Jesus' foreknowledge was not as complete as John indicates elsewhere, or that Jesus was troubled by the prospect of imminent suffering.

Judas, possessed by Satan, nevertheless immediately obeys Jesus and leaves the meal. John writes that none at the table understood Jesus' words, some thinking that as Judas had the money box he had been instructed either to buy something for the coming feast or to give something to the poor. These thoughts might have reminded them of the incident when Judas challenged Mary's anointing of Jesus with costly ointment (12.2-8). Certainly the reader is reminded of the way John has sought to characterize Judas, who, after receiving the morsel, 'immediately went out. And it was night.'

This 'night' may well be historical, but at least as important is its symbolic import. This is the night that will end Jesus' work (cf. 9.4 'night comes, when no one can work' and 12.35 'Walk while you have the light, lest the darkness overtake you'). Hoskyns suggests that '...Judas is banished from the light, and passes out into the darkness under the judgement of God.'[80] This 'night' will seal the fate of both Jesus and Judas, bound together as they seemingly are 'in order that scripture may be fulfilled' (13.18). They are to meet once more, in the garden across the Kidron valley (18.1) where Jesus will lead his disciples from the supper table. Before then, Jesus will mention Judas just once, during the farewell discourse or prayer of chapter 17 that has already been discussed.

1.5 Gethsemane – encountering Judas

All the texts examined so far have wrestled with interpreting Judas' actions in handing over Jesus. The difficulties involved in such interpretation have by now been well rehearsed, so much so that the texts dealing with the handing over itself do not raise any fresh issues, as will be seen in the exegesis of this section. This does not imply that the accounts are straightforward (e.g. the significance of the kiss recorded in the synoptic Gospels is hard to assess), but this is not surprising given that the actions they record are precisely those that the New Testament writers have been struggling to interpret thus far.

Matthew (26.36) and Mark (14.32) indicate that after the supper Jesus went with his disciples to a place called Gethsemane. In Luke (22.39) the location is described as the Mount of Olives, in John (18.1) as a garden across the Kidron valley. Matthew and Mark describe Jesus praying three times. He is 'sorrowful and troubled' at Matthew 26.37b and 'greatly distressed and troubled' at Mark 14.33b. After the third time he returns to his disciples and says 'Are you still sleeping and taking your rest?' followed by:

---

80 Op cit. p443. (Cf. John 3.19 'And this is the judgement: the light has come into the world, and people loved the darkness rather than light because their deeds were evil').

Matthew 26.45b
'See, the hour is at hand, and the Son of Man is *betrayed* into the hands of sinners.'
Mark 14.41b
'It is enough; the hour has come. The Son of Man is *betrayed* into the hands of sinners.'

Both Matthew and Mark mention the 'hour', which is 'at hand' and 'come' respectively. Now is the Son of Man given over/betrayed 'into the hands of sinners'. Here is the fulfilment of Mark 14.21 and Matthew 26.24 ('the Son of Man goes as it is written of him, but woe to that man by whom the Son of man is *betrayed!*'). Both use the passive voice of παραδίδωμι, which, as Holleran observes, 'emphasizes not only that Jesus is delivered up by one of his own disciples (14.21) but also that he is delivered according to God's design, since the "reverential passive" is often used absolutely in place of the active voice with the divine name.'[81] The passive, therefore, adds to the use of παραδίδωμι in connoting the providence of God. Tödt writes that the 'one who subordinates his will to the Father's will is in so doing delivered into the hands of sinners. The one who is not overwhelmed by the power of darkness is delivered up by God.'[82]

Much commentary space is given over to the possible meanings of the Greek word ἀπέχει in Mark 14.41, here rendered 'It is enough', for which there is no obvious translation.[83] Nearly every suggestion, being necessarily speculative, is conditioned by the dramatic context in which the word is found. Brown's comment on his suggestion, 'The money is paid', can speak for many: 'I have no assurance that this is right, but it does fit in with the immediacy of what follows.'[84]

---

81 J. Walter Holleran *The Synoptic Gethsemane – a critical study* (Roma: Universita Gregoriana Editrice, 1973) p63. This description should be understood in the light of the work of Daube and Derrett discussed earlier.

82 H.E. Tödt, *The Son of Man in the Synoptic Tradition* (London: SCM, 1965) p200.

83 It may be that Matthew omitted the word because he too failed to understand it. It means something like 'have from' (being a compound of the verb 'to have' with the preposition 'from'), or alternatively 'avoid, be distant from'. Exegetes vary in their translations between supplying a subject, most commonly Judas, and the generality exemplified by Jerome in the Vulgate and repeated in the English Standard Version of the Bible and elsewhere: 'It is enough.' It is not necessary for the purposes of this book even to summarise all the scholarly suggestions, which range from mistranslation from Aramaic to scribal misreading. There can be no certainty about any of them.

84 Op cit. p1383. Of interest here are those who suggest Judas as the subject for ἀπέχει, on the grounds that it usually has a personal meaning which is justly supplied by the context. De Zwaan's translation begins 'Judas did receive the promised money. The hour is come, the Son of Man is betrayed...' (de Zwaan, J 'The Text and Exegesis of Mark xiv.41 and the Papyri' *Expositor*, 6th series, 12, 1905, p470. See also E.A. Smisson, 'Mark xiv.41: apechei' *The Expository Times* 40, 1928-29, p528) Boobyer builds on this with reference to the six occasions in the New Testament that forms of ἀπέχει have the meaning 'to receive', as in Philemon 15 ('that you might *receive* him...'). Arguing that ἀπέχει must be related to the handing over and arrest that is shortly to occur, he considers that the word must have the same subject; that is, Judas. As Philemon concerns the receiving of one person by another, so here Judas is about to

Both Matthew (26.46) and Mark (14.42) continue with, 'Rise, let us be going, see, my *betrayer* is at hand'.) In Mark they are the last words Jesus speaks to his disciples, in Matthew the last spoken before the resurrection. In both Matthew 26.46 and Mark 14.42 the form of παραδίδωμι has a different sense from the previous verse, here indicating the agent of the said 'giving over'. At the corresponding point in Luke the word is not used. There the disciples are asked to 'Rise and pray that you may not enter into temptation' (Luke 22.46b). There is no mention of the approach of Judas, as in Matthew and Mark. Nor are the disciples reproved for being asleep. They are simply enjoined to pray; for Luke the only adequate response in such a time of difficulty. In that Gospel, therefore, the 'hour' is primarily not that of Judas' actions (as it is for Matthew), but of prayer. In Luke alone a strengthening angel appears to Jesus (22.43), whose anguish is correspondingly less than the portrayal of lonely resolve in Mark, which in turn is only marginally softened in Matthew. In John there is little sign of internal struggle. Conflict is hinted at in 16.33 – '...be of good cheer, I have conquered the world' – and in Chapter 18 Jesus faces Judas and the accompanying 'band' with greater confidence even than in Luke.

Jesus' encounter with Judas is found in all four Gospels, but as has been seen, prior to their accounts of this meeting there has been much variation in the information given about this 'one of the twelve.' Neither Mark nor Luke mention the name of the deliverer/betrayer in their portrayal of the last supper. None of the synoptics mention anyone leaving, or say anything specific about either the inclusion or exclusion of Judas in the events described. All three mention money but only Matthew gives an exact sum (26.15), the amount being relevant to his later account of Judas' death. Matthew and John both identify Judas in the last supper, and it is clear in both that Jesus knows the identity of the one who will do the 'handing over'. John shares with Luke the ascription of satanic influence on Judas, and has a longer description of Jesus' prediction of the delivering up/betrayal than any of the synoptics (as well as more references to money).

Brown argues that a 'mysterious, villainous figure' like Judas must have generated 'folkloric tales' that influenced the Gospels.[85] However plausible this may be (and his use of 'mysterious' is more justified than 'villainous'), the nature of such material remains speculation; it cannot be known precisely how the Gospel writers arrived at their accounts. Certainly John attempts a fuller account of Judas than the synoptics by, for example, recording Judas' departure from the supper. Yet he, unlike the synoptics, has not described any previous meeting with the

---

receive or even 'possess' Jesus. Therefore Boobyer offers the following translation: 'Still resting? He is taking possession of (me)! The hour has come...' (G.H. Boobyer, 'APECHEI in Mark 14.41' *New Testament Studies 2*, 1955-56, p48). Such a translation, or that of de Zwaan, while impossible to conclusively disprove, is clearly open to the criticism of finding rather too much in ἀπέχει than is evident from the passage as a whole. Both also depend on finding a meaning in the context of the passion narrative, when at least some critical opinion argues that 'the Gethsemane account may have been altogether independent of its present context...' (Holleran, op cit. p56).

85 Brown, op cit. p242.

Jewish authorities to account for the apparent speed with which Judas is able to procure 'a band of soldiers and some officers from the chief priests and the Pharisees' (John 18.3).

At the beginning of Chapter 18, John describes Jesus and his disciples entering the 'garden' across the Kidron valley, immediately (without any prayer) encountering 'Judas, who *betrayed* him', who 'also knew the place, for Jesus often met there with his disciples'.[86] At verse 5 Jesus, in the face of the lanterns and weapons, identifies himself as the one they seek. Judas, who is not the leader of the band he has procured (they have a 'captain' [18.12]), has no particular role once the garden and Jesus have been located. Not even required to identify Jesus, the last words about him in John are simply 'Judas, who *betrayed* him, was standing with them' (18.5). With these words of passive complicity Judas passes out of John's account.

In the synoptics, Judas arrives as Jesus is speaking. In Mark, Jesus says that his 'hour has come', his betrayer is 'at hand', and 'immediately, while he was till speaking, Judas came' – verses 14.41, 42 and 43 respectively. The 'hour' for Mark is therefore apparently not quite identical with the handing over, for it has begun before the 'betrayer' has arrived. In the parallel passage in Matthew 26.45 and 46 the words are 'at hand' are repeated, suggesting that the Matthean 'hour' is that of the handing over, for the 'hour' and Judas are described in identical fashion.

At Mark 14.41b Jesus' words, 'The Son of Man is *betrayed* into the hands of sinners' strike an eschatological and universal note;[87] now at 14.42 they refer to a particular person: '...see, my *betrayer* is at hand.' The passive is used once again, with the implication that even here Judas is part of God's purposes.[88] The encounter between Jesus and Judas is described thus:

Matthew 26.47-50

While he was still speaking, Judas came, one of the twelve, and with him a great crowd with swords and clubs, from the chief priests and the elders of the people. 48Now the *betrayer* had given them a sign, saying, 'The one I will kiss is the man; seize him.' 49And he came up to Jesus at once and said, 'Greetings, Rabbi!' And he kissed him. 50Jesus said to him, 'Friend, do what you came to do.' Then they came up and laid hands on Jesus and seized him.

Mark 14.43-46

And immediately, while he was still speaking, Judas came, one of the twelve, and with him a crowd with swords and clubs, from the chief priests and the scribes and

86 The reference to the journey across the Kidron is reminiscent of II Samuel 15.23 where David flees from Jerusalem 'across the brook Kidron' having been deserted by his trusted counsellor Ahitophel. David proceeds to the Mount of Olives where, unlike the Johannine Jesus, he weeps and prays to God, indicating that the passage forms part of the background to the synoptic accounts also.

87 Holleran, op cit. p67.

88 It is also worth noting that the form of παραδίδωμι is identical to John's last reference to Judas as quoted above.

the elders. [44]Now the *betrayer* had given them a sign, saying, 'The one I will kiss is the man. Seize him and lead him away under guard.' [45]And when he came, he went up to him at once and said, 'Rabbi!' And he kissed him. [46]And they laid hands on him and seized him.

Luke 22.47-48, 54a

While he was still speaking, there came a crowd, and the man called Judas, one of the twelve, was leading them. He drew near to Jesus to kiss him, [48]but Jesus said to him, 'Judas, would you *betray* the Son of Man with a kiss?'

[54]Then they seized him and led him away, bringing him into the high priest's house, and Peter was following at a distance.

All the Gospels agree that Judas came with a group hostile to Jesus (though not on the exact makeup of that group), which had gathered quickly once darkness had fallen. They agree that Jesus needed identifying, even though he announces himself in John. At Mark 12.12 it is stated that the chief priests and scribes 'were seeking to arrest [Jesus], but feared the people'. At Mark 14.1 'the chief priests and scribes were seeking how to arrest him by stealth and kill him...' (this and the previous text is paralleled in Matthew and Luke). Now, through the agency of Judas, this is achieved. Judas' function is to guide the arresting party to the right place and then to identify Jesus. Though some question the plausibility of this, neither is obviously unreasonable. For example the accounts are clear that it was dark and Jesus was surrounded by disciples.

Here the reader is helped by understanding the primary meaning of παραδίδωμι as 'hand over', for it seems that here 'Judas gave Jesus over by making it possible to arrest him; there is no evidence he betrayed secrets.'[89] The identification, in the synoptics, is made through a kiss. In Mark the kiss is the focus of the narrative, being a prearranged signal. In Matthew, Judas announces the 'sign' there and then, before coming up to Jesus, greeting him, and kissing him. In Luke no signal is explicitly mentioned (indeed Judas does not speak at all, nor is it certain that the kiss actually takes place) but it is implied in what happens. Jesus mentions the kiss himself in the context of a question about the handing over of the 'Son of Man', thereby alluding to earlier predictions of the passion in 9.44, 18.31-2 and 22.22.

In Mark, the first word Judas speaks to Jesus is, 'Rabbi' (14.45). In the context of that Gospel the greeting is ordinary enough, while in Matthew the same word has different connotations. At 23.7 Jesus has criticised the use of 'Rabbi' as a title, and at 26.25 Judas is the only disciple at the last supper to refer to Jesus in this way (the others use 'Lord'). To the alert reader his use of 'Rabbi' at Gethsemane might indicate one already separated from the other disciples.[90]

The significance of the fact that identification is achieved through a kiss is hard to assess. Nowhere else in the Gospels are Jesus and his disciples recorded as exchanging a kiss. The 'kiss of peace' between Christians, and the kiss between

---

89 Brown, op cit. p751.

90 Further, his use of 'Greetings' to prefix it could seem ironic in that the Greek word used is derived from the verb 'to rejoice'.

Rabbi and pupil in Rabbinic Judaism, both developed later. If it were simply a normal greeting, that would fit with the attempt to arrest Jesus by stealth, without fuss. If, however, the kiss had implied special affection then Judas would seem to be acting disreputably.[91] Since the likelihood of one or the other is not known, there is little theological point in speculating on possible implications. In Luke, Jesus questions Judas' action ('Judas, would you *betray* the Son of Man with a kiss?'). He speaks to Judas by name, the only time this occurs in all four Gospels. The question can be read as a rebuke, as indicating surprise, or indeed as an 'implicit appeal for repentance'.[92] Luke's account is too brief to shed much light on which is the 'correct' reading; the reader does not even find out if the kiss was carried out (the text states only that Judas 'drew near').[93]

Both Matthew and Mark use the word κατεφίλησεν for the kiss, a more elaborate expression than that used by Luke. Brown comments that this usage is 'no more than vivid narrative',[94] but F.W. Belcher and others have speculated on its significance without being deterred by lack of scriptural evidence.[95] In Mark no response is recorded to Judas' kiss. Those supplied in Matthew and Luke 'would

---

91 Brown's 'malevolent hypocrite' (ibid. p255) is too strong for the context, however.

92 Ibid. p259.

93 The Codex Bezae has '...and having come near, he kissed Jesus. This one had given them a sign: 'Whomever I shall kiss, he is (the one).' Certainly this is one way of reducing the ambiguity in Luke, but equally clearly the Bezae text cannot be given priority here (cited in Brown, op cit. p258). Luke's understatement notwithstanding, it is likely that the gospel writers would have been aware that describing a moment of handing over/betrayal in the context of a kiss was powerfully dramatic, and would not have been altogether surprised that it has 'entered the repertory of Christian imagery' (ibid. p254). If they had meant the passage to be read in the light of Proverbs 27.6 ('Faithful are the wounds of a friend; profuse are the kisses of an enemy') this would undercut the downplaying of Judas' moral status in the previous paragraph, but as there is no direct reference to this text this cannot be known one way or the other.

94 Op cit. p253.

95 Belcher compares the use of κατεφίλησεν (Mark 14.45 and Matthew 26.49) and φιλῆσαι (Luke 22.47) in the Septuagint and New Testament, concluding that the 'former has a sense of intense emotion, while the latter lacks this quality' (F.W. Belcher, 'A Comment on Mark xiv.45', *The Expository Times*, May 1953, p240). Examples of κατεφίλησεν in the Septuagint include the departure of Orpah from Naomi (Ruth 1.14) and the meeting of David and Jonathan in 1 Samuel 20.41. In the New Testament Luke uses it in the parable of the prodigal son (15.20). Belcher's case is well made, but he goes beyond the texts in suggesting that Judas did not repent after Jesus' condemnation but at the moment of the kiss. He calls it a 'kiss of repentance' although there was 'such a conflict going on in Judas' mind that he could not retract from the deed...' (ibid. p257).
P.B. Emmet argues that Judas is worried about Jesus escaping in the darkness and confusion, and yet 'cannot bring himself to violently seize Jesus. And so with guile he goes up to Him as a friend, and puts his arms around Him kissing Him ardently, thus not only identifying Him but making it impossible for Him to escape without a struggle. The kiss is not a merely gratuitous addition to the treachery, but part of the deep-laid scheme to prevent the escape of Jesus.' (P.B. Emmet, 'St Mark xiv.45' *The Expository Times* 19, 1938-9, p93).

have the effect of countering any suggestion that Jesus did not know what Judas planned and thus safeguarding [his] exalted character'.[96] In Matthew 26.50, Jesus says words that have been much discussed without agreement as to their intent: 'Friend, do what you came to do'. The Greek word here usually translated 'friend' (Ἑταῖρε) is more straightforward than what follows. It means companion, partner or comrade; and this is the only time Jesus uses it (John 15.15, where he calls his disciples 'friends', uses a different word in Greek). There are, however, two previous uses in Matthew that help to explain its usage here. In the parable of the labourers in the vineyard, the householder responds to one of the grumblers by saying 'Friend, I am doing you no wrong' (20.13). And then in the parable of the marriage feast the king notices a man without a wedding garment and says to him 'Friend, how did you get in here...' (22.12) before having him cast out into the darkness. In both of these examples the individuals spoken to have failed to respond adequately to the situation, and the irony in the way they are addressed may be implicit in relation to Judas as well.[97]

The literal meaning of the Greek translated above as 'do what you came to do' is ambiguous, meaning something like 'for which you are here.' The difficulty is that the phrase is grammatically incomplete, and commentators cannot agree even on the sense in which this is so, let alone the precise wording that would make sense of the ambiguity.[98] In Brown's view the varying suggestions should not disguise the fact that the range of meaning is narrow. He rules out the possibility of a question, on the grounds that Jesus already knows why Judas is there, favouring an ironic interpretation over an inferred anger or sadness.[99] Deissmann, however, points out that the old Latin and Syriac versions have understood the words of Jesus as a question, and reckons that later rejection of this

---

96 Brown, op cit. p256.

97 It is also worth citing Psalm 55.12-13 (alongside Psalm 45.9, discussed earlier) as representative of the Old Testament dread of being attacked by a friend: 'It is not an enemy that taunts me – then I could bear it... But it is you, my equal, my companion, my familiar friend.' Brown raises the possibility of Sirach 37.2 ('Is it not a sorrow unto death when your companion and friend is turned enemy?') underpinning Matthew 26.38 ('My soul is very sorrowful, even to death...'), though his conjecture that it is Judas as friend turned enemy that is the main cause of Jesus' sorrow is surely incorrect (ibid. p257). Firstly, the cup (of suffering) of the next verse is a better candidate. Secondly, the use of psalms in the gospels is more to do with indicating that the events are in fulfilment of scripture (especially apologetically 'difficult' occurrences such as Judas' actions) than with reflecting Jesus' feelings.

98 The main suggestions are along the following lines: that the pronoun implies a non-existent antecedent (e.g. ' "that is the identifying kiss" for which you are here'); that the phrase is an aposiopesis (broken off in the middle because of the circumstances); that a verb or verbal construction needs to be supplied by the translator (the commonest suggestion being simply ' "do that" for which you are here'); the pronoun has the weight of an interrogative, making the phrase a question ('for what are you here?'); or a colloquialism meaning ('that's what you are here for').

99 Ibid. p1388.

is explained by the passing of those who had a feel for the living language of New Testament Greek in favour of those understanding was 'atticistic'.[100]

As so often in such discussions, Deissmann mixes technical argumentation with assumptions about what must (in his eyes) be going on in the passion narrative. In criticising translations other than his preferred 'Friend, wherefore art thou come?' he writes that

> ...one of the most genuine and wonderful words of the Saviour has fallen sacrifice to 'atticism'. It is an unintentional self-revelation of the one betrayed, which glitters as a last star before the traitor in the night of rejection: comrade, companion, friend has he yet called the one who has sunk to such depths! How can the Gospel of the Passion forego this human, this superhuman word unless it is absolutely necessary?[101]

However impassioned this may be, Deissman's reading clearly cannot be accepted on these grounds alone.[102] Brown's argument that a question is unlikely because Jesus already knows why Judas is there is no certainty either, especially his contention about ironic intent, but it does fit better with the overall narrative movement.

In John's Gospel the difficulty is not problematic texts regarding Judas, but that the one he has portrayed as a 'thief' does so little. How is the absence, for example, of any reference to a kiss to be interpreted? That John knew nothing of even so vivid a tradition? Or that he deliberately chose not to include it in his account? Certainly in John's passion narrative it is always Jesus that has the initiative, and the inclusion of Judas' action would have detracted from that. As has been pointed out, Jesus identifies himself; further, at 18.8 he asks for the disciples to be allowed to leave. This request is to 'fulfil the word that he had spoken, "of those whom you gave me I have lost not one" ' (18.9). This 'word' refers to 17.12: 'I have guarded them, and not one of them has been lost except the son of destruction, that the scripture might be fulfilled'. By implication Judas is included when 'they [the crowd] drew back and fell to the ground.' (18.6) Brown uses the inclusion to argue that the breadth of Jesus' power is being demonstrated here.[103] After all, Satan has entered into Judas (13.27) and the 'son of destruction' is described in 2 Thessalonians 2.4 as the one who exalts himself to the level of God. If the intention is to show even the 'prince of this world' prostrating himself before Jesus, such a portrayal is immediately undermined by the realisation that even such power, as incarnate in Christ, nevertheless falls short of being able to

---

100 Adolf Deissmann, 'Friend, wherefore art thou come' *The Expository Times* 33 (1921-1922) p491.

101 Ibid. p493.

102 His technical arguments are not helped by his addition (in a footnote) of a question mark to the Greek text, with no indication given that this is not to be found in any original manuscript.

103 Op cit. pp261-2.

save Judas Iscariot from being 'lost'. Or, once again, is it rather that Judas must bear such a fate so that 'scripture might be fulfilled'?

Finally, having rejected the violence of Peter, saying that he must drink the cup the Father has given him (18.11), Jesus is arrested and bound by the soldiers and the officers of the Jews (18.12). In Luke also it is at the end of the encounter in the garden that Jesus is seized (22.54). In Mark, however, Jesus has hands laid on him immediately following Judas' instructions and the kiss. In 14.44 Judas has stated that his kiss will identify the wanted man, who is to be seized and led away either 'securely' or 'safely' (the Greek could mean either). This ambiguity (found only in Mark) is perhaps symptomatic of the difficulty in fathoming Judas. Is Judas concerned for Jesus' safety, or simply that in no circumstances should he be allowed to escape? Or perhaps even something of both?

In Matthew 26.48 it is also Judas who issues an instruction ('seize him') and again Jesus has hands laid on him and is seized (26.50). In Matthew's Gospel alone the reader does not have to wait very long to find out what happens to Judas (27.3-10). John and Mark make no further reference to him; nor does Luke in his Gospel (though Acts 1.15-26 contains an account of Judas' death and the selection of his apostolic successor).

1.6 The death of Judas

Chapter 26 of Matthew's Gospel has Jesus make three prophecies concerning his disciples: that they would flee (v56), that Peter would deny Jesus three times (vv69-75), and that the one who handed over the Son of man would have been better unborn (v24). While all the synoptics agree on the fulfilment of the first two, only Matthew introduces material to do with Judas' death into the account of the 'handing over' of Jesus from the chief priests to Pilate. Three reasons can be adduced for this placing. Firstly, that Matthew wished to emphasize the connection between Judas' actions and his fate. Secondly, that to recount a suicide in the resurrection narratives would have been to strike a wrong note of negativity and failure. Thirdly, and arguably most importantly, describing Judas' death later in the narrative would bring it into close proximity with the death of Jesus, an association Matthew might not wish to encourage lest the two seem too closely bound up together in the economy of salvation. Luke, who does offer a rather different account of Judas' end, does so not at the end of his Gospel but at the beginning of the *Acts of the Apostles.*

Three verses (27.3-5) are sufficient for Matthew to tell what happens to Judas:

> Then when Judas, his *betrayer*, saw that Jesus was condemned, he changed his mind and brought back the thirty pieces of silver to the chief priests and the elders,
> 4saying, 'I have sinned by *betraying* innocent blood.' They said, 'What is that to us? See to it yourself.'
> 5And throwing down the pieces of silver into the temple, he departed, and he went and hanged himself.

The following five verses describe the chief priests' purchase of the potter's field with the returned silver, and will be discussed shortly. In the above the first thing to note is an omission: Judas is not referred to as 'one of twelve' as he was in Gethsemane. Here he is simply 'his *betrayer*', and has by implication placed himself outside the disciples. The realisation of Jesus' condemnation, however it occurred (the text is not explicit), has wrought a change in Judas. Once again something absent from the text is worthy of attention, for instead of the usual word for 'change of mind' or 'repentance' in the New Testament (μετάνοια) Matthew uses μεταμεληθεὶς. Matthew has used this word before (at 21. 29, 32) to describe the son who first says he will not obey his father and then changes his mind, and then the failure of the chief priests and elders to heed the message of John the Baptist. These uses do not indicate very clearly that μεταμεληθεὶς means something less than 'full' repentance, although Brown argues that it might.[104] Later writers divide on this matter, and those who argue that Judas' repentance was not genuine might take some encouragement from this untypical word. Abbott-Smith, however, says that any supposed distinction between μεταμεληθεὶς and μετάνοια is 'difficult to maintain by usage',[105] a view supported by the definitions found in Arndt and Gingrich as well as Danker.[106]

In context the meaning seems reasonably clear. Judas is so repentant that he goes away and hangs himself. Whether later writers are correct to attribute despair to Judas (as will be discussed in Chapter 5) is a moot point, however. He admits that he has 'sinned in *betraying* innocent blood', commenting only on his own sin, not that of the chief priests who have also 'handed Jesus over'. His statement focuses on Jesus' innocence rather than that he was Judas' rabbi. In this way he has witnessed to the chief priests concerning Jesus' lack of guilt, so challenging their actions, and has acknowledged his own guilt. As will be seen later in this book, many writers from at least Origen onwards are prepared to write favourably about Judas' actions here; though even more disagree, as will be seen. Matthew, however, states no more than has already been set down. He offers no comment on the acceptability or otherwise of Judas' penitence. The balance of evidence, however, must fall on the side of its unacceptability, for the verses cited may be seen as a fulfilment of Jesus' prophecy or curse of 26.24: 'Woe to that man by whom the Son of Man is betrayed...'. The picture of genuine repentance proving unacceptable to God alongside Judas' part in the economy of salvation is an uncomfortable one, however.

---

[104] Ibid. pp638-9.

[105] G. Abbott-Smith, *A Manual Greek Lexicon of the New Testament* (Edinburgh: T.&T. Clark, 1986) p287.

[106] Liddell and Scott translate the word Matthew uses (μεταμεληθεὶς) as 'repent at, change one's line of conduct' (op cit. p1114), while Arndt and Gingrich have 'regret, repent, change one's mind' (op cit. p511) and Danker 'be very sorry, regret, change one's mind' (Frederick William Danker, *A Greek-English lexicon of the New Testament and other early Christian literature* [based on Arndt and Gingrich, revised and edited by Danker], Chicago, London: University of Chicago Press, 2000) p639.

It is nevertheless true that what Judas repents of, the handing over of 'innocent blood', is a serious matter. The Hebrew understanding of the *masor* has been discussed earlier in the chapter, and indeed the verses under discussion here have resonances with many Old Testament texts. Examples include the death of Abel, where God says to Cain that 'now you are cursed from the ground, which has opened its mouth to receive your brother's blood from your hand' (Genesis 4.11).[107] Moreover this particular 'innocent' is acclaimed 'Son of God' by Roman soldiers before the end of the chapter (verse 54).

It cannot be known what Jesus might have said had Judas offered penitent words to him. The chief priests are certainly less than sympathetic. Their reply is so brief in the Greek that translations have to flesh it out: 'What [is that] to us? See [to it] yourself.'[108] Judas' response is dramatic. He throws down the pieces of silver in the temple/sanctuary and leaves.[109] Even more dramatically, Judas then goes off and hangs himself.[110] Some later writers have found this almost a noble act, but it seems unlikely that Matthew intended such a portrayal. His attitude is not explicit, though Brown points out that Matthew's final words about Judas contrast unfavourably with those about Peter at 26.75: 'And he went out and wept bitterly.'[111] It is often argued that the Hebrew attitude to suicide was that it was an unacceptable act towards the Creator God.[112] Malina and Rohrbach, however, argue that Judas hung himself as 'a public sign of repentance and to redress lost honor'.[113] Keener contends that 'Roman society, as well as many others in

---

107 Other examples include a Mosaic commandment at Deuteronomy 28.25 – 'Cursed be he who takes a bribe to slay an innocent person'; and God's judgement on Manasseh 'for the innocent blood that he had shed; for he filled Jerusalem with innocent blood, and the LORD would not pardon.' (2 Kings 24.4). See also Psalm 106.38-9; 1 Samuel 19.5; Jeremiah 7.6, 19.4, 22.3, 26.15.

108 Pilate speaks similarly at 27.24, saying, 'I am innocent of this man's blood; see to it yourselves.'

109 It is not certain if the reference is to the inner sanctuary, the treasury, or even the entire temple precinct. Certainly, however, Judas' action picks up Zechariah 11.13 (11.12 has been cited earlier with reference to its 'thirty shekels of silver'), where at God's command the shepherd of his flock says that he 'took the thirty shekels of silver and cast them into the foundry/treasury/to the potter in the house of the LORD.' The Septuagint has 'foundry', the Masoretic text 'potter' (which in Hebrew is close enough to 'treasury' for some scholars to state this as the meaning). This latter option is certainly closest to Matthew 27.6, but the resonance with Zechariah is clearly not dependent on this reading.

110 Matthew's language is similar to II Samuel 17.23, where Ahitophel (whose story has been referred to previously in sections six and nine), seeing that the revolt against David would fail, 'went off home to his own city. And he set his house in order, and hanged himself...'. The vocabulary for 'went off' and 'hanged himself' is the same in the Septuagint and Matthew.

111 Op cit. p644.

112 Brown cites the Mishna Sanhedrin 10.2 as arguing that Ahitophel has no place in the life to come (ibid. p644).

113 B.J. Malina and R.L. Rohrbaugh, *Social Scientific Commentary on the Synoptic Gospels* (Minneapolis: Fortress Press, 1992) p162.

Mediterranean antiquity, regarded suicide as an honorable and noble way to die, and in some circumstances many Jews in this period concurred.'[114]

That the chief priests consider the silver pieces 'blood money' (v6) and use it to buy a 'potter's field' (v7), anticipates the scripture attributed to Jeremiah in verses 10-11. Not suggested by that scripture is that the field is to 'bury strangers in' (v7) and known as the 'Field of Blood to this day' (v8), presumably because blood money has been used to purchase it. It therefore stands as a reminder of the innocent blood of Christ.[115]

Just as the death of Judas seems to have fulfilled Jesus' words at 26.24 ('The Son of Man goes as it is written of him...'), so Matthew wishes to show the theme of 'blood money' as fulfilling texts from Jeremiah. At 26.31 he cited Zechariah 13.7 as follows: 'I will strike the shepherd, and the sheep of the flock will be scattered.' This is placed in the mouth of Jesus following the last supper as he sets out with his disciples for the Mount of Olives, and is one example amongst fourteen where a 'fulfilment formula' is used. While the Zechariah citation is more or less accurate, however, the words used by Matthew at 27.9-10 (attributed to Jeremiah) cannot be found in the Old Testament: 'And they took the thirty pieces of silver, the price of him on whom a price had been set by some of the sons of Israel, and they gave them for the potter's field, as the Lord directed them.' Zechariah 11.13 comes closest, despite the Jeremiah attribution. Just why Matthew cites Jeremiah has been the subject of much writing, without any possibility of certainty on the matter.[116]

What is clear is that Matthew has gone to a lot of trouble in attempting to show that even these most difficult aspects of the passion, Judas' actions and those of the chief priests, had their place within the working out of God's purposes. Lindars emphasises the importance of the final phrase of the quotation ('as the Lord directed them'), however it has been arrived at. That the Lord has 'directed' is indicative of the demonstration 'that every detail of the known history of Judas was prefigured in Scripture, so that the whole falls into the divine plan'.[117]

---

[114] Craig S. Keener *A Commentary on the Gospel of Matthew* (Grand Rapids, Michigan: Eerdmans, 1999) p658.

[115] 'To this day' is a phrase often employed in the Hebrew Bible where place-names are explained, for example Beersheba at Genesis 26.33 and the Valley of Achor at Joshua 7.26. The phrase serves to indicate that the story comes from an early tradition. The name of the land indicates judgement on the one who delivered Jesus, and thereby that the actions of Judas do not invalidate Matthew's proclamation of Jesus as Messiah.

[116] It does seem that the quotation is a conglomeration, mainly taken from Zechariah but perhaps influenced by Jeremiah, particularly 32.9-14 ('And I bought the field at Anathoth from Hanamel my cousin, and weighed out the money to him, seventeen shekels of silver') which has no counterpart in Zechariah. Lindars argues that Matthew is using the work of an earlier exegete, and in arriving at his compound quotation has incorporated exegetical comment, even to the point where 'text and comment change places' (op cit. p120). Whether or not Lindars is entirely right, it does seem certain that complicated textual work has gone on in order to arrive at the quotation Matthew gives in 27.9-10.

[117] Ibid. p121.

Albright and Mann comment that, 'Matthew's purpose is not to provide information for the sensation monger, but once again to call attention to "fulfilment".'[118] Here, at the point where a tragic reading of Judas might seem the most appropriate, Matthew is at pains to attempt to place the events within the providence of God.

As has been seen, Matthew has consistently added to the Marcan passion narrative.[119] Now Matthew has an entire scene not found in Mark, a scene which clarifies his overall negative judgement on Judas. It now remains to examine the other New Testament narrative of Judas' death, namely Acts 1.16-20. These verses form part of Peter's speech to about 120 Christian brethren (that the amount is ten times the number of apostles is no coincidence), leading up to the selection of Matthias to take Judas' place amongst the apostles:

> 'Brothers, the Scripture had to be fulfilled, which the Holy Spirit spoke beforehand by the mouth of David concerning Judas, who became a guide to those who arrested Jesus. For he was numbered among us and was allotted his share in this ministry.' (Now this man bought a field with the reward of his wickedness; and falling headlong he burst open in the middle and all his bowels gushed out. And it became known to all the inhabitants of Jerusalem, so that the field was called in their language Akeldama, that is, Field of Blood.) 'For it is written in the book of Psalms,
>
> > "Let his habitation be desolate,
> > and let there be no one to live in it";
>
> and
>
> > "Let another take his office." '

Peter's speech is delivered in between the narratives of the Ascension and Pentecost, and clearly offers a substantially different account of Judas' death to that found in Matthew. Here there is no repentance, no mention of the chief priests, no suicide by hanging, and only indirect reference to money. Rather the manner of his death is spelt out in gruesome detail. There is agreement on the suddenness of the death, however, and on the acquisition of a field and the name of that field. Above all there is a similar emphasis on the fulfilment of scripture, which provides the framework for the passage.

The relevant scripture is that spoken by the Holy Spirit through the 'mouth of David' (1.16) in the 'book of Psalms' (1.20), specifically Psalm 69.25 and 109.8.[120] What was said of the enemies of the Psalmist was ascribed to those

---

[118] W.F. Albright, and C.S. Mann, *Matthew – Introduction, translation and notes* The Anchor Bible (New York: Doubleday, 1984) p340.

[119] Mark 14.11 mentioned silver paid to Judas, but it is Matthew who specifies that it is thirty pieces (26.15; 27.3). In Matthew Judas asks two questions not found in Mark; namely 'What will you give me if I *deliver* him over to you?' (26.15) and 'Is it I, Rabbi?' (26.25), and receives an additional comment/question (depending on the translation) from Jesus: 'Friend, do what you came to do/why are you here?' (26.50).

[120] Bruce points out that even before the time of Christ many of the Psalms were interpreted in a Messianic sense. This was particularly true of the 'royal' Psalms, and for those who had faith that Jesus was the Messiah many of them, ascribed to David,

opposed to Christ, as in the references to Psalm 41.9 already discussed in section 1.5. What Judas has done to merit such treatment was to be 'guide' to those who arrested Jesus' (1.16). This sounds rather prosaic given the language of betrayal/handing over and satanic influence found in Luke's Gospel. Only here is Judas so described. The phrase 'one of the twelve' is noticeably absent also, but Peter says that Judas was 'numbered among us' and was 'allotted his share in this ministry.' (1.17) The fact that this is no longer the case is immediately explained in verses 18 and 19. It is recounted that Judas bought a field with the money from the chief priests, the 'reward of his wickedness'. There he 'burst open in the middle and all his bowels gushed out'.[121] This field becomes well known, and is described in 'their language'[122] by the Aramaic name of Akeldama meaning 'Field of Blood'.

As Wilcox notes, it is the fact that Judas was one of 'the twelve' that 'underlies the enormity of his failure and the resultant need for his replacement'.[123] 1.23-26 explains how the 'lot' falls to Matthias. Later in Acts no replacement is found after the death of James the brother of John (killed by Herod 'with the sword' at Acts 12.2), emphasizing that it is the nature of Judas' actions and death as understood in relation to scripture that necessitates his replacement. Events that might be read as simply tragic, as wrecking Christ's symbolic calling of 'the twelve', are seen to be recoverable and within God's providence. Now that Judas has received his 'reward', God's purposes continue with 'the twelve' returned to full strength. Once the election of Matthias has emphasized this fact, he is never mentioned again.

This emphasis on providence can be seen in the way that Luke makes use of the psalms. For example he quotes Psalm 69.25 at verse 20a. Lindars points out that when compared with the Septuagint version of the Psalm, it becomes apparent that a plural has been changed to a singular (in this case a 'their' to a 'his' indicating the adaptation of the verse to apply to a particular individual.

'were understood as prophetically applicable to Jesus.' (F.F. Bruce, *Commentary on The Book of the Acts*, Grand Rapids, Michigan: Eerdmans, 1954, p48).

[121] In an influential article, F.H. Chase argues that the account of Judas' death in Acts includes a 'a medical term denoting a disease' ('ΟΝ ΠΡΗΝΗΣ ΓΕΝΟΜΕΝΟΣ IN ACTS 1.18' *Journal of Theological Studies* 13, 1911-12, p279) and relates it to the vocabulary used in Papias' account of the death of Judas. He marshalls a variety of internal and external evidence to justify this, but Lake's judgement on the article seems fair, namely that there 'is too much extant Greek literature for us lightly to accept a new meaning for a well-known word…'. (Kirsopp Lake, *The Beginnings of Christianity – Part I The Acts of the Apostles*, London: Macmillan, 1933, p29).

[122] The reference is to the 'inhabitants of Jerusalem'. Peter is hardly likely to have used the phrase 'their language', which indicates the possibility of a piece of traditional material placed by Luke at this point in the speech.

[123] Max Wilcox, 'The Judas Tradition in Acts 1.15-26' *New Testament Studies* 19 (1972/3) p448. Wilcox points out that the Hebrew for 'portion and share' can be translated by the same Greek word used for the 'share' in the ministry that had belonged to Judas (Acts 1.17).

There is also now an emphasis on the 'desolate' place being a vacancy as well as a punishment for that individual. As Lindars writes, there is

> ...thus a progressive exegesis here. First the conduct and subsequent fate of Judas is explained by the quotation; he had ranged himself with the enemies of Jesus, and so his death is the first example of these prophetic warnings coming true. Then secondly it can be applied to the practical matter of the need for scriptural warrant for the election.[124]

Indeed the election is then immediately justified by a second quotation, from Psalm 109.8.

While Psalm 69 is the most widely cited of all the psalms in the New Testament, Psalm 109 is used only in relation to Judas Iscariot. Verse 8b ('may another take his office') is used straight after 69.25, at Acts 1.20b. In its original setting 8b is part of a series of curses (vv6-15) which could be applied to all those who crucified Christ ('For wicked and deceitful mouths are opened against me...', 109.2) as well as to Judas, before verse 8 is used in relation to the election of a new apostle. Lindars comments that the 'application of these cursing psalms (whether 69 or 109) to Judas points to the apologetic necessity of explaining the defection of one of the closest friends of Jesus'.[125] It is worth restating at this point that the psalms have been quoted several times in connection with Judas, on each occasion to help explain the difficult fact that Jesus shared his ministry and

---

[124] Op cit. p103.

[125] Ibid. p109. While the apologetic concerns of the New Testament writers lead them to constantly refer to the Hebrew scriptures, it has been argued by writers such as Lake and Harris that in this matter of the death of Judas their sources are more widespread. Harris' article of 1900, 'Did Judas really commit suicide?' was written following the publication of the ancient story of Ahikar, the grand vizier of Sennacherib, which includes an account of the death of the traitorous Nadan, who 'swelled up, and burst asunder.' (J. Rendel Harris 'Did Judas really commit suicide?' *American Journal of Theology*, July 1900, p491). Harris goes on to argue that this story influenced the shape of the earliest legends about Judas which were later adapted by Matthew, Luke and Papias. For him the influence of the Ahitophel story and the psalms is secondary. He also refers to the death of Herod the Great as recounted by Josephus (Antiquities 17), which is another 'swelling up and bursting'. Brown, on the other hand, sees the deaths of Ahitophel and Antiochus Epiphanes as underlying the accounts in Matthew and Acts respectively (op cit. p1445). Lake offers a careful verdict on the significance of the story, arguing that 'attempts to prove any conscious literary dependance of Matthew, Acts or Papias on any one source, such as for instance the story of Ahikar, are to be deprecated. The truth probably is that there was a loose tradition of the way in which the death of a traitor ought to correspond to his offence. One writer put in one detail, the next added another, until nearly all had been incorporated.' (Kirsopp Lake, *The Beginnings of Christianity* – Part I 'The Acts of the Apostles', London: Macmillan, 1933, p30). To be fair to Harris, he does not focus entirely on the story of Ahikar and Nadan, as implied by the reference to Josephus above, even if he is perhaps over dependent on it. He also refers to some interesting Hebrew material from writers such as Solomon of Bassara and Procopius that links Judas with the serpent of Genesis 3.

his table with the one whom gave him up to crucifixion. As well as the psalms discussed here, each of the Gospels draw on Psalm 41.9 in their particular 'Jesus/Judas' narratives. Lindars argues that this is a secondary development in the use of such psalms, following on from their initial 'general use to explain our Lord's sufferings and death'.[126] The theme of fulfilment and providence, as we have seen, is returned to again and again, and while this is a feature of the Gospels as a whole, it is a particular feature of the treatment of Judas. One only has to examine texts relating to another apostle who failed Jesus, Peter, to see that this is so.

It has been taken as read during this discussion of the death of Judas that no harmonization between Acts and Matthew is possible. Rather, the similarities, differences, and complexities of the narratives have been examined. One thing above all has been clear: that for the authors of these passages the death of Judas cannot be read as 'tragic' as it was in accordance with scripture and therefore the purposes of God. Their very insistence on this is an indirect witness to the difficulty of understanding the actions of Judas, one of the twelve, as within the purposes of God.

1.7 Issues and conclusion

It remains in this chapter to summarize the nature of the treatment of Judas found in the New Testament, and to reiterate some of the themes and issues that have arisen from the preceding exegesis. To begin with, it has been seen that in their pre-passion narrative material all four Gospels agree that Judas should be described as 'one of the twelve' and that he had the name 'Iscariot'. Further, they agree that he handed over/betrayed Christ and received money for this action. The money receives more elaborate treatment in Matthew (in relation to the fulfilment of scripture) than Mark or Luke, and in John avarice and thievery are overtly introduced, so characterising Judas in partial explanation of his later actions. In both Luke and John, Judas falls under the influence of Satan.

In terms of the way the relationship between the four Gospels is conventionally understood, there is a progressive increase in material concerning Judas from Mark to John, and that this material is of an increasingly negative nature. A reading of Mark alone, in Greek, gives a picture of one of the twelve named Judas Iscariot, whose role is to hand Jesus over to the chief priests in order to fulfil what has been said about the fate of the Son of Man (9.31 and 10.33). In the main it is a picture less negative than the weight of later associations would indicate, although hardly neutral given Judas' contact with the chief priests (14.10-11) and the important text at Mark 14.21 ('...the Son of Man goes as it is written of him, but woe to that man by whom the Son of man is *betrayed*...').

---

[126] Op cit. p110.

Matthew parallels this text (at 26.24), and elaborates on Mark in various ways, naming Judas at the last supper and having him ask, 'Is it I, Rabbi?', describing Judas as issuing the command to seize Jesus in Gethsemane, and so on. Again, in relation to the use of παραδίδωμι, much of what is said of Judas is in relation to his role and its part in God's purposes (evidenced also by the references to the fulfilment of scripture) and not as overtly negative as English translations of the Bible make it appear. Yet there is also the story of the death of Judas, including his repentance, as well as fulfilling the 'cursing' text mentioned at the beginning of this paragraph.

Luke 6.16 introduces the noun 'traitor', and ascribes satanic influence to Judas actions – although once again forms of παραδίδωμι are widely used. He also tells of Judas' death at the beginning of the *Acts of the Apostles*, and although there are major differences with Matthew, they are agreed on the importance of scriptural fulfilment in understanding the events described. Whether or not eschatological salvation remains open for Judas cannot be deduced with any certainty. Certainly Judas dies without explicit forgiveness, in circumstances that underline the unpleasantness of his fate, but Matthew and Luke say no more than that. Their accounts of his death do have a finality about them, but are silent about Judas in relation to the last judgement. If Matthew's mention of Judas' repentance is taken as a small hint towards the possibility of eschatological salvation, John's introduction of the phrase 'son of destruction' (or 'perdition') and his insistence that Judas is 'lost' might be taken the other way. In the end, the New Testament is not conclusive on this issue.

To continue with John's Gospel, there is agreement with Luke about satanic influence, and pre-passion material concerning Judas' role as treasurer. John's treatment is distinctive in terms of the apparent instruction from Jesus for Judas to proceed with the handing over (13.27) and the lack of a role for Judas in the garden (18.1-12).

This brief setting out of the 'progression' of Judas material in the Gospels may seem straightforward enough. But what is to be made of it? That Judas was originally 'friend' to Jesus, performing an essential part in the necessary death of Christ, and that by the time John's Gospel came to be written Judas was regarded as the 'betrayer', a thief and a 'devil'? Such a case could be plausibly made. But if the Gospels are read carefully, it is clear that such a reading is inadequate. For example in Mark there is the not inconsiderable matter of 14.21 ('...woe to that man...'). And in John there is the use of παραδίδωμι rather than προδίδωμι throughout, as well as his emphasis on Jesus' foreknowledge, in accordance with his portrait of Christ as always 'in control'. This raises the possibility that Judas was chosen precisely to fill a particular role in the passion. Once he has done so no further mention is made of him, and there is no account of his death to emphasize his fate.

A difficulty running through all the Gospels is maintaining, or failing to maintain, an apparent distinction between what Judas does, and who he is. Westcott perceptively observed, in relation to the use of παραδίδωμι, that Judas' act is 'regarded in relation to the Lord's Passion, and not to his sin'.[127] The use of the word draws attention away from Judas as a 'person' to the actions he carries out and their part in the passion. As has been pointed out, the use of παραδίδωμι, particularly in the passive, carries the connotation of the will of God.[128]

The close reading of the New Testament texts concerning Judas and his relationship with Jesus attempted in this chapter, has indicated the issues and problems that prevent any clear and simple view about Judas emerging. The texts are too dense for that. And if the Gospel writers have not bequeathed to us an entirely clear and coherent picture of the significance of Judas in relation to Jesus, this is because they did not have one. Their texts indicate a sense of struggle and tension in relation to Judas and the implications of his actions for understanding Jesus. For example Judas participates in the last supper and the footwashing, but without any discernible impact on his actions. As was argued earlier, the way the incarnate Christ should be understood is at issue here. Should Jesus be understood as a powerful, all knowing figure, capable of all things, or is this a form of docetism highlighted when Jesus' relationship with Judas is focused on? If the latter, this might indicate that the self-limitation of the incarnate Son be taken seriously, as indicated by Mark 13.32: 'But concerning that day or that hour, no one knows, not even the angels in heaven, nor the Son, but only the Father.'[129]

An important theme has been the way the Old Testament material has entered the discussion, in particular the Psalms. It could be argued that these are examples of a wider Old Testament motif of 'betrayal', including the betrayal of the covenant by the Hebrew people, that is inevitably reflected in the New Testament. Whatever validity this argument might be taken to have, a unique factor in the Gospels is that Judas is 'lost' (unlike, for example, Judah, who hands over Joseph but is later reconciled to him). The 'fulfilment of scripture' has been discussed both in relation to specific texts such as Zechariah 11.12b, and in a general sense such as Mark 14.21 and parallels. In the latter, it is unclear which texts are being referred to. In the former, it is often not obvious what relation the texts might have to Judas, and on occasions ingenuity is needed to make such texts

---

127 B.F. Westcott *The Gospel According to St John – The authorized version, with introduction and notes* (London: John Murray, 1903) p110.

128 Barrett, for example, does not even mention Judas in his discussion of 1 Corinthians 11.23 ('in the night in which he was *handed over...*'), assuming that God is the one who 'hands over'. C.K. Barrett *A Commentary on the First Epistle to the Corinthians* (London: A & C Black, 1971) p266. Mark's gospel clearly comes closest to portraying Judas in terms of his action alone. Once again 14.21 affects the picture, with its emphasis both on what Judas does and as 'the man' who is cursed. There is also the designation 'one of the twelve' to ponder. Does this heighten the possibility that God's will was being done, or emphasize the reason for the curse, as one 'who ate of my bread has lifted his heel against me'? Westcott's comment was made in relation to John's gospel, and yet it is John who has the most material describing Judas the individual. Moreover, despite describing Judas in ways seemingly designed to delineate a plausible human character, John also apparently understands Judas as 'evil incarnate'.

129 This is a theme discussed in Chapter 7.

'fit' (such as Matthew's conglomerate text from Zechariah and Jeremiah at 27.9-10). Here the use of scripture for apologetic reasons is clear. The Gospel writers strive to place the role of Judas, with all the difficult questions it raises, within God's purposes. For if it is not within those purposes, the overall thrust of the narrative is undermined. On the other hand, that God's providence involves the designation of Judas as 'better unborn' is uncomfortable as it raises the dissonant note of tragedy.

Enough has been said to illustrate the truth of Balthasar's words with which this chapter began, 'The handing over of Jesus in the Passion remains a mystery...'. The issues relating to Judas that emerge from an examination of the New Testament material have been identified, and include the following:

1. The attributions given him (e.g. 'one of the twelve' and 'thief').
2. The significance of the New Testament usage of παραδίδωμι, and in particular the way this verb and its various uses indicate the workings of divine providence.
3. The way in which Judas' actions are understood in relation to the fulfilment of scripture; i.e. that they are part of God's purposes. The most difficult text here is Mark 14.21 and parallels, with its pairing of necessity and culpability.
4. The nature of Judas' participation in the last supper and footwashing, and the implications for his exclusion or inclusion in the redemption wrought by Christ.
5. The nature of his 'repentance' and death, and whether or not eschatological damnation is the implication of the relevant texts.
6. The extent of moral responsibility Judas bears for his role in the passion (the relevant factors including divine necessity, and the will of Satan, and including the possibility of the intersection of both).
7. The way Jesus should be understood (i.e. the most appropriate Christology) given the way his particular relationship with Judas develops, from the initial call to the handing over, and the proximity of their deaths.

Running through all these are questions relating to the person of Christ and the providence of God as they relate to Judas. From the way Judas is identified in the apostolic lists, to the frequent references to Jesus' foreknowledge and scriptural fulfilment, the Gospel writers can be seen to be wrestling with these questions through the issues highlighted above. There is a constant sense that if Jesus had not foreknown about Judas, this would damage the claims the Gospel writers are making for him. The possibility that in relation to Judas, Jesus was mistaken or indeed fails in his redemptive purposes, is troubling and difficult. Such issues are worth struggling with, for if it is possible that the apostolic 'insider' is in some measure a defeat for Jesus, even finally remaining 'outside' salvation, does this indicate that when God becomes incarnate, one consequence is the revelation of tragedy and intractability in the world? Is this, to begin to use explicitly trinitarian language, because the incarnation is a self-limitation of God the Father, in which He does not will to intervene when God the Son experiences (and in an important sense creates) such a 'loss' from amongst these he pledged to protect?

In the succeeding chapters the Christological questions that have arisen through this examination of the biblical texts relating to Judas will be explored further. Chapter 2 will take up the most regularly occurring theme of this chapter, as time and time again it has been seen how the New Testament writers struggle to show that Judas' actions and fate, which could be understood in terms of tragedy, are in fact within the providential purposes of God. The theological exploration begun here will continue with reference to two key writers who have wrestled with the New Testament texts concerning Judas and explicitly addressed this theme: Karl Barth and Donald MacKinnon.

Chapter 2

Judas and the Tension between Providence and Tragedy

Particular attention must be paid to the remarkable calm with which the New Testament speaks of Judas Iscariot.[1]
Karl Barth

There is no solution offered in the Gospels of the riddle of Iscariot... The problem is stated; it is left unresolved, and we are presented with the likeness of the one who bore its ultimate burden... .[2]
Donald MacKinnon

The previous chapter showed that the key questions arising from an examination of the place of Judas in the New Testament centre around the providence of God and the person of Christ. This chapter will explore the tension between providential and tragic readings of Judas Iscariot, as exemplified in the writings of Karl Barth and Donald MacKinnon. These two theologians have been chosen because their contrasting approaches to the range of issues and questions surrounding Judas set out the boundaries of the available theological 'landscape'. While many writers and theologians have touched on the theological and Christological issues arising from a consideration of the place of Judas in the New Testament, as will be seen later in this book, few have given them the prominence that Barth and MacKinnon do, and fewer still can match them for insight and profundity. Part of the argument of the chapter is that it is not simply their abilities as theologians that lead them to attend to the density of the relevant Gospel texts in the way that they do, but also their context as European writers living in the shadow of two world wars, and in particular the Holocaust.

In this context it is increasingly widely accepted that some of the roots of anti-Semitism are to be found in the Gospels themselves.[3] There is an awareness

---

1 §35.4 'The Determination of the Rejected' *Church Dogmatics* II.2 (Edinburgh: T.&T. Clark, 1957) p459.

2 'Order and Evil in the Gospel', pp90-96 of *Borderlands of Theology and other essays* (London: Lutterworth Press, 1968) p92.

3 There are, however, many differences of view as to how direct the line is between Christian anti-Judaism and the Holocaust. See, for example the opposing views on this topic as expressed in essays by Emanuel Tanay and Judith Hershcopf Banki in *Holocaust Scholars Write to the Vatican*, edited by H.J. Cargas (Westport, Connecticut: Greenwood Press, 1998).

that what happened in the Holocaust is related to the fact that Jews have been 'identified both with Judas, the disciple who for money betrayed his Master with a token of love, and with the devil, the very opposite of all that Christ stands for'.[4] Certainly both MacKinnon and Barth are alert to the fact that the role and fate of Judas in the New Testament is related to the experience of the Jewish people in subsequent centuries, although they understand this relation in different ways. Their contrasting methodologies and conclusions, each with their own strengths and shortcomings, are in some measure responses to this insight.

2.1 Barth's 'calm' excursus on Judas

In his preface to Volume II, Part 2 of the *Church Dogmatics*, dated Whitsuntide 1942, Barth writes that in 1933 'the affairs of Europe and finally of the whole world hurtled with ever increasing violence into the crisis which still engulfs us.'[5] It is in such a context, involved both in writing dogmatics, and what he describes as 'the Third Reich and the German-church conflict', that Barth composed an intricate and detailed forty eight page small print excursus devoted to a consideration of Judas. Its extraordinary mixture of conceptual analysis and biblical exegesis has been the focus of at least two significant books on Barth's hermeneutics, by David Ford and Paul McGlasson.[6] McGlasson attempts the deliberately limited task of describing and analysing Barth's exegesis (arguing that it is methodologically pluralistic), while Ford relates this exegesis to Barth's overall theological schema and raises questions about the way the former is made to support the latter. Both have something to contribute to the particular approach of this book, which is to attend to Barth's treatment of the Judas texts in the New Testament and his theological conclusions about the place of Judas in Christology.

The excursus is to be found in Chapter VII of *Church Dogmatics II.2*, entitled 'The Election of God'. In the chapter Barth first discusses the election of Jesus Christ, then the election of the community, and finally the election of the individual. For Barth, election cannot be understood apart from rejection; the two are always in tension, for outside Jesus Christ all are rejected. He argues that in Christ is manifested both the difference between the elected and the rejected, and what they share. Both are determined by the same will of God, and defined in

---

Holocaust Scholars Write to the Vatican, edited by H.J. Cargas (Westport, Connecticut: Greenwood Press, 1998).

4 *Approaches to Auschwitz – The Legacy of the Holocaust* Richard L Rubenstein and John K Roth (London: SCM, 1987) p38. See also Hyam Maccoby, *Judas Iscariot and the Myth of Jewish Evil* (New York: The Free Press, 1992).

5 *Church Dogmatics* II.2 (Edinburgh: T&T Clark, 1957) pix.

6 David Ford's doctoral thesis was published as *Barth and God's Story – Biblical Narrative and the Theological Method of Karl Barth in the Church Dogmatics* (Frankfurt am Main: Verlag Peter Lang, 1981); Paul McGlasson, *Jesus and Judas – Biblical Exegesis in Barth* (Atlanta, Georgia: Scholars Press, 1991).

relation to God. So it is that for Barth the rejected one is understood as having an improper or dependent existence, in the sense of having isolated himself from God by resisting election.

Barth argues that this rejection is the plight from which the elect have been saved, and continually tend towards. Indeed, he writes, the rejection of the world and the individual is what Christ bore on the cross, and it is through Christ that the elect know the rejected most fully. The elect are also 'implicated'[7] in the godlessness and rejection of their neighbour. Here the meaning of the Gospel is to be found, for the horror of rejection is seen to be limited and bounded by God:

> It is for this man, for his replacement and transformation, that Jesus Christ died and rose. It is this man whom the elect confronts in himself and others. It is to this man that the Gospel is addressed as the Word of Truth.[8]

The purpose of the Gospel is to give the one without a future, the rejected, a future in covenant with God. This applies to Israel, the Jewish people, but above all in the New Testament to Judas. For Barth, Judas is never simply an individual who acts in a particular way, but always a representative figure, a type, whether of the rejected as a totality, Israel, or the apostolic group. So it is that he begins his excursus by noting the repeated Gospel insistence that Judas was 'one of the twelve', so that (as in the Old Testament, but even more so) the rejected is found in close proximity to God. This, he argues, witnesses both to the effectiveness of the devil, and that this effectiveness can only find expression under the dominant power of the Lord who knew from the beginning who would *betray* him (John 6.64). It is in this sense that Barth writes of the 'remarkable calm' of the New Testament in relation to Judas; a calmness that is related both to the combination of 'the paltriness and tremendous consequences of this event...', and that as portrayed in the Gospels Judas comes across as a 'planned figure with a planned role'.[9] Here are clear indications as to why Barth's analysis of Judas can be accurately characterized as 'providential'.

The notion of 'calmness' in relation to Judas' treatment in the Gospels is striking and unusual, however, so unusual, in fact, that the onus is on Barth to make a strong case for the validity of his claim. McGlasson argues that the purpose of Barthian exegesis is 'simply to halt before the biblical text, to allow it a voice, to invite and encourage the reader simply to notice *what is there...*'.[10] In many ways this view is supported by the excursus under discussion, particularly in its attention to uses of the verb παραδίδωμι, but it can be challenged in certain respects, as will be seen later once Barth's overall argument has been more fully set out.

---

7 Ibid. p452.
8 Ibid. p455.
9 Ibid. p460.
10 Op cit. pp119-20.

Central to Barth's argument is the continuity between Judas and the other apostles, as is indicated by his awareness that the Greek vocabulary of παραδίδωμι, which describes Judas' actions, is inadequately translated by 'betray' and parallels the actions of others, and indeed of God. McGlasson comments that:

> To my knowledge, no other expositor, ancient or modern, has used this word and concept to make the exegetical points that Barth makes... . Moreover, not only would a proficient knowledge of Greek (and a good Greek concordance) be necessary to read these texts the way Barth does, but so would the precise control that he has of the doctrinal issue under discussion and the way the texts address that issue. That is to say, Barth's reading is a technically brilliant achievement... .[11]

It is this technical proficiency that underlies the use Barth makes of texts containing παραδίδωμι, such as his argument that Israel and the apostles all share the guilt of 'handing over' Jesus to trial and crucifixion, and moreover that if this were not so they could not receive what God wanted them to receive. Judas represents what the church has in common with rejected Israel and the world, and therefore what the apostles need to be cleansed *from*. The election of the apostles depends on this:

> And the apostle Judas Iscariot is the special agent and exponent of this handing-over [which enables Christ's cleansing death] as it was decreed to be necessary in the counsel of God.[12]

Barth is aware that texts on the guilt of Judas such as '...woe to that man by whom the Son of Man is betrayed! It would have been better for that man if he had not been born' (Mark 14.21 and parallels) hardly give a sense of 'calmness'. He acknowledges that Judas is *the* sinner of the New Testament, and proceeds to examine the nature of this sin. If by this Barth means that his is the worst sin, this view can be challenged, as William Klassen has done with reference to Peter.[13] Against this it can be argued that Peter was able to make restitution, and that Barth at least distances himself from the vituperative aspects of the Christian tradition. He is careful to locate Judas' sin in the initiation of a chain of events which includes the high priests and Pilate, and to argue that he was guilty of a 'minimum of hostile activity' rather than a maximum.[14]

---

11 Ibid. p143. McGlasson may not be aware of the writings of such as Augustine and Aquinas on this point (to be discussed in Chapter 4), but even if he is the point is well made.

12 Op cit. p461.

13 For example Klassen argues (in *Judas – Betrayer or Friend of Jesus*, London: SCM, 1996) that, 'Compared with Peter or with the other disciples, Judas comes out relatively well' (p91), and quotes T. Weeden (from *Mark: Traditions in Conflict*, Philadelphia: Fortress Press, 1971) to the effect that all the obtuseness and hostility of the disciples is crystallised in Peter (p79).

14 Op cit. p460.

Barth goes on to note that for Judas 'the presence and protection and vigilance of Jesus were in vain',[15] and that he is not simply 'unclean', but *representative* of the uncleanness of all the apostles. The key moment is the anointing at Bethany (John 12.1-8). Mary's prodigal act of giving is contrasted with Judas' insistence that another purpose is more important that glorifying Jesus in his coming death. Whether or not Judas was dishonest in a narrow financial sense, Barth argues that Judas 'robs' Jesus and the other apostles in his concern to preserve his own initiative. Judas has turned to Jesus, but not yielded to Him, and this incomplete allegiance enabled him to hand Jesus over.

In this Judas represents not simply the other apostles, but also 'the Jews' (Barth notes Judas' name), doing what Israel has always done in relation to Yahweh.[16] He argues, somewhat speculatively, that Judas wants to be an apostle without the obedience that goes with it, just as Israel wanted to enjoy being the people of God without the responsibility thereby implied.[17] Judas' kiss in the garden,[18] and subsequent repentance, must be seen in this light. Barth goes on to write that it is because Judas shows the guilt of both the apostolic group and Israel that his repentance cannot alter Jesus' 'woe to that man...'. Neither can Judas make restitution for the process that he has begun.

It seems that for Barth Judas both *shares* in the sins of Israel and the Apostles, and in some sense *bears* particular responsibility for these in the manner of his death. Barth does not argue that Judas' repentance is a closed book, however. He writes that according to the New Testament it is 'left an open question which is not met or heard or answered by a promise of grace...'.[19] It occurs the wrong side (that is, before) of the salvific event of the cross, and its 'incompleteness' corresponds to the incompleteness of his surrender to Christ. As Judas has rejected grace, argues Barth, so there cannot be grace for him in repentance. In summary, therefore, 'no promise of grace could be held out for Judas, and no genuine penitence was possible.'[20]

Barth does not explain at this point why Judas' repentance, on Matthew's account apparently a genuine turning away from acknowledged guilt, is unacceptable. Nor is it yet evident how the 'question' of Judas' repentance remains open, particularly as Barth emphasises that his suicide is primarily a judgement making clear that he has no future as an apostle or in the church. As

---

15 Ibid. p461.

16 Ibid. p 464. Cf. Hyam Maccoby's argument in *Judas Iscariot and the Myth of Jewish Evil* (New York: The Free Press, 1992).

17 Barth argues that although the accounts of Judas's death in Matthew and Acts disagree in externals, they agree in 'material content' to the effect that both Judas and Judah (Israel) have 'no future as such and in and for themselves' (Ibid. p469).

18 Barth also writes that 'the treacherous kiss by which Judas distinguishes Jesus from the surrounding disciples at the arrest is the sign of the gratitude of lost man for the existence of Him who now wills to intervene for him' (Ibid. p502).

19 Ibid. p466.

20 Ibid. p467.

the account of his death in the *Acts of the Apostles* graphically indicates, Judas dies from an 'internal contradiction'[21] which reflects that of Israel, taking the consequences of free choice to their uttermost in rejecting the very Messiah for whom the nation waited. Barth writes that his actions and his death belong to the night, and to Satan, and are deserving of the horror expressed in the New Testament:

> There can be no doubt that here at the very heart of the New Testament we are confronted by the problem of the rejected, by the question: What is the will of God for him? What has God determined concerning him? And we meet this question at the same central place where the New Testament also raises the question of the elect.[22]

These are not easy questions to answer, as Barth readily acknowledges. It is hard to say if there is any redemptive significance for Judas in the Lord's supper, the footwashing, or indeed in Jesus' death. Since Judas, as Barth continually affirms, made manifest what was concealed in all the apostles (and to some extent seen in Peter), it would be 'an unspeakably hard affirmation... that Jesus died in vain for him',[23] and that he alone was excluded from the 'Father, forgive them, for they know not what they do' (Luke 23.24). On the other hand the New Testament gives little indication that Judas was anything other than lost, even if it is not entirely conclusive on this issue. Here Barth's typological exegesis, emphasising Judas as a representative figure, comes up against the brief put powerful condemnatory texts from the synoptic Gospels ('woe to that man...') and John 17.12 ('none of them has been lost but the son of destruction').

Barth wants to argue, however, that the New Testament does not tell us the final outcome. He contends that Judas exists in a heightened form of the situation between Jesus and all people: 'the open one of proclamation' in which the Church preaches not universalism but both the reality of human wickedness and the overwhelming power of grace.[24] Here Barth makes an intriguing and innovative move, arguing that although Matthias is elected to Judas' place at the beginning of Acts, given the overall shape of that work 'we can hardly deny that it is really Paul who took over Judas' place and the work abandoned by him.' As a persecutor Paul had been like the 'ghost of Judas'[25] in his attitude to the church, but following his conversion he lived out the possibilities of the new Israel, fulfilling what Judas tried to reverse – the faithful handing over of Jesus to the Gentiles. By Jesus' death 'the Judas in Paul dies',[26] so that he (along with all the subsequent bearers of apostolic tradition) is no longer capable of what Judas did.

---

21 Ibid. p470.
22 Ibid. p471.
23 Ibid. p475.
24 Ibid. p476.
25 Ibid. p478.
26 Ibid. p501.

This is a remarkable notion coherent with Barth's examination of the uses of παραδίδωμι in the New Testament. It must be said, however, that no other commentator has linked Paul and Judas in this way. Can it be that Barth has seen an aspect of 'what is there' in the New Testament texts no one had noticed before him? Or has Barth imposed his fondness for what Balthasar calls 'correlative pairs of reprobate and election'[27] such as Cain and Abel, Esau and Jacob, and Saul and David? Again, this is a crucial question that will need to be returned to, but at this point it is necessary to attend further to what Barth sees as the possible implications for understanding Judas:

> How, then, does it stand with Judas, even though, of course, his picture can only negatively reproduce that of Paul? Is not Judas also, in his own place and after his own fashion, the outstanding apostle? Is he not the holy one among them – 'holy' in the old meaning of the term, the one who is marked, branded, banned, the one who is burdened with the divine curse and thrust out, the one who is thus brought into remarkably close proximity to Jesus himself? ....For all the dissimilarities, is it possible to overlook the likeness in which Judas alone of the apostles stands face to face and side by side with Jesus? Or the more than chronological proximity of his very different death to the death of Jesus? *Mutatis mutandis*, could not the famous utterance of the high-priest in Jn.11.50: 'It is expedient for us, that one man should die for the people, and that the whole nation perish not,' be said of Judas too in his relationship to the other apostles? ...he too, like Jesus, suffered his death in the place of others; that Jesus actually did not go alone to the death which the sin of all the apostles made necessary. And although lacking the power of His death, there went with Him this one apostle, and represented in the person of this one there went all the dead of the old covenant which Israel had continually broken... .[28]

The quotation could be read as arguing that Judas' death in some measure shares in the atoning significance of Jesus' death, but Barth states that it does not, and that in its 'utter darkness' it emphasises the light and life offered by the crucifixion of Christ. This unique function, witnessing to the divine rejection that Christ bore away through his death, is possible for Judas alone of all the apostles. Paul, conversely, witnesses to the divine election. Between the two of them is the figure of Christ, for 'Apart from him Judas would not be Judas, just as apart from Him Paul would not be Paul.' Here Barth recognises that Judas' rejection is bound up with the impact Jesus had upon him, although he cannot see this (as MacKinnon will later argue) as pointing to tragedy. Here, rather, is seen the fact that in the place of any rejected person, 'an elect will one day stand.'[29] This does not alter Judas' rejection, and Barth has no time for those who credit Judas with hidden ideas and intentions in order to make him righteous (a criticism that he might have extended to those who vilify him). His only justification (as with Israel) is as the

27 Hans Urs von Balthasar *The Theology of Karl Barth* (San Francisco: Ignatius Press, 1992) p182.

28 Op cit. p479.

29 Ibid. p480.

occupier of a place to be filled very differently by another. Both can in this sense be seen not merely as negative but as 'uniquely positive' figures.[30]

For Barth it is in the triumvirate of Judas, Jesus and Paul that the primary meaning of Judas is to be found. He also emphasises, however, that in Judas is seen a 'co-operation... in the task of the apostolate and the Church',[31] though this occurs only through the grace of Christ and against Judas' will. In a careful and sensitive exegesis of uses of παραδίδωμι in the Gospels, he argues that it means the handing over of a free person into the power of those who wish to do him harm. Judas' sin was to do just this; to deliver Jesus to sinners, rather than sinners to Jesus. Here the devil's words to Jesus in the wilderness, that all authority and glory 'has been *delivered* to me' (Luke 4.6) appears to be fulfilled. It is nevertheless true that Judas' action, as well as serving the devil, also lies behind the positive handing on or delivery of the faith which is the apostolic task – as in I Corinthians 11.23: 'For I received from the Lord what I also *delivered* to you, that the Lord Jesus on the night when he was *betrayed*...'.

McGlasson' judgement on the brilliance of Barth's achievement has already been noted. He does qualify this by arguing that although the text is peppered with such terms as 'obvious', Barth's reading is in fact anything but; with the result that the 'persuasive power of his rhetoric is minimal.'[32] McGlasson does not consider the extent to which his own surprise at Barth's understanding may be influenced by the emphasis in the tradition on 'betrayal' rather than 'handing over', but he does raise an important issue here. Is Barth's reading original in the sense of genuinely shedding light on a mainly neglected aspect of the texts, or is he imposing a predetermined theological schema?

According to Barth, the interrelation of the 'handing over' of Judas and the apostles is more than a semantic accident. It is not simply that the latter rectifies the former, for the two are also continuous; the apostles carrying on what Judas began, albeit in a rather different way. So it is, argues Barth, that 'active participation in the positive task of the apostolate'[33] cannot be denied even to Judas.

Barth goes on to give examples of God – and Paul – 'handing people over', as in Romans 1.18f where sinners are three times spoken of as *given up* to the consequences of their own evil, and in 1 Corinthians 5.5 and I Timothy 1.20 where Paul writes of *delivering* an immoral man and two blasphemers to Satan. This can only be described as rejection or abandonment, and the best that those thus 'handed over' can hope for is that even as Judge, God will not cease to be their God. There is more to say than this, however, for Barth discerns in Paul 'a final possibility – or, rather, an entirely new possibility beyond the completed judgement'.[34] For example in the second half of the verse at 1 Corinthians 5.5 Paul writes that the reason for delivering the man to Satan is 'for the destruction of

30 Ibid. p484.
31 Ibid. p480.
32 Ibid. p144.
33 Ibid. p488.
34 Ibid. p486.

the flesh, that his spirit may be saved in the day of the Lord Jesus.' Here it is seen that the power of Satan is limited by the power of God, in order that the man's 'spirit' should be saved.

Barth argues that there is a new beginning even for those apparently utterly lost. God, he asserts, 'will awaken them from this death which they must die... the revelation of God's wrath does as such aim at this eschatological possibility of faith...'. Barth holds that in all such New Testament texts there can be found the possibility of salvation for those handed over and utterly lost. He does not say that Judas is never spoken of as 'delivered' in the New Testament (though Barth writes of him in these terms), nor that there is little suggestion of Judas' salvation. Rather Barth bases his case on the relation between the 'handing over' of Judas and the apostles, the correspondence with the divine 'handing over', and his proposal that Judas should be understood in relation to Paul. For example he argues that in view of 'the relation between the delivery of Paul and Judas', the 'objective justification of Judas'[35] can be spoken of.

Moreover, because Judas' handing over of Jesus into the power of others is but a pale reflection of God's self-deprivation for the sake of His creatures, the consequences of his action in Gethsemane and at Golgotha take place within the overall purposes of God. What happens, Barth asserts, has 'nothing to do with human tragedy or the like, but... had to happen, as the will of God'.[36] So although Judas is rightly threatened with hell, this threat is 'a reality which is necessarily limited by faith in Jesus Christ... Jesus triumphs over hell so that 'it would never again be able to triumph over anyone.'[37] Barth is clear that no-one is entirely abandoned by God but Jesus Christ himself, who is lost and found again so that no-one should be eternally lost.

This has nothing to do with any restitution on the part of Judas. Barth emphasises, against Matthew 27 and his own reference earlier in the excursus to the repentance recorded there, that Judas died without even the possibility of a saving repentance. It is only because there is a limit, an eschaton, 'which confronts the status and fate of the rejected absolutely externally, and encounters them as an absolutely new factor' that there is any hope for Judas. This eschaton is the handing over of Jesus, which Judas participated in, for the sake of the world. The result is that Christians should 'not lose sight of the hope of the future deliverance of the rejected at the very frontier of perdition'.[38]

Barth ends his excursus with a discussion of the parallelism between the 'handing over' of Judas and God. He observes that Judas brought Jesus into circumstances where only God could help Him, and in so doing confirmed that the human world had become the kingdom of Satan. The crucial point for Barth, however, is that 'the more profoundly and comprehensively we attempt to formulate the sin and guilt of Judas... the more nearly his will and deed approach

35 Ibid. p488.
36 Ibid. p493.
37 Ibid. p496.
38 Ibid. p497.

what God willed and did in this matter...'.[39] He writes that while Adam wished to be like God, in Judas is seen an 'assault' upon God. This is a strange choice of word, particularly given his careful exegesis of παραδίδωμι, and arguably not in line with the New Testament texts. It does serve to heighten the paradox of an 'assault' willed by God in order to liberate humanity from Adam's sin. For this is Barth's understanding, and he therefore argues that the act of Judas cannot:

> ...be considered as an unfortunate episode, much less as the manifestation of a dark realm beyond the will and work of God, but in every respect (and at a particularly conspicuous place) as one element of the divine will and work. In what he himself wills and carries out, Judas does what God wills to be done... In one sense Judas is the most important figure in the New Testament apart from Jesus. For he, and he alone of the apostles, was actively at work in this decisive situation, in the accomplishment of what was God's will and what became the content of the Gospel. Yet he is the very one who is most explicitly condemned by the Law of God.[40]

Barth even expresses some sympathy with the Cainite reverence for Judas, and dismisses the vituperative writing on Judas by Abraham Sancta Clara and Carl Daub – just as he dismissed vituperation aimed at the Jews in his own time.[41] His point is that contempt is as misplaced as veneration. The paradox is rather that 'the divine and human [handing over] cannot be distinguished in what Judas did'[42] and that in his case 'sin is made righteousness, and evil good.'[43] For Judas alone, despite the fact that his act was one of sin and guilt, became the servant of Jesus' reconciling work, and he alone died with Christ. Barth writes that

> ...the power of the matter entrusted to the apostles is so great that even Judas is not exempt from its positive service, but subject to it; and... an outstanding function is indeed allotted to him in this service. But this is something that we must affirm, because, according to the New Testament, it is just as undeniable as his sin and guilt.[44]

Here Barth relates Judas to Israel (noting that passages about Judas often make reference to the fulfilment of Old Testament texts), arguing that neither could

---

39 Ibid. p501.

40 Ibid. p502.

41 He later regretted that he had not done this more strongly. Writing in 1968 about the Barmen declaration, so crucial to the Confessing Church, he felt that its one major failing was that he had not made the 'Jewish question' a decisive enough feature of his draft of the text: 'Of course in 1934 no text in which I had done that would have been acceptable even to the Confessing Church, given the atmosphere that there was then. But that does not excuse me for not having at least gone through the motions of fighting.' ('Brief an Eberhard Bethge' *Evangelische Theologie*, 1968, p555; quoted in Eberhard Busch, *Karl Barth – His life from letters and autobiographical texts*, London: SCM, 1976, p248).

42 Ibid. p502.

43 Ibid. p503.

44 Ibid. p504.

nullify the divine tasks entrusted to them despite their sinfulness. Jesus died for Judas, for Israel, and for all the rejected – and therefore the question of the future of the former two is always open, and can never be understood outside of the 'situation of proclamation'.[45] For Barth's final point is that God wishes the rejected, the non-elect, to hear the Gospel which proclaims the promise of their election.

It is clear that throughout his excursus Barth has attempted to hold together the nature of Judas' sin with the greater power of salvation as found in Christ. Ford argues that in this Barth is finally unsuccessful because his exegesis, which depends on 'a use of typology which presupposes a certain sort of providence',[46] goes substantially beyond the New Testament texts concerning Judas. By 'certain sort of providence' Ford means that Barth's typological exegesis, whereby events or characters in the biblical narrative can interpret other events or characters independently of authorial intention, depends on an understanding of God as unifier of the parts and the ultimate author of meaning. Barth assumes that when he finds parallels, such as in the various uses of παραδίδωμι these are significant because they are part of a providential order. His exegesis becomes a response to the problem of evil, in that God is shown as bringing about His own ends through even the most destructive of human actions. The meaning Judas gave to his actions, whatever this might have been, is given a final meaning by God. Ford argues that in trying to show this, 'Barth presses his method to the point of producing contradictions.'[47] For Ford the crucial point is that the New Testament, 'with its two stories of [Judas'] death, both smacking of the most bitter finality, gives no hint'[48] of any such resolution. Barth, he considers, has therefore attempted to impose a 'system' on the Gospel stories in a way that needs correction in the light of his own stated intention to hear what the Bible is saying.

It can be argued that this is unfair to Barth, who in fact affirms the rejection of Judas. It is rather that he finds this rejection to be contained within the Judas/Jesus/Paul triumvirate, and eschatologically limited. For Barth, if there is a 'calmness' to the New Testament treatments of Judas, it is both because the New Testament can be correctly identified as fundamentally eschatological in character, and that it is traversed by a series of related 'handings over' which give a context to Judas' actions. Here, however, he does seem open to Ford's criticisms, as Barth cannot offer any Gospel text unequivocally indicating 'calmness'.[49] His case rests on an overview of the New Testament material that the individual writers could

---

45 Ibid. p506.

46 Op cit. p91.

47 Ibid. p91.

48 Ibid. p92. In a subsequent essay entitled 'Barth's Interpretation of the Bible' Ford writes that 'Barth presses the typology of Judas with Paul so as to support the possibility of an ultimately favourable verdict on Judas. Yet the two grim New Testament accounts of Judas' death clearly make no attempt to remove in this way the sting of finality from Judas' fate.' (S.W. Sykes, editor, *Karl Barth: Studies of His Theological Method*, Oxford: Clarendon Press, 1979, p85).

49 One possibility might have been the Johannine 'It is finished!' (John 19.30).

not have had. Ford might have strengthened his case by making more of the unusual nature of Barth's treatment of παραδίδωμι and the exegetical points he is thereby able to make. The correlation of Judas and Paul is dependent on this treatment, although the fact that Barth was predisposed to 'see' such a pairing does not necessarily invalidate this particular piece of exegesis. Barth must indeed be given credit for a sensitivity to the particular nature of the New Testament texts concerning Judas, and the possible parallelism between different passages opened up by attention to the Greek vocabulary, that is almost unique in the tradition.[50]

More than this, if the difficult questions relating to Judas' actions, death and ultimate fate are not simply to be left hanging in the air, some theological response is necessary, as Barth has clearly seen and attempted to provide. However, the nexus of questions focusing around the fact that in the Gospels Judas apparently fulfils scripture in the positive sense of facilitating Christ's salvific death, and yet finds condemnation, can be responded to in more than one way. Barth's argument is very different from, indeed in many ways opposed to, the writing of Donald MacKinnon as this relates to Judas. For MacKinnon, attention to Judas does not so much reveal the providence of God, as indicate the presence of the tragic at the heart of the New Testament. It is to his contrasting approach to the issues and questions surrounding Judas that the book now turns.

2.2 MacKinnon's elusive remarks on the tragedy of Judas

In 1961 Donald MacKinnon delivered his Inaugural Lecture as Norris-Hulse Professor of Divinity at the University of Cambridge.[51] During the lecture he expressed his sympathy for those who 'distrust any doctrine, any image of the relation of the world to God which blurs the reality of evil, both physical and moral...'. He went on to argue that in relation to moral evil

> ...we have to acknowledge that the New Testament itself leaves altogether unresolved the questions inevitably raised by the action and the role of Iscariot. The Son of Man goes indeed the way prescribed for him in the scriptures he is concerned to fulfil; but woe to that man by whom he is handed over to his foes. 'It were good for that man that he had not been born.' It would be hard to find anywhere a sharper enunciation of the existence of sheer discontinuity in a world in the same utterance represented as providentially ordered.[52]

MacKinnon would periodically return to these 'unresolved questions' for the rest of the decade, particularly in his writings on Christianity and tragedy. While the

---

50 William Klassen is correct to say that the subsequent work of W. Popkes, referred to in Chapter 1, should also be recognised here. Op cit. p193.

51 The lecture is the title essay of *Borderlands of Theology and other essays*, edited by George Roberts and Donovan Smucker, in which it is reprinted (London: Lutterworth Press, 1968) pp41-54.

52 Ibid. p49.

latter category is not explicitly evoked here, the phrase 'sheer discontinuity' comes close. The difficulty for the reader is that MacKinnon's remarks, as above, are usually (in stark contrast to Barth) brief and suggestive rather than carefully spelled out. In order to explore further the import and validity of MacKinnon's insight it is necessary to trace other references in his writing on this theme.

In doing so two hypotheses based on the paragraph quoted above can be tested. First, it seems that MacKinnon does not quote scripture because his first concern is with biblical exegesis, but is focused on what he describes as 'the existence of sheer discontinuity in [the] world'. He takes Mark 14.21 to be a 'sharp' enunciation of a reality contiguous with twentieth-century experience, contained within the context of a Gospel 'utterance' whose import is apparently providential. Second, that the elusiveness of his Inaugural Lecture is representative, and his intuitive sense of the density of the Gospel text, full of potential insight, is unlikely ever to be fully worked through and expressed in his writing.

Both of these hypotheses can explored through an examination of a series of eight (unpublished) lectures on 'Evil'[53] MacKinnon delivered in 1962 and 1963. Those who had attended his Inaugural Lecture, and noted the paragraph quoted above, would not have been surprised to find him beginning his series with a discussion of tragedy, and an analysis of the role of Judas in the economy of salvation. In characteristically interrogative style, MacKinnon states his disagreement with the contention of Professor D.D. Raphael that neither Christianity nor Judaism have any place for the tragic.[54] If this were so, he argued,

---

53 Here I am using lecture notes taken by Professor Frances Young when she was a postgraduate at Cambridge. I have reconstructed the lectures with her assistance. Extracts from these are contained in an Appendix to this book. I am grateful to Dr Peta Dunstan, librarian at the Cambridge Divinity School, for the information that MacKinnon lectured twice on the subject of 'Evil', in the Lent terms of 1962 and 1963. The Inaugural Lecture referred to above indicates something of the background to these lectures, as do the broadcast talks 'Our Contemporary Christ' (1962) and 'Order and Evil in the Gospel' (1963), both published in *Borderlands of Theology and other essays*, ibid. pp82-96. In the former, MacKinnon argues (against theologians such as Loisy and Bultmann) that, 'Christianity faces men with the paradox that certain events which could have been otherwise are of ultimate, transcendent import; and this without losing their character as contingent events.... [Jesus'] judicial murder, its pain and its end, form the substance of the confession of faith' p87.

54 Here MacKinnon has in mind Raphael's 1959 Mahlon Powell lectures, published as *The Paradox of Tragedy* (London: George Allen & Unwin Ltd, 1960), though an outline of Raphael's views was also broadcast on the BBC Third Programme (to which station MacKinnon was an occasional contributor). In Chapter 2 of *The Paradox of Tragedy*, Raphael first argues that tragedy 'deals with evil and the effects of evil. Above all, all the great tragedians are disturbed by injustice, and are led to wonder whether the power that moves the world is just' (p.37). Thus far MacKinnon would broadly agree, but Raphael goes on to state that 'there are two reasons why the path of tragedy tends to diverge from that of religion as we understand it in our Biblical tradition' (p37). These are that tragedy points out the problem of innocent suffering without providing a solution, and that the tragic hero is often more sublime than the

it would mean that the 'Christian view of human existence has no place for the sheerly intractable – for that which in the end defeated moral effort, making of the story of such effort a "sound and fury signifying nothing".'[55]

Immediately MacKinnon has indicated the nature of some of his fundamental concerns; with ethical and moral issues, and attention to the darker aspects of human experience. He characterizes the most difficult aspects of this experience as the 'intractable', a term crucial to his understanding of tragedy, and here defined as that which 'defeats moral effort'. This particular focus is but one amongst many possible understandings of tragedy, as the work of the many 'theorists of tragedy' – from Aristotle to Hegel, Nietzsche, Bradley and Nussbaum – illustrates.[56] Therefore the status of MacKinnon's characterisation needs further elucidation. This can partly be achieved by exploring the ways in which MacKinnon utilises his understanding of the 'intractable'.

In the lecture under discussion MacKinnon elaborates his argument with reference to both *Oedipus Rex* and the Christian Gospels. His interpretation of the former is that Oedipus was involved in guilt simply because he sought to avoid it. If he had stayed in Corinth, rather than attempting to give the lie to the oracle by fleeing, he would not have precipitated the events that led to tragedy. MacKinnon does not accept that this kind of situation is alien to Christianity. He argues rather that it is as human beings try to avoid the intractable that they are thrown into guilt, and that this problem is raised at 'a new level of intensity' in Christianity. He proceeds to illustrate his meaning with reference to Mark 14.17ff. Here Jesus eats the last supper with his disciples, and tells them that one of the twelve will betray him. Verse 21 is a text that fascinated MacKinnon, the 'woe to that man' saying quoted in his Inaugural Lecture, and already much discussed in this book.

MacKinnon contrasts his understanding of the text with that found in the writing of Vincent Taylor.[57] He agrees with Taylor that Judas has an important

---

power he opposes, which in religious terms means being more sublime than God. Raphael does acknowledge the power of the 'suffering servant' motif, and acknowledges that the story of Jesus does have tragic qualities. He continues his argument, however, by stating that as soon as you 'add the Christian doctrine of the divinity of Jesus, and of the redemption secured by his passion [and] at once the situation ceases to be tragic.' (p54) What Raphael might have made of MacKinnon's view of a self-limiting triune God, enduring defeat for the salvation of the world, cannot be known.

55 Here, and in subsequently unfootnoted references, I am quoting from the reconstructed lectures as explained in footnote 53. An Appendix gives the text I have been working from of the first two lectures, and the final section of the eighth, which contain most of the references to Judas cited here.

56 See Morris Weitz's excellent discussion in his entry on 'Tragedy' in *The Encyclopaedia of Philosophy* Volume 8 (New York: MacMillan, 1967) pp155-161.

57 In *The Gospel according to St Mark* (New York: St Martin's Press, 1966; first edition 1952) Vincent Taylor makes the following comments on Mark 14.21: 'It suggests that, while the death of the Son of Man is in accordance with the divine purpose, the responsibility of Judas remains. Behind the moral and religious issue stands the philosophical problem of the relation of divine causality to human activity, but it is the

role to play in the path willed by God for Christ, who freely accepted this path. While Taylor is content to argue, however, that Judas both played a part in God's destiny and yet was also morally responsible, MacKinnon points to what he sees as the paradox involved in such a claim; that Judas apparently acted as a morally responsible agent whilst also playing such an indispensable role in the divine purpose that God could have been 'activating an automaton'. This is a rebuff to both Taylor and Barth, and the crudity of the phrase indicates MacKinnon's resistance to any suggestion that Judas' actions can be straightforwardly explained as providentially determined by God in order to further His redemptive purpose.

The paradox pointed to here, important though it is, is not the heart of the argument, which MacKinnon introduces with a quotation from George Moore's poem *Germinal* ('In the lost boyhood of Judas, Christ was betrayed').[58] This is that Jesus was defeated as far as Judas is concerned: 'He was not *Christus Victor* for him.' It can be argued both that this defeat was freely accepted by Jesus, and that this acceptance was willed by God. Yet this 'free acceptance' is conditional on the existence of Judas, of whom it is written 'better for that man if he had not been born.' If, however, he had not been born, his birth not willed by God, the scriptures could not have been fulfilled. MacKinnon thus points to what he means by 'sheer intractability', and even the possibility of an ultimate dualism. He goes on to ask, 'Or must we – if we deny the element of intractability that limits divine power – be compelled to lay the damnation of Judas at the door of the omnipotent Himself?' MacKinnon goes on to imply that the incarnation *contributes* to this intractability in the consequences that the coming of Christ have for Judas.

Here, verbally at least, MacKinnon has partially clarified the thinking hinted at in his Inaugural Lecture. It seems that he is arguing that in Mark 14.21 and parallels (for these are the texts he has in mind) the sense of 'sheer discontinuity' lies in the juxtaposition between the first part of the verse, which emphasizes the providential fulfilment of scripture ('For the Son of Man goes as it is written...'), with the remainder ('but woe to that man by whom the Son of Man is *betrayed!* It would have been better for that man if he had not been born'). The second half of the verse points to Judas, presumably born by the providence of God and somehow acting freely within a pattern of scriptural fulfilment, paradoxically being declared better unborn. If he was literally 'better unborn' this

---

former which more immediately arises in the saying. The responsibility of Judas is affirmed because what will befall Jesus is not remorseless fate but a destiny willed by God, but freely chosen and accepted by Jesus Himself. As such, it finds its expression in a course of historical events with which the act of Judas is connected and for which he is responsible in his own degree. He is not the blind instrument of fate. Such appear to be the implications of the saying. The "woe" pronounced over him is not a curse, but a cry of sorrow and of anguish: "Alas! for that man," and the saying, "It were better, etc" is not a threat, but a sad recognition of facts' pp541-2.

58 I am able to identify the source of the quotation because it appears in the entry on 'Judas Iscariot' in *A Dictionary of Biblical Tradition in English Literature*, edited by David Lyle Jeffrey (Grand Rapids, Michigan: Eerdmans, 1992) p420. The original poem has proved elusive despite a search in many libraries.

implies that there are contingent events outside God's providence, and yet if Judas had never existed he could not have played his part in the Son of Man going 'as it is written'.

In his lecture, MacKinnon focuses his thinking into the following questions: 'Was Judas' act in the providence of God? If it were, what are we to say?' In what way (if any) can it be said, 'better for that man if he had not been born'? MacKinnon's argument is that his questions are illustrations of what he describes as the 'problem/mystery' of moral evil. Certainly his question concerning providence is a key one. For example, if Judas' actions took place within the providential purposes of God, what MacKinnon means by 'defeat' needs greater explication. In fact he is not explicit about what he means by 'defeat', except in so far as he links it to Judas' damnation. In this MacKinnon is expressing what he takes to be the judgement of the Christian tradition on Judas, as he quotes no texts beyond Mark 14.21. He might have mentioned the act of betrayal/handing over as well, for 'defeat' could imply that Judas acted contrary to Jesus' intentions: the fact that 'one of the twelve' could 'betray' his Master, particularly in the sacramental context of the last supper and footwashing.

Once again, MacKinnon does not spell out the argument that he has implied or intuited. He does not fully express what the alert reader might infer from attending to his arguments: that either both Judas' birth and future actions in some way 'defeat' God's providential purposes, or that providence is seen to operate in a morally reprehensible way. If the former, Judas illustrates that a birth which in God's purposes would never have taken place, in fact did so. The reason for him being 'better unborn' is that he is beyond Jesus' salvific powers, and indeed plays a crucial part in ending Jesus' ministry. If the latter, Judas is allowed, even encouraged (cf. John 13.27, 'What you are going to do, do quickly') to act in certain ways that will fulfil scripture, but result in his suicide and damnation.

In his second lecture MacKinnon again asserts that in Judas is seen the 'problem/mystery'[59] of moral evil. He discusses the possibility of justifying the ways of God to humanity – theodicy – and the assumptions underlying attempts to do so. The following summary of theodicy is offered: 'out of the unquestionably evil, good comes whose attainment is inconceivable without evil, but of such magnitude as to justify evil.'[60] Judgements about some individual human lives

---

59 While MacKinnon does not use this phrase in his published writings, its accordance with his subsequent thought can be seen in the following quotation from his 1967 essay 'Atonement and Tragedy' (*Borderlands of Theology*, op cit., pp97-104), where he argues that the 'lesson to be learnt from tragedy [is] that there is no solution to the problem of evil; it is a lesson which Christian faith abundantly confirms, even while it transforms the teaching by the indication of its central mystery' p104.

60 It should be noted that this is hardly a straightforward dictionary definition of theodicy, which, like tragedy, is understood in a variety of ways. Here MacKinnon seems to have in mind Protestant thinking as, for example, found in the Lutheran philosopher Leibniz. However he also discusses the *privatio boni* argument at length, of which Augustine and Aquinas are the key advocates in the Christian tradition. For a perceptive discussion of the variety of approaches to 'theodicy', see Kenneth Surin's *Theology and the Problem of Evil* (Oxford: Blackwell, 1986) particularly pp1-70.

might support such a view, he argues, but the wider implication is something rather harder to sustain – that through the providence of God this is a universal regulative principle.

MacKinnon therefore labels the assumptions underlying theodicy as *monism* and *determinism.* He does not define these terms, which is unfortunate as his use of them, particularly the former, does not entirely follow from his definition of theodicy. Monism is a philosophical position that sees the universe as a harmonious unity, where what may *appear* evil from the vantage point of humanity is not so when seen from a cosmic perspective.[61] The root meaning of determinism is that there is an inevitability or necessity to events, which militates against the common Christian understanding of free will.[62] MacKinnon questions the very possibility of attaining a monistic point of view, from which it could be plausibly argued that the contribution of evil to the articulation of good can be discerned as a fundamental law. He prefers what he calls a 'common-sense pluralism' in which there is a way of redemption seen in Christ, but one that includes defeat and in which the 'traitor' is unredeemed. What remains undiscussed is the difference between this kind of 'pluralism', and a metaphysical dualism.

In his third and fourth lectures MacKinnon continues to discuss theodicy, with reference to the suggestion that God does not 'will' sin, but 'permits' it. This, he suggests, brings to mind a God whose first purposes being 'defeated', embarks upon the strategy of redemption (used in this way, MacKinnon is unhappy at ascribing the word 'defeat' to God). He then introduces an analysis of the 'language of ontology', being particularly concerned with the *privatio boni* argument which he traces from Plotinus through Augustine to Aquinas. Analogous to his arguments on theodicy, MacKinnon raises questions about the sustainability of this argument as an all encompassing explanation. He cannot accept, for example, that the concept of evil as a 'deprivation of the good' is adequate to the suffering of the Holocaust, or the creative quality that human malice often exhibits. While MacKinnon does not explicitly mention Judas at this point, the implication is that it is not adequate to say that Judas' actions were simply 'permitted', as the Gospels portray them as having a necessary quality within the economy of salvation. Whether or not Judas could be seen in terms of *privatio boni* is more open to question, however.

See also Part II of John Hick's *Evil and the God of Love* (London: MacMillan, 1985) and Jurgen Moltmann's entry on theodicy in *A New Dictionary of Christian Theology* (London: SCM, 1983) pp564-566.

61 See John Hick's discussion of monism and dualism in *Evil and the God of Love,* op cit. pp15-33.

62 See, for example, St Augustine, *De libero arbitrio voluntatis*, translated as 'The Free Choice of the Will' in *The Fathers of the Church* series, volume 59 (Washington: Catholic University of America, 1968). There is a tension between the arguments of this relatively early work, and Augustine's later emphasis on the overwhelming priority of grace.

A further implication is that the 'problem/mystery' of evil, as manifested in Judas' role in the Gospels, is not a subject best written about propositionally. A more effective idiom or manner of discourse is the 'logic of the Gospel' (it is partly because Karl Barth takes this 'logic' so seriously that he is the most effective opponent of the 'tragic' viewpoint MacKinnon argues for). In his seventh lecture MacKinnon describes the Gospel as a 'story told in descriptive prose that expresses a whole series of contingent propositions... the ultimate theodicy is the story of Jesus...'. The paradox, he argues, is that the particularity and precariousness of what can be said about Jesus is what enables it to operate as a 'theodicy' aware of its own limitations. Here MacKinnon comes close to collapsing atonement into theodicy.

In his eighth lecture, MacKinnon argues that the Gospels show Jesus grappling with the physical illness and suffering of others, but suggests that the most important issues of human life lie elsewhere. They show that the mission of Jesus is fundamentally concerned with moral evil, and the sin under which the human race is labouring. Immediately his argument brings MacKinnon back to Judas and the observation that the coming of Jesus was 'appalling ill-fortune for some of those who came in contact with him.' Once again he quotes Moore's line about the 'lost boyhood of Judas', arguing that this upbringing would never have born such 'bitter fruit' without Jesus. For MacKinnon this is one of the burdens that Christ bore on the cross, as is the fundamental contradiction between justice and mercy. What is most significant for MacKinnon is that Jesus was prepared to endure defeat. Jesus' own achievement of the moral life could not in itself resolve the mystery of evil, and yet in his endurance the significance and salvation of Christ is most clearly to be seen.

It is evident that MacKinnon's analysis in his lectures on 'Evil' circles around a cluster of issues relating to Judas, the implications of which are at best partially elucidated. The second hypothesis mentioned just prior to the beginning of this section, that MacKinnon's intuitive sense of the importance of these issues was never fully worked through and expressed in writing, has received some support. The following summary attempts to spell out the interrelated issues and assertions arising from the lectures:

1. The role of Judas in the economy of salvation represents a defeat for Jesus. In that Judas defeats the 'moral effort' of Jesus, he witnesses to the 'intractable' in human life – by which is meant that which is resistant to every effort (even by God in Christ) to overcome it. Judas cannot be guided, managed or persuaded into salvation, but through his actions finds condemnation.
2. The nature of the 'defeat' Judas represents, and his subsequent fate, indicates either that God is ultimately responsible for his damnation (as a kind of 'by-product' of the salvific process), or that God is limited by the existence of the intractable in human life.
3. The nature of the moral responsibility Judas bears is unclear, given that his actions were crucial to the economy of salvation.

4. The underlying assumptions of theodicy are hazardous, and the ontological *privatio boni* argument unsatisfactory. Whatever insights these traditions of analysis may offer, they cannot be the all-embracing arguments their proponents intend them to be. Therefore a 'common-sense pluralism' is to be preferred, in which it can be asserted that in Christ there is indeed a 'way of redemption', but one which contains genuine defeat and intractability – and that therefore Judas is unredeemed. This kind of approach is best exemplified in a Christological discourse informed by the insights of tragedy.
5. Mark 14.17 ff. (and parallels), but particularly 14.21, are the key Gospel texts. This is because MacKinnon senses in them a significant discontinuity or tension between providence and tragedy, with Judas acting within a pattern of scriptural fulfilment, yet paradoxically being declared better unborn.

These issues and assertions can be focused into one key suggestion diametrically opposed to Barth: that the life and actions of Judas Iscariot are more accurately described as evidence of the tragic at the heart of the Gospels, than as revealing the providence of God.

Nearly ten years after the lecture series just discussed, MacKinnon asked the following question in a seminar: 'Was there that which Jesus alone could do under the conditions in which it had to be done which was of such import for humanity that the risk was justified, the cost well spent?' The continuity in thinking is apparent, and it is significant that this is evident through a *question* rather than a statement. Nicholas Lash, who jotted down the question word for word, argues in a perceptive obituary of MacKinnon that attention to it defined his work.[63] Lash asserts that the Second World War and attendant horrors had a decisive impact on MacKinnon, leaving difficult questions to be faced about both God and humankind. It was in this context that exploration of the 'tragic vision' became central to his writing, with the Holocaust being particularly important.

His work did not explicitly deal with the relationship between tragedy and theology until the nineteen sixties. Glimpses of the intellectual process that led to this focus, so apparent in the Cambridge lectures and subsequent publications, may be found in his 1957 book *A Study in Ethical Theory*. There, for example, he considers Kant's approach to radical moral evil, arguing that Kant took the intractability of the world seriously – but as a barrier to moral obedience, not the starting point for a new metaphysics or ethics susceptible to the temptations of an 'heroic' view of life. What mattered was the sense, if any, that could be given to the nature of this 'barrier' or 'horizon' in aiding comprehension of the character of human experience.[64] MacKinnon also admires Hegel's insight into the human predicament with reference to the individual in relation to society. For Hegel, he writes, there 'was a sense in which the dialectical opposition of principles of conduct and policies of life was but the reflection of a deeper tragic opposition in

---

[63] Nicholas Lash, 'The stuff of legend' *The Guardian*, Saturday March 5 1994.

[64] *A Study in Ethical Theory* (London: A. and C. Black, 1957) p86.

which men were involved at the level of their personal and collective existence'.[65] This opposition was not superficial, but something intrinsic to the nature of human life.

In *A Study in Ethical Theory* there is none of the detailed reference to particular plays or the passion narratives that will be evident within a decade. Here, however, can be seen what remains true – MacKinnon is not interested in tragedy for primarily literary reasons, but as offering insight into the characterisation of human ethical experience. The urgency of this enquiry has to be understood against what Lash describes as the 'decisive impact' of the Second World War, particularly the Holocaust. At some point between this book and his Cambridge lectures he began to see tragedy as likewise offering insight into the nature of the Gospels, and the crucial relationship between Christ and Judas.

MacKinnon's 1963 broadcast talk called 'Order and Evil in the Gospel', discussed in the introduction, hovers on the edge of a discussion of tragedy. It speaks of the appalling cost of Christ's victory, for 'there is no solution offered in the Gospels of the riddle of Iscariot',[66] and the healing that comes from Christ's endurance and bearing of this burden. His 1965-66 Gifford lectures dealt extensively with tragedy, but were not published until 1974. The first published essay explicitly on the subject is entitled 'Theology and Tragedy',[67] and in it MacKinnon writes of a 'multiple complexity' in the family of works described as tragedies. He discusses the reasons for the ancient quarrel between the poets and the philosophers that began with Plato. He considers the result to have been that even those who are not Platonists regard tragedy as secondary in understanding the world, with primacy being given to more general, propositional forms of discourse.

MacKinnon contests this, and argues further that the 'open textured' quality of tragedy can be related to the Christian story. He reminds his readers of the anti-Semitism in the Gospels, and the contribution made thereby to the cultural conditions that made possible the Holocaust. He argues that Jesus chose not to use his influence to work against the movement of the Jewish people towards the catastrophe of A.D. 70. Finally, he states, whilst the passion of Christ is of ultimate significance, it is also a literal failure. This failure is focused in the figure of Judas where 'the tragic quality of his mission becomes plain, "Good were it for this man if he had not been born" '.[68] Yet through his actions the Son of Man goes the way chosen in Gethsemane: 'There is no solution here of the problem of the moral evil; there is nothing moreover which the Easter faith somehow obliterates.' For Christ is subsequently revealed to his own, not to the world, and those who accept the empty tomb can see it as 'no more than a sign pointing'.[69]

---

65 Ibid. p220.

66 Op cit.

67 First published in the journal *Religious Studies* (April 1967). Reprinted in *The Stripping of the Altars* (London: Fontana, 1969) pp41-51.

68 Ibid. pp168-9.

69 Ibid. p169.

MacKinnon concludes that the term 'tragic' has much to offer to the 'system of projection' appropriate to Christianity, and needs careful consideration. He therefore takes up some of these themes in an essay entitled 'Atonement and Tragedy', originally delivered at a Colloquium on the philosophy of religion in Rome (1967).[70] MacKinnon begins by recognizing that fundamental theology will always reflect the assumptions and prejudices of the theologian. Nevertheless, he argues, the risk of evaluating Christ's work in ethical terms is necessary. From his work as a moral philosopher MacKinnon is aware that some such evaluations are profound explorations of the human condition, whilst others are 'morally horrifying'. Part of the problem, he suggests (in an important sentence that sums up something of his theological method), lies in 'a failure to find the form of moral reflection least wholly inappropriate to the analysis of the Christian material'.[71] This is partly due to Plato's victory for the philosophers over the poets (just discussed), and in particular the tragedians. He now seeks to ask the question: can the work of Christ receive effective theological treatment when represented as tragedy?

It is asserted, MacKinnon writes, that tragedy is incompatible with Christianity because it witnesses to 'the intractable surd element in the scheme of things'.[72] And yet in Racine, Sophocles, and Shakespeare there is a paradoxical affirmation both of human freedom and of that in the world which brings moral fidelity to nothing. Their works of imagination portray the 'freedom of open possibilities' as well as the reality of moral evil that makes the 'comfortable musings' of many theologians and philosophers seem trivial.

The Gospels, argues MacKinnon, should not be read as orientated to a happy ending, as though to wipe out the memory of their more sombre events. Indeed, in the Gospels one sees 'the authors trying to come to terms with a revelation of the ways of God with men too strange to admit of decisive comprehension or representation'.[73] The Gospels are certainly apologetics, but many theologians have been slower to recognize that they are also a reaching back to the past in the attempt to come to terms with it. In that past is Christ's presence to the intractable, and his betrayal (with its consequences for Judas as well as Christ). Here the 'surd element in the scheme of things' has a face and a name, and the very revelation of God has a tragic aspect.

MacKinnon argues that through the paradox of Christ's manifestation as both judge of the world and condemned man, have arisen both subjective and objective understandings of the atonement. But, he writes, these are doctrines in a different sense to that of the Trinity,[74] in that they refer to an historical deed. They

---

70 *Borderlands of Theology*, op cit. pp97-104.

71 Ibid. p100.

72 Ibid.

73 Ibid. p102.

74 It can of course be argued that since the doctrine of Trinity has both an immanent and an economic dimension, it cannot be entirely separated from Christ's historical actions. MacKinnon later wrote that, 'It is to engage in the task of reconstructing the doctrine of the Ultimate that the form of Jesus' ministry, his life, his death, and his being

will fail if they do not attend to the sheer waste and failure involved. Could Jesus have done more to avert the Jewish catastrophe less than forty years away? Could he have avoided involving his contemporaries in a terrible guilt that provided the excuse for later anti-Semitism? In the events of Good Friday the judgement of the world and the foundation of its hope are glimpsed, but part of the price was Christian acquiescence in the 'final solution'. For it is necessary to come to terms not only with the work of Christ but what the church has made of it.[75]

The discussion so far has seen much that is characteristic of MacKinnon. He prefers paradox to synthesis, alert to the temptation of comforting falsehood – so no 'solution' to the problem of evil. In this light he reads the Gospels, and so foregrounds[76] for his readers particular aspects of their narrative. He emphasizes Christ's contingency, his self-emptying, and the disclosure of a tragic reality, seen most clearly in the fate of Judas and the Jews, that is not wiped out by the resurrection. It is also characteristic that his allusive style has nowhere offered a clear definition of tragedy, nor spelled out explicitly just what it is that makes Judas and texts such as Mark 14.21 'tragic'.

There have been some indications as to why MacKinnon considers 'tragedy' an appropriate 'system of projection', but once again the reader is left to spell out the substantive point. For one of the features of tragedy is the unforeseen consequences of human action, however well intentioned. In this sense the fate of Judas in relation to Jesus not only mirrors but contributes to later treatment of the Jews, from the destruction of the temple to the Holocaust. This point is strongly made by MacKinnon's Cambridge colleague and friend George Steiner, in his 1995 essay 'Two Suppers'.[77] In it Steiner elaborates the connection between the treatment of Judas in the Gospels and the tragedy of the Holocaust in a way that arguably expresses the implications of MacKinnon's position, although it goes beyond anything MacKinnon wrote.[78] Unlike MacKinnon, who tends to focus on the synoptics, Steiner discusses John 13, particularly verse 27: 'Then after the morsel, Satan entered into [Judas]. Jesus said to him, "What you are going to do, do quickly." ' First pointing out that Judas is the only disciple with a specifically

---

brought again from death to boundless life, is found in God as He is in Himself' *Themes in Theology – the threefold cord* (Edinburgh: T. & T. Clark, 1987) p154. The quotation comes from an essay entitled, 'The Relation of the Doctrines of Incarnation and Trinity', pp145- 167.

75 Op cit. p103.

76 I use the term 'foreground' in the sense described in Harold Bloom's *Shakespeare – The Invention of the Human* (London: Fourth Estate, 1999) – to indicate that which draws attention to, or makes prominent, particular features of a written work (see p737ff).

77 'Two Suppers', The Priestley Lectures, University of Toronto, April 1995. Published in *No Passion Spent – Essays 1978-1996* (London: Faber, 1996) pp390-419.

78 Steiner calls the strongest expression of this connection found in MacKinnon's writing, in the essay 'Atonement and Tragedy' discussed earlier, a 'classic statement' ('Tribute to Donald MacKinnon', pp2-9 *Theology* January/February 1995) p6.

Jewish name,[79] and then the contradiction or tension with John 6.70, where Judas is described as a 'devil', Steiner writes that in the second half of the verse:

> A terrible humanity comes through: that of a man scarcely capable of countenancing the horrors to be visited on him, yet wishing to 'be done with them.' To my mind, the abyss of truth in this pericope precludes literary invention... .[80]

Steiner goes on to argue that whereas Jesus and Judas may understand what is happening, the Gospel makes it plain that the other disciples do not know why Jesus has spoken as he has, but think that as Judas has the money box, he is being enjoined either to buy what is needed for the feast, or to give something to the poor (vv28-9). Steiner argues that while neither motive would do Judas any dishonour, the 'concatenation is catastrophic. It enmeshes the person and destiny of the Jew with that of money...'.[81] This and the thirty pieces of silver mean that the 'daemonic ambiguities of money... will cling to the Jew like leprosy.'[82] In verse 30 the Gospel records that 'after receiving the morsel, [Judas] immediately went out; and it was night.' Steiner writes of this in the strongest terms possible:

> Judas goes into a never-ending night of collective guilt. It is sober truth to say that his exit is the door to the Holocaust. The 'final solution' proposed, enacted by National Socialism in this twentieth century is the perfectly logical, axiomatic conclusion to the Judas-identification of the Jew... . That utter darkness, that night within night, into which Judas is dispatched and commanded to perform 'quickly', is already that of the death-ovens. Who, precisely, has betrayed whom?[83]

Thus Steiner turns the anti-Semitic notion of the Jews as 'Christ killers' on its head. The suggestion is made that the responsibility for later horrors, including those of the Second World War that provide the foreground to MacKinnon's writing, lies with Christ. And whilst even MacKinnon never writes in such stark terms, such indeed are the implications of his argument that the coming of Jesus has something tragic about it both for Judas and the Jewish people. As a Christian theologian, however, he cannot leave the matter there. He does conclude that the 'lesson to be learnt from tragedy [is] that there is no solution to the problem of evil', but goes on to say that this 'is a lesson which Christian faith abundantly confirms, even while it transforms the teaching by the indication of its central mystery'.[84] In Christ, he contends, the conflicting claims of truth and mercy are reconciled by deed, not word, in a way beyond human comprehension, requiring description and redescription. The bitterness of the deed is beyond any formula,

---

79 This point is central to the argument of Hyam Maccoby's book *Judas Iscariot and the Myth of Jewish Evil* (New York: The Free Press, 1992).

80 Ibid. p416.

81 Ibid.

82 Ibid. p417.

83 Ibid. As indicated at the beginning of this chapter, what Steiner describes as 'sober truth' is contested territory by Holocaust scholars (see footnote 3).

84 'Atonement and Tragedy', op cit. p104.

for (and these are the final words of the essay), 'Here is the revelation of God, but here also is that human deed in which the abysses of existence are sounded and the ultimate contradictions of life plumbed and explored.'[85]

MacKinnon is fond of this kind of peroration,[86] but it must be said that 'sounding' and 'exploring' the abysses and contradictions of life do not amount to what Christian doctrine describes as the economy of salvation. It could be said that the misfortune for Judas was to have his heart 'sounded', and that MacKinnon has not shown how this is good news. The Gifford Lectures referred to earlier offer the most likely source of further elucidation, as they are MacKinnon's most extended treatment of the themes under discussion, particularly in chapters eleven and twelve of what was eventually published as *The Problem of Metaphysics.*[87] Chapter Eleven is titled 'The transcendence of the tragic', and once again finds MacKinnon contesting the claim that Christians and the Christian religion have moved beyond tragedy. There is a rare acknowledgement of the strong human wish for a 'solution' to the problem of evil,[88] but for him this wish is not best served by avoiding the complexity of what is at stake.

There are few new arguments relating to the questions under discussion, however. MacKinnon does include a favourite reference, quoting the Duke of Wellington on the tragic quality inherent in victory. He recalls Wellington's statement that 'a victory is the most tragic thing in the world, only excepting a defeat',[89] which helps him to see the tragedy inherent in Romans 9-11 and the passion narratives. In the former is the question all the Gospel writers dealt with, and which in a sense was their 'problem of evil' – the rejection of the Messiah by the people to whom he came. Once again this is a theme with powerful resonances in relation to the anti-Semitism of subsequent centuries. For MacKinnon the key temptation is to see the catastrophic course of events, including the horrors of the twentieth century, as providential and therefore bearable.[90] He simply cannot accept that the events of his own lifetime were 'bearable'. Neither could he accept

---

85 Ibid.

86 For example his 1967 essay 'The Future of Man' ends as follows: 'Yet obstinately we can still claim that Christ is greater than any institution claiming monopoly of his secrets, and that it may in the end be made plain that in his faithfulness unto death is the healing of our human hurt, and in his mystery the secret of our ways' (*Explorations in Theology 5*, London: SCM, 1979) p10.

87 *The Problem of Metaphysics* (London: Cambridge University Press, 1974). That these lectures were published at all (and this in a revised form) is attributed to some of MacKinnon's postgraduate students retrieving the notes from his study. The delay in publication can reasonably be attributed to MacKinnon's sense of the incompleteness of his work.

88 Ibid. p24.

89 This quotation is referred to in *The Problem of Metaphysics*, pp126 and 131, and in *Explorations in Theology 5* op cit. pp44, 192 and 194.

90 It is arguable that even Jürgen Moltmann, who seeks to face the horrors of Auschwitz in *The Crucified God* (London: SCM, 1974), attempts to make these horrors 'bearable' by arguing that they are 'taken up into the grief of the Father, the surrender of the Son and the power of the Spirit' (p278).

the kind of Christian apologetic that found in the *Pax Augusta* the divinely ordered setting for the spread of the Gospel, forgetting the means by which it was imposed and upheld.[91]

MacKinnon concentrates particularly on Luke's Gospel, where he does not find a picture of a developing ministry, crowned with glory after a superficial defeat. Rather, he argues, Christ endures a searching temptation, and yet refuses the prospect of a bloodless victory gained by throwing himself from the temple parapet, or coming down from the cross. In so enduring, Jesus is able to remain free to associate with the disreputable, to receive the confession of the penitent thief, and demonstrate his perfect obedience to his Father. In his supreme hour, MacKinnon writes, one might say that miracle is 'ethically out of place'.[92] In Luke there is not the 'tragic irony' of John, but there is a sense of a deeply tragic reality, of victory achieved at appalling cost. Christians have tended to shy away from acknowledging this, but MacKinnon wonders whether

> ...Christianity, properly understood, might provide men with a faith through which they are enabled to hold steadfastly to the significance of the tragic, and thereby protect themselves against that sort of synthesis which seeks to obliterate by the vision of an all-embracing order the sharper discontinuity of human existence.[93]

He is suggesting that 'tragedy regarded as a form of discourse, itself [provides] a way of representing the relation of the familiar to the transcendent',[94] in that the very ruthlessness of its interrogation enables the projection of our ultimate questioning in ways unavailable through any alternative.

In such projection the conflicts of duties, ambiguities and self-deceptions of human life are saved from trivialisation and given some sort of significance. Tragedy touches issues to do with the intractability of human life and the limits of rationality. Yet, MacKinnon regrets, few have had the courage to read the Gospels as tragedies. Part of the reason is the complexity of the resurrection narratives. Certainly these evidence a victory, in that Jesus' way is affirmed as that of God, but it is not a victory that is free of a tragic quality for, 'The surd element remains.' A key example of this is that

> ...the Son of Man has gone his appointed way, and the one who has made it possible for him to take that journey 'has gone to his own place'... . Indeed, increasingly one sees that the reality of Christ's humanity resides in the fact that as he lived he was

---

91 MacKinnon often quoted Father R.M. Benson's remark that the conversion of Constantine 'was the greatest single disaster which the Christian Church ever sustained.' See, for example *Themes in Theology* (Edinburgh: T. & T. Clark Ltd), pp98 and 142.

92 Op cit. p133.

93 Ibid. p135.

94 Ibid.

> confronted with real choices, fraught, in consequence of the way in which he chose, with disaster as well as achievement in their train.[95]

For MacKinnon, therefore, tragedy and Christology are bound together. For him Christ is both the One through whom the world is created, and the one crucified in plumbing the depths of that world. In that sense the person of Christ, whose identity is constituted by God, can be seen as taking the consequences of his own creation, which is shown in his passion to be capable of the deepest tragedy. Those who have made possible such a 'reading' of the Gospel stories, the tragic writers, help to make possible the insight that if there can be any 'solution' to the existence of evil in the world it is to be found not in propositional discourse, but in the historical Christ who encounters the worst that the world can give, and out of that experience offers illumination and healing.

This 'healing', however, has a terrible cost, as is seen in the immediate fate of Judas, and the subsequent traumas of the Jewish people. It is a hard and painful 'solution', fragmentary, difficult to assimilate; but given the intractability of the world (in MacKinnon's account) no other way is possible. This is shown in the resurrection, whereby the life of Jesus is made accessible to contemporary human beings. This life is so crucial not because it is that of a 'superman', but because in its receptivity and self-abandonment is revealed the triune God. The unity of Christ with the Father emerges out of an historical engagement exhibiting all the ambiguity and precariousness of a human life, and the impossibility of determining the future effects of that life. In the contingent events of Jesus' life, death and resurrection are seen this uncontingent unity.

Here it is important to recognize, as Kenneth Surin has written, that MacKinnon does not have a comprehensive doctrine of the Incarnation, but 'provides the reader with a series of clues which point to those features that would have to be present in any account faithful to the Gospel narratives and the Christological traditions of the Church.'[96] Moreover the coherence of the 'clues' can be questioned. MacKinnon's insight into the role of Judas are fascinating, and yet he never properly explores their implications. Can he really be suggesting that the world as created in Christ is of such a nature that individuals can be destroyed within the redemptive process? MacKinnon has no doctrine, or 'clue' to suggest anything like an Augustinian account of the 'fall' that is the proper context for understanding *privatio boni.* He clearly finds any form of monism unacceptable, but the question of an ultimate dualism is neither resolved nor ruled out. For 'tragedy' itself is not innocent of ontological claims, and these are not faced by MacKinnon in any sustained way.

---

95 'Ethics and Tragedy' (a lecture delivered at the University of Stirling in February 1971), *Explorations in Theology 5* (London: SCM, 1979) p194.

96 'Some aspects of the "grammar" of "incarnation" and "kenosis": reflections prompted by the writings of Donald MacKinnon', pp93-116 in *Christ, Ethics and Tragedy – essays in honour of Donald MacKinnon* edited by Kenneth Surin (Cambridge: University Press, 1989) p93.

In a 1989 *Festschrift* for MacKinnon, Brian Hebblethwaite offers some pertinent criticisms of MacKinnon's arguments on evil and tragedy.[97] Hebblethwaite is prepared to agree that glib 'answers' to the problem of evil are to be avoided, but suggests that if there were no answer at all, aspects of the Christian faith such as a personal or moral God would have to disappear. He also agrees that the Christian faith must face up to the kinds of disaster that defeat human goodness, which is one definition of what 'tragedy' means. He does not accept, however, that the story of Christ bears witness to 'ultimate, eternal failure and an absolutely irredeemable corruption of the good'.[98] He argues that 'it is extremely difficult for the Christian mind to concede that any situation or person is ultimately and finally irredeemable for all eternity' and that Christianity is committed to faith in a final consummation in which both victims and perpetrators can participate.[99]

Hebblethwaite therefore will not concede the 'ineradicability of the tragic' to MacKinnon. He argues that despite historical tragedies, no human being can remain irredeemable for all eternity. The fact that there are many unresolved tragedies in human life does not mean that there is no future resolution. In this sense tragedy can have no finality, because all 'victims will participate in the resurrection, transformation and consummation of all things', including Judas.[100] For Hebblethwaite, MacKinnon's emphasis on the failure of Christ with regard to Judas, and the subsequent contribution of the Gospel to anti-Semitism, are indeed important questions – but they do not point to the final ineradicability of the tragic because Christianity affirms the reality of eschatological redemption.

MacKinnon might well respond that all that can be known of redemption is what has been seen in Christ, whose very redemptive victory nevertheless retains the quality of the tragic. The key point is that in MacKinnon's trinitarian discourse the failure of God the Son is not incompatible with the triumph of God the Father, but defeat remains part of Christ's history and so of the Godhead. Hebblethwaite cannot offer an alternative account of the role of Judas in the passion narrative, or challenge MacKinnon's analysis of their finality in relation to him, simply arguing that even Judas must be redeemed in the end. He goes on to agree with MacKinnon that explanations and eschatological hopes must not be used to downplay evil in the world, but conversely argues that moral outrage and practical imperatives should not be allowed to do away with the quest for answers. If this quest is abandoned there will be an avoidance of the consequences of understanding the problem of evil as insoluble.

Again, MacKinnon might respond that his argument is that the problem of evil 'remains intractable by any of the methods traditionally employed to solve or dissolve it'.[101] It is theodicy as a method that is being rejected in favour of Christology – indeed a very different idiom, but a kind of 'answer' nevertheless. Hebblethwaite's strongest counter to MacKinnon is his remark that the 'charge of

---

97 'MacKinnon and the problem of evil', Ibid. pp131-145.

98 Ibid. p140.

99 Ibid. p142.

100 Ibid. p141.

101 *Explorations in Theology 5*, op cit. p193.

evasion can be pressed in more than one direction'.[102] By this he means that the theological consequences of declaring the insolubility of the problem of evil and the ultimacy of the tragic, as well as collapsing theodicy into atonement, have not been adequately attended to by MacKinnon. While Hebblethwaite does not explicitly relate these remarks to Judas, they are highly relevant. For, as has been indicated, on MacKinnon's account it does begin to look as though the death and damnation of Judas are the 'price' of salvation. He has used the category of tragedy to pinpoint the weaknesses in the arguments of others; here, perhaps, is seen how the tragic resists being written into even a theology that seeks to embrace something of it. For example, MacKinnon is acute in pointing out difficulties with the doctrine of *privatio boni* but the problems do not disappear when it is rejected. Perhaps the main point of the doctrine is the avoidance of ontological dualism, and therefore the main danger in rejecting it is the possibility of accepting some form of a heresy which has disturbing implications for the whole of Christian doctrine. The danger can only be heightened if one is attempting to articulate 'Christian tragedy', and MacKinnon never explicitly attends to such issues.

MacKinnon's theological idiom is complex and many-sided, relying on a profound intuition and sense of moral purpose for much of its richness and effectiveness. A question mark must be raised by the extent of its incompleteness, however, if not its 'evasion'. It may well be that, as MacKinnon wrote of Kierkegaard, he teaches best not by a doctrine but by a method.[103] In this regard, his struggle to find 'the form of moral reflection least wholly inappropriate' is significant.

2.3 Conclusion

MacKinnon admired the work of Karl Barth, whom he called 'the one living theologian of unquestionable genius',[104] although strangely he seems never to have read Barth's writing on Judas Iscariot. First published in English in 1957, it could have provided MacKinnon with a necessary counterpoint to his own argumentation. As has been seen, Barth argued that the actions and fate of Judas had 'nothing to do with human tragedy or the like, but... had to happen, as the will of God'.[105] MacKinnon, on the other hand, has asserted that in the role of Judas in the Gospels is seen 'the intractable surd element in the scheme of things' where God in Christ experiences a measure of defeat in redeeming the world.[106]

Each can find a measure of support in scripture and tradition, and their writings lay bare issues and questions present in all writing concerning Judas in the Christian tradition. To reiterate the crucial difference between the two: Barth

---

[102] Op cit. p143.

[103] 'Some notes on Kierkegaard', *Borderlands of Theology*, op cit. p128.

[104] *Borderlands of Theology*, op cit. p54.

[105] Op cit. p493.

[106] *Borderlands of Theology*, op cit. p100.

cannot see Judas as having anything to do with human tragedy, as MacKinnon does. He shows his awareness of the 'reading' MacKinnon points to by his insistence that what Judas did, and what happened to him, was not an 'unfortunate episode' but in every respect part of the will of God. Perhaps the key question, therefore, is whether the 'logic of the Gospel' suggests tragedy (MacKinnon) or providence (Barth). It is the contention of this book that in fact it suggests a necessary tension between the two. In the previous chapter it was seen that this tension arises in the New Testament itself, as the writers struggle to articulate how Judas' actions come within the providence of God. In this chapter it has been seen that there are problematic aspects in focusing primarily on one aspect of the providential/tragic polarity.

For Barth, as has been seen, Judas is not amongst the elect but one of the 'rejected'; though he states that the two can only be understood in relation to each other. He understands Judas both as a representative of Israel, and of what the other disciples and the church have in common with Israel. Barth considers that the protection of Christ was 'in vain' as far as Judas was concerned, and yet that it was precisely the 'rejection' of Judas and others that he bore on the cross. It is for the rejected that Christ died and rose again, in order that Israel and Judas might have a future with God. Barth does not deny the horror of rejection, but argues that it is nevertheless limited and bound by Christ. MacKinnon for his part shares with Barth the view that attending to Judas is important in understanding what Christ bore on the cross, but for him this is a 'defeat' which has a bitter finality about it.

MacKinnon never describes Judas as 'representative', though he does link Judas and the Jewish people in the sense of both being casualties of the incarnational economy. He is more overtly concerned with 'what happened', with contingent history, than Barth. For MacKinnon the New Testament texts about Judas witness to a struggling to comprehend a disturbing reality, and have no sense of 'calmness' about them. His key text is Mark 14.21, while Barth focuses on the language of 'handing over' and John 6.70, where Jesus identifies Judas as a 'devil' from the first. While Barth draws the other apostles, Paul and Israel into his excursus, MacKinnon focuses only on the paradox of 'better unborn' and Judas' death and damnation. Barth, therefore, has attempted to 'read' Judas in the sense of the totality of the drama in a way MacKinnon never does. Nevertheless MacKinnon's intuitive sense of where the heart of the matter lies has an undoubted power, and the possibility remains that he has pointed to a flaw in the superstructure of Barth's argument capable of bringing it tumbling down.

Barth's reading of παραδίδωμι takes up the questions raised in the previous chapter about the parallelism between Judas' actions and those of others, such as the high priests, and even the purposes of God. A related question is for both Barth and MacKinnon at the heart of the New Testament: what is the will of God for Judas? Barth finds it hard to say if there is any redemptive significance for Judas in the Lord's supper, the footwashing, and Jesus' death, and equally cannot accept that Jesus died in vain for him. MacKinnon also finds the latter problematic, yet it is the implication of his use of the word 'defeat'. Accepting his tragic reading opens the way to the suggestion that in the incarnation is seen the self-limitation of the triune God, a self-limitation carried through to the point of enduring intractability and defeat.

It can be seen that the contrasting 'readings' of Barth and MacKinnon have brought to light a series of interrelated questions and issues relating to Judas. These concur with the issues identified at the end of the previous chapter, and focus the theological issues at the heart of this book:

1. Was Judas a 'defeat' for Christ, or are his actions and death limited and bound by Christ? If Judas does demonstrate such a defeat, does this indicate that when God becomes incarnate, one consequence is the revelation of tragedy and intractability in the world? Is this because the incarnation is a self-limitation of God the Father, in which He does not will to intervene when God the Son experiences (and in an important sense creates) such intractability in 'plumbing the depths' of the human condition?
2. Do the last supper, the footwashing and Jesus' death have salvific power as far as Judas is concerned, or not? This focuses the question relating to the nature of Judas' participation in these events identified in the previous chapter.
3. Does the possibility of eschatological salvation remain open for Judas - or is he eternally damned? Is MacKinnon right to argue that the death of Judas is 'final', and there can be no further hope for him? Or can the possibility of election still be held out to him, as Barth insists?
4. MacKinnon points to the paradox of moral responsibility in relation to the divine will and purpose. What is the relation between the actions of Judas and the fulfilment of scripture? Are Judas' birth, actions, and death within the providence of God, or not?
5. Is the place of Judas Iscariot in the economy of salvation better explicated by a Barthian 'providential' excursus, or the more fragmentary allusiveness of MacKinnon's emphasis on tragedy? Or, as is the argument of this book, by attending to the tension between these opposed interpretations? Further, might attending to this tension furnish clues about the 'least inadequate' idiom for struggling with issues of evil and suffering (including the consequences of the connection between the Gospels and anti-Semitism) in the contemporary world?

Such are the significant questions and issues. Arising as they do out of an examination first of the biblical texts themselves, and then of the opposed readings of Barth and MacKinnon, they offer a paradigm for approaching the multifarious writing on the theme of Judas in the Christian tradition. The next four chapters will demonstrate that the issues identified above are key to approaching the tradition in a way that will best explicate the nature of the arguments found there. The first issue to be examined concerns the nature of Judas' participation in the footwashing and last supper, and the implications for his exclusion or inclusion in the redemption wrought by Christ.

Chapter 3

Judas' Participation in the Footwashing and Last Supper

Indeed, since [Judas] was such as he was, and incorrigible besides, it was not fitting to keep him within the company any longer.[1]

John Chrysostom

One of the themes identified in the opening two chapters is the nature of Judas' participation in the last supper and footwashing. Of particular concern is their salvific efficacy as far as Judas was concerned, and whether or not Judas represents a 'defeat' for Jesus. These questions will be addressed in this first thematic chapter, as implicit within them is the issue of why Judas was included in the original twelve at all. As will be seen, when exegetes consider the Gospel accounts of the footwashing or last supper, the way in which these are understood to reveal the difference between Judas and the other disciples often leads them to discuss the nature and interpretation of his calling by Jesus.

The point has been made that the way the sacraments are understood has important Christological implications, and this is true also of Jesus' call to Judas. Both raise questions of limit, providence and tragedy. For example the questions of the extent and nature of Jesus' foreknowledge, and his judgement of others, are raised. The nature of Judas' inclusion in the twelve generally, and his participation in the last supper and footwashing particularly, are indicative of God's will and purposes for him. The issues are not straightforward, however. As was seen in Chapter 2, even Karl Barth's providential reading of Judas recognizes that it is difficult to say if there is any redemptive significance for Judas in the Lord's Supper, the footwashing, or indeed in Jesus' death.

The difficulty noted by Barth is raised in a particular form early in the Christian tradition, through the formulation of the question of whether or not Judas participated in the footwashing or last supper. Such a question would hardly be warranted on the basis of scripture alone, even though it most commonly occurs in exegeses of John 13, but arises in relation to the kind of Christological questions that have emerged in the opening chapters of this book. This chapter begins with a contrast between the writing of Origen, who argued that Judas was excluded from the footwashing, and that of Chrysostom and Augustine. In this way it is possible

---

1 *Commentary on St John the Apostle and Evangelist*, Homilies 48-88, *Fathers of the Church*, Volume 41 (Washington: Catholic University of America, 1960) Homily 72, p272.

to achieve a clear sense of the theological issues at stake, without analysis of every patristic text on the subject. Augustine's writings are in turn important for understanding a medieval debate between Rupert of Deutz and Alger of Liège, with Rupert using a form of Origen's argument. The topography of the arguments involved is completed by reference to Aquinas and Abelard. The final section of the chapter focuses on the writing of Jonathan Edwards, who struggles with the kind of position adopted by Origen and Rupert. He does so in a way that points towards both the attractiveness and the difficulty, for the theologian, of excluding Judas either from the footwashing or the sacrament of Christ's body and blood.

The arguments of all of the writers considered here, in the main found in commentaries on John's Gospel, witness to an awareness of the difficulty of interpreting the figure of Judas in the light of their dominant understanding of Jesus. Furthermore, it is striking that even those who disagree with Origen, Rupert and Edwards about Judas' exclusion, find other ways to argue for his *difference* from the remaining disciples (despite the New Testament emphasis on Judas as 'one of the twelve'). They do not see Judas as a representative figure, in Barthian fashion, the only exception being in relation to his Jewishness.

In what follows the question of *limit* is a recurring theme. In Chapter 2 this was a concept discussed in relation to MacKinnon's emphasis on Judas as a 'defeat' for Christ, in which Christ the Son is understood as revealing, even creating, the intractability and tragedy inherent in the created order. In MacKinnon's allusive work the incarnation is a self-limitation of God the Father, in that He does not intervene as Christ plumbs the depths of human evil and malevolence. The limitation of Jesus' powers, in the sense that his perception and insight operated within the parameters of the rest of humanity, is an intrinsic part of such a Christology. The argument of this book is that attending to the tension between the latter, and Christologies that emphasize Jesus' foreknowledge of God's providential purposes, is the most fruitful way of explicating the issues. It will be seen that while this tension is *perceived* by many writers, the attempt is nearly always made to minimise or deny it. This only results in the creation of fresh difficulties and incoherences, so strengthening the case this book is seeking to sustain. The first writer in whose work this will be demonstrated is Origen.

3.1 Origen on Judas as 'holy but changing for the worse'

Origen (c.185-c.254) is the first major Christian writer 'to deal with the tremendous historical and theological problems of the event of the betrayal'.[2] Before him, much of the earliest consideration of Judas was restricted to popular legend and apocryphal works. This may have been, as Laeuchli argues, because the Gospel accounts of Judas 'remained a rather dark spot for the young church, which was in constant self-defence against the manifold powers of the pagan

2 Samuel Laeuchli, 'Origen's Interpretation of Judas Iscariot', pp259-268, *Church History* Volume XXII (December 1953) p253.

world'.[3] In his *Commentary on the Gospel according to John*, Origen considers the role of Judas at some length in an exegesis of John 13.[4] It is here that he argues that Judas was excluded from the footwashing described in that chapter. In order to appreciate the theological significance of his argument, it is first necessary to sketch something of Origen's overall understanding of Judas.

Origen writes that all good actions, and all sins, are 'taken up into the Gospel' either to be recognized in heaven or for the accusation of those at fault. This is why, he argues, Judas' betrayal and those who crucified Jesus are included.[5] On the question of whether or not Judas was in some sense predestined to such acts, Origen strikes a note at variance with much patristic and apocryphal writing. First, he discusses whether or not Judas was against Christ from the start. He considers whether Judas had ever 'been [Christ's] and had fallen away' (32.154), and argues with reference to Scripture that Judas had good qualities. He notes that the disciples do not know of whom Jesus speaks when he says that one of them will hand him over (32.240). Psalm 41.9 makes 'it clear that Judas had once genuinely believed' (32.159)[6] and that 'Judas was holy and changed for the worse' (32.247).[7]

The question of what Origen refers to as 'foreknowledge' is an important one in relation to Judas. In *Contra Celsum*[8] he tackles the question of whether or not such foreknowledge means that events happen *because* they have been predicted, as Celsus claims. Origen argues that the one foretelling an event does not thereby cause that event. Foreknowledge does not mean, 'This shall infallibly happen, and it is impossible that it can be otherwise.'[9] Origen writes elsewhere

---

3 Ibid.

4 Origen, *Commentary on the gospel according to John*, Books 1-12 and Books 13-32 (*Fathers of the Church*, Volumes 80 and 89; Washington: Catholic University of America Press, 1989 and 1993).

5 Ibid. Book 1.68, p48.

6 Here Origen must mean the first part of the verse, 'Even my bosom friend in whom I trusted...'.

7 Ibid. p388. Origen also writes that 'I would not think that [Judas] would have been entrusted with the money box if he were a thief from the beginning. He was trusted with it, therefore, because he was worthy of being trusted, although it was foreknown that he would fall away' (32.161). Furthermore, 'Jesus once had high hopes in him... [who] shared the most nourishing secret teachings with the apostles...' (32.162-3, p373). In his commentary on Matthew, Origen notes that Judas is included when Jesus takes the twelve aside to tell them what is to happen in Jerusalem (*Matthew Commentary*, XVI.2), and ten of the disciples are indignant with the sons of Zebedee (*Matthew Commentary*, XVI.8).

8 *Origen Contra Celsum* 2.11, translated by Frederick Crombie, Volume II of *The Writings of Origen*, Volume XXIII of the Ante-Nicene Christian Library (Edinburgh: T.&T. Clark, 1872) Book II, Chapter XX, p26-27.

9 Ibid. p27. To support his argument Origen refers to Psalm 109, where he understands that 'Judas is spoken of by the mouth of the Saviour...' (as Augustine and others assume also). He writes as follows: 'Now, if you carefully observe the contents of the psalm, you will find that, as it was foreknown that he would betray the Saviour, so also was he considered to be himself the cause of the betrayal, and deserving, on account of

that the condemnatory aspects of Old Testament predictions about Judas do not mean that he had of necessity to become a traitor.[10]

For Origen, Satan plays a crucial part in Judas' 'change for the worse'. He writes that Jesus is familiar with 'the lower or higher powers which work in men', and if someone gives place to the devil, 'Satan enters him, just as Judas gave place when the devil had put it into his heart to betray Jesus, wherefore Satan also entered him after the morsel.'[11] Judas' fault, says Origen, lies in that he did not reject what the devil put into his heart. The most that can be said at this point is that Judas' faith in Christ and resistance to Satan was lacking in some way, a rather different view to the observation made later in the commentary on John that Judas 'was not concerned for the poor, but was a thief...' (32.109).[12]

It can be seen that, for Origen, Judas is a figure who develops and changes (a view that is surely related to his affirmation of a final *apocatastasis*, in which all people will be saved). Origen's solution to the question as to how Jesus could choose a disciple whom would 'betray' him is not to appeal to Jesus' foreknowledge, but to say that Judas originally had good qualities Jesus recognized. As soon as this question relating to Jesus' choice has been dispelled, however, another arises: how to account for Judas' moral deterioration whilst within the apostolic circle. Because Judas *changes*, he implicitly becomes a figure over whom Christ and Satan do battle. Therefore Origen is left with the problem that in the end it is Satan who 'wins', introducing a note of discordance and tragedy into the narrative (not least in that Judas becomes a site of struggle *because* of his proximity to Jesus).

In the 'struggle' between Christ and Satan, the events of John 13 have a crucial place. So it is that in Book 32.19 of his commentary on John, Origen

---

his wickedness of the imprecations contained in the prophecy. For let him suffer these things, "because," says the psalmist, "he remembered not to show mercy, but persecuted the poor and needy man." Wherefore it was possible for him to show mercy, and not to persecute him whom he did persecute. But although he might have done these things, he did not do them, but carried out the act of treason, so as to merit the curses pronounced against him in the prophecy.'

10 In his *Commentary on the Epistle to the Romans*, Books 6-10 (*Fathers of the Church*, Volume 104, Washington: Catholic University of America Press, 2002) Origen writes that, 'Judas did not betray because the prophets had predicted it, but because he was going to be a traitor the prophets predicted these things he was going to do out of the wickedness of his own purpose. For surely Judas had it within his power to become like Peter and John had he wanted to; but instead he chose the desire for money rather than the honor of the apostolic society' (7.8.6, pp90-91).

11 Op cit. Book 10.321-2, p327. Origen chooses his words carefully, aware of the ambiguity in John as to just when Judas 'belonged' to Satan. As will be seen later, 'gave place' is not the same as 'entered' in Origen's terms, but the first of two distinct stages.

12 In Origen's commentary on Matthew avarice is made the root of Judas' actions. The embezzling of money intended for the poor damages his soul, so giving the devil an opportunity. (*Matthew Commentary*, XI. 9)

argues, against the Gospel account (e.g. John 13.12, 'When he had washed their feet...') that Jesus 'did not wash Judas' feet'. He tries to justify this with reference to Jesus' words to Peter, 'If I do not wash you, you have no part of me' (13.8). The argument seems to be that as 'the devil had already put it into his heart to betray the teacher and Lord, since the devil found him not clothed in the full armour of God...', Judas was not one with Christ and therefore could not be washed. No explanation is given as to why Judas was not 'fully clothed in the armour of God.' This is striking within Origen's overall portrayal of Judas, for as has been seen, he certainly did not regard him as wholly bad.

The reason that Origen argues thus is his sensitivity to the Christological implications of Judas' *inclusion* in the footwashing. The sacramental action would be reduced in power, in Origen's eyes, if Judas had been included. This is because Judas' 'change for the worse' is apparently not affected or halted. Judas changes, and Jesus bears a portion of the responsibility for the manner in which he does so. This implies limitation in Jesus Christ, and it is evidently unacceptable for Origen that Judas' feet were washed because lack of effect on Judas would emphasize that implication. In John 13, the proximity of the footwashing to Satan entering Judas with the morsel is simply too stark. The effect of Judas' exclusion, however, is simply to raise further questions. There are now two main interpretative possibilities: either that Jesus excluded Judas because he knew the footwashing would be ineffective in his case, or that only people already worthy of the sacramental action were included.

Origen takes the latter position, commenting that the eleven disciples were 'clean', and that 'Jesus adds to their cleanness also the washing of their feet. He would have washed neither those who had not bathed nor those who were not wholly clean...' (32.73). This is soon qualified, however, as he allows the possibility that 'perhaps it was to take up the filth on the disciples' feet into his own body... . For he himself bears our infirmities...' (32.83). But Jesus does not, apparently, bear the infirmities of Judas, 'wounded' (32.25) by the devil but not yet, on Origen's account, fully possessed by him.

This exclusion is heightened by Origen's sense that Judas is linked with the 'good goal' of the 'economy of suffering', and that Jesus has from God the capacity to have 'all things... under his control.' (32.25, 34) Clearly Origen wants to read John 13 providentially, and he will not allow this reading to be disturbed by any implication of limit in relation to the footwashing. It is this avoidance that leaves his attempt to give a coherent account of Judas in relation to Jesus in difficulty.

To his credit Origen does appear to be struggling with this issue of limit in relation to Christ and his salvific power, although he never fully articulates it. For example he writes (at 32.23) that, 'the food and wine of this supper could not exist in a heart that had been struck by the devil...'. This might be because the sacrament is simply ineffective due to demonic influence, or, as Paulinus of Nola puts it, that 'Judas is not worthy of Christ's blood, for he cannot have as redeemer

One whom he preferred to put up for sale.'[13] According to Paulinus, Judas has excluded himself by his own unworthiness. Origen has chosen to safeguard the efficacy of the sacrament by including only those who are worthy enough to receive it. The result is unsatisfactory for his overall argument, however, in that the question of limit is not so much resolved as displaced. Jesus' effectiveness in teaching and formation is seen to have its limits, as Judas has 'changed for the worse' whilst under the particular influence of Christ as 'one of the twelve'.

Here is where the 'contest' with Satan is relevant. As has been stated, on Origen's account, Satan first 'wounds' Judas by putting into his heart thoughts of betrayal. Then, at the supper, it is after the giving of the morsel that Satan 'enters' Judas: 'He had not been able to enter earlier...' (32.281). Origen's explanation of this is that 'it was necessary, by the gift of the morsel, to take back that better gift from the unworthy man, which he seemed to have, for even what he seems to have will be taken from him who does not have' (32.282).[14] It seems, therefore, that when Jesus offers Judas something good (the morsel, signifying peace) that goodness returns to him and Judas loses even the 'peace' that he still has. Once again, Judas is seen as 'unworthy of bread' because he 'gave [Satan] a place to enter' (32.285).[15] As to whether or not Judas actually consumed the morsel, Origen is unable to decide.[16]

Origen later takes a different line, stating that Satan feared the morsel's 'beneficial power' (32.308), though he cannot say for certain if Satan therefore prevented Judas from eating (32.312), or if the morsel was not for salvation (as it was for the other disciples) but judgement, 'because Satan entered [Judas] after the morsel' (32.309). This indecision witnesses once again to the difficulties Origen finds in constructing a coherent account of Judas in relation to Jesus. Origen sees the sacrament as having 'beneficial power' and yet knows that John describes Satan as entering Judas. This, he senses, implies one of three possibilities: that the

---

13 *Letters of St Paulinus of Nola*, (*Ancient Christian Writers*, Westminster, Maryland: Newman Press, 1967) p38.

14 Here he is clearly referring to Matthew 25.29 or Luke 8.18 ('...even what he thinks he has will be taken away') and he goes on to relate the morsel to Luke 10.6 ('if there is not a son of peace there, your peace shall return to you...').

15 Origen may have had a text such as 1 Corinthians 11.29 in mind: 'For any one who eats and drinks without discerning the body eats and drinks judgement upon himself.'

16 Later, Ephrem, in commenting on John 13.26, speculated that the morsel was deconsecrated by being dipped in water before being given to Judas, presumably because he was concerned at the implication that Judas had received eternal life. Isho'dad comments on this 'deconsecration' that 'there is no likelihood in it' *Fragments of the Commentary of Ephrem Syrus upon the Diatessaron*, translated by J. Rendel Harris (London: C.J. Clay & Sons, 1895) pp84-5. A writer such as Cyril of Jerusalem has no difficulty in stating that Judas both drinks from the 'cup of blessing' and receives the 'blessed gifts' before going out into the night. (Catechesis XIII, *The Works of St Cyril of Jerusalem, Volume 2, Fathers of the Church*, Volume 64, Washington: Catholic University of America Press, 1970, pp7-8).

power of sacrament must be limited, or Judas never received it, or that the benefits were closed to Judas because of his unworthiness.

Origen comments that none of the disciples except Judas dipped into the dish with Jesus, for Judas 'wished to have equality with him' (32.292). But now it is not simply devilish thoughts that Judas is contending with; rather he has been so overcome that when Christ says 'what you are going to do, do quickly' it is unclear whom is being addressed – the words could have been said 'either to Judas himself, or to Satan', thereby either 'summoning the opponent to the battle, or summoning the betrayer to render his service to the economy [of suffering] that was to bring salvation to the world' (32.295). In what follows Origen continually refers to Judas and Satan together. He 'beheld the one who entered and the one who received' and commands speed so that he may 'prevail against the wicked one for the salvation of men' (32.298). Judas (here alone) obeys Jesus, 'going out' from him in every sense of the word, but this exit into the night is also attributed to Satan's inability to remain in Christ's presence.

For Origen this 'night' is an image of the night in Judas' soul. Judas is now 'filled with darkness' (32.316) to such an extent that after his words of repentance it is Satan who leads him to the noose and hangs him, and touches his soul. Judas was such that God could not speak of him as he had of Job, 'But touch not his soul' (32.317). Christ is no longer with Judas. He would not have said 'I am with you' (32.381), not even when he dipped the morsel, 'for what concord is there between Christ and Belial?' (32.382). Here is evident another difficulty in Origen's conception of Judas. In places he has portrayed him as acting freely in his role in the passion, not acting under some kind of divine necessity. Yet he also understands Judas' actions as part of a cosmic struggle between Christ and Satan. As Laeuchli puts it, if 'it is the devil who has possession of Judas, how can he still be the responsible actor?'[17] If Origen intended the crucial moment of decision to be when Judas allowed the devil to 'put into his heart to betray the teacher and Lord, since the devil found him not clothed in the full armour of God' (32.19), he spends very little time considering the nature of this moment.

Origen's discussion of Judas, it can be seen, runs into a number of difficulties. He has argued that Judas did not have his feet washed, but in doing so only displaces the question of limitation in relation to Christ. The question moves from the efficacy of the footwashing, to the effectiveness of Jesus' influence on his disciple from the time of the call to the events of the passion. Origen states that Judas acted freely and could have done differently, yet also hints that he had an important role to play in the divine economy, and furthermore contends that he was taken over by the cosmic power of Satan. Adding to his indecision over whether or not Judas received the morsel, is his argument that 'what you are going to do, do quickly' refers either to summoning an opponent, or to someone serving the economy of salvation (32.295). It appears that Origen is prepared to countenance the idea that Judas has some role to play in the divine economy, even

---

[17] Op cit. p263.

if he does not develop this idea in his *Commentary*, and places it as a possibility next to 'summoning the opponent to battle'. In relation to Judas, however, it seems that the battle has been lost and Jesus defeated.

Origen rarely holds such contrasting, even contradictory, perspectives together; considering the matter first from one perspective, then another. In the end the different perspectives are left, as Laeuchli puts it, 'in a dialectical confrontation, and this probably will happen whenever Christians think about the theological implications of the betrayal, behind which lies the question of the reality of evil in its relation to God'.[18] In considering Judas, Origen is frequently inconsistent, yet this very inconsistency, or interpretative range, witnesses to his determination to take the Gospel texts seriously in their density where Judas is concerned. His inconsistency witnesses to the tension he felt between different exegetical and interpretative approaches. That Origen has not achieved coherent answers to the theological and Christological questions raised by John 13 is unsurprising in relation to the argument of this book, but he does at least recognize the issues and difficulties and take them seriously.

3.2 Chrysostom on the 'incorrigibility' of Judas

John Chrysostom (347-407) makes an instructive contrast with Origen, and witnesses to the importance of the Christological issues raised in the preceding analysis, particularly with regard to limit. To begin with, Chrysostom's tone is very different from Origen's. For example, in his *Commentary on St John* he writes of Judas as 'bestial and crazed', suffering from the terrible vice and disease of covetousness (Homily 65), 'brazen' (Homily 70), and 'a sacrilegious wretch and a thief' (Homily 71).[19] Therefore Christ

> ...had reason to despise him most of all. Yet see how kindly Christ received him and washed his feet. He did so, for He wished by this action to restrain the betrayer from that evil deed... He did not wish to force him, but to draw him away from the betrayal by his own free choice. And that is why he washed his feet. Yet that wretched and unhappy man was not even shamed by this.[20]

Here Chrysostom and Origen agree on Judas' 'free choice' but come to opposing conclusions about the footwashing. Chrysostom accepts that Judas' feet were washed in an attempt to change him, but this failed.[21] Indeed he does not express

---

18 Op cit. p266.

19 *Commentary on St John the Apostle and Evangelist*, Homilies 48-88 (*Fathers of the Church*, Volume 41, Washington: Catholic University of America, 1960) pp211-12, p255 and p261.

20 Ibid. p251 (Homily 70).

21 Thomas More (1478-1535) has a similar argument to Chrysostom. He writes that the nearer Christ came to death, the more tenderly he thought particularly of his twelve apostles. This is why he would not cast out 'Iudas the traytour, tyll he caste out hym self, but for all his traiterous purpose, tenderly wente about to mende hym, and broughte

this as a 'failure' for Christ, but places the blame squarely on Judas. Origen, conversely, is aware of the implications of the efficacy (or lack of it) of the footwashing for the way *Christ* is understood and this leads him to take a different line. By excluding Judas from the footwashing he avoids the danger of Christ being seen to fail, but misses out on the strength of Chrysostom's argument – that Judas was at least given a chance. Here, then, is a stark example of the difficulty of adequately portraying Judas.

Chrysostom's understanding of Judas, in contrast to Origen's, is likely to encourage his readers to despise the 'traitor'. Unlike the New Testament, he uses προδίδωμι as liberally as παραδίδωμι, with a resultant emphatic shift in tone. That his polarisation of Jesus and Judas might have this effect does not seem to have occurred to him, as indicated by the end of Homily 71 where he first says that John's Gospel mentions Psalm 41 ('...has lifted up his heel against me...') because Christ 'wished to affirm the treachery and deceit and covetousness of the plot' and then immediately writes that 'these details have been recorded that we may not bear ill will against those who wrong us, but may reproach them and weep over them...'. He concludes the homily with a summary of his argument so far:

> Nothing so pleases God as not returning evil for evil... . We have been enjoined to return the opposite, in fact: namely, good works, prayers. That is why Christ repaid the man that was going to betray Him with just the opposite. For example, He washed his feet, reproved him in private, inspired him with fear sparingly, ministered to him, allowed him to share in His table and His kiss. Yet, though he did not become better because of these things, He himself persevered in His course of action.[22]

A further, no doubt unintended, consequence of Chrysostom's polarisation is that the best of Christ's redemptive efforts are seen to fail with the worst of human wickedness (which Judas is assumed to represent). Chrysostom goes beyond scripture in praising Christ, yet for all the human resources available to his divinity, from the washing to reproving and inspiring, are seemingly ineffective. This impression is deepened in Homily 72, where Chrysostom portrays Christ as troubled that Judas will not share in the gifts of endurance and hospitality he foresees for the other disciples. Christ says that 'one' will betray, and goes as far

---

him to the supper with hym.' ('A Treatise Upon the Passion' *The Complete Works of St. Thomas More*, Volume 13, edited by Garry E. Haupt, New Haven and London: Yale University Press 1976, p103) More emphasises that Jesus still hopes that Judas might 'mend', and continues to give Judas' 'highe stubborne hert, occasyon to relent and repent & amend if it wolde be...' (p106). The washing of the disciple's feet is what might achieve this, for to More this is a cleansing of the 'affections' that carry us to good works or bad. The humility of Christ in including Judas is made much of, but the ineffectiveness of the washing is simply noted: More writes that Christ, although showing great humanity in 'washing the traitours fylthy feete, hadde not cleansed hym...' (p108).

22 Homily 71, op cit. p265.

as indicating who it is by saying 'It is he to whom I shall give this morsel...' (John 13.26). This is intended to shame Judas, for 'whom would it not win over to receive the morsel from Him. Yet it did not win Judas. Therefore "Satan entered into him", deriding him for his shamelessness.'[23] For Chrysostom Satan has not entered the picture until now, so intent has he been on portraying *human* wickedness. He also reckons that Satan did not dare to possess Judas whilst he was one of the disciples, and that Christ's actions make diabolic influence possible by indicating that at last Judas is cast out from the twelve:

> Indeed, since he was such as he was, and incorrigible besides, it was not fitting to keep him within the company any longer. And that is why Christ at last keeps him out; then, when he had been cut off, Satan seized him. Leaving his companions, the traitor went out into the night.[24]

Chrysostom's argument is striking. He says he cannot imagine who could not be won over by Christ, and yet Judas is apparently just such. Since this is simply the way Judas is, and Christ is unable to change this 'incorrigible' man, Christ abandons his efforts and delivers him to Satan. Chrysostom has come close to identifying what MacKinnon later calls 'intractability', and yet he is so intent on emphasizing the power of Christ that he cannot offer any overt suggestion of limit, preferring to characterize Christ as persisting in love and tolerance, not until he can do no more, but until he 'cuts Judas off'.[25] No longer, it seems, is it sufficient 'not to return evil for evil' as he urged in Homily 71.

It has been seen that Origen and Chrysostom differ over whether or not Christ washes Judas' feet. Both converge, however, in that the implication of their writing is that Christ's redemptive powers are limited. For Origen, Christ cannot wash a disciple who is not at one with Him. For Chrysostom, the washing simply fails to change Judas, and in this example at least, it is he who seems closest to the Gospel. Origen, however, does show a greater willingness to struggle with the tension between providence and tragedy that runs through the theme of this chapter, and in this sense his exegesis can be judged the more successful. This is, paradoxically, because his very inconsistency reflects the complexity of the issues, rather than because his exclusion of Judas from the footwashing can be accepted.

---

23 Homily 72, ibid. p271.

24 Homily 72, ibid. p272.

25 In Homily 81 Chrysostom refers to John 6.37 ('him who comes to me I will not cast out'), a particularly difficult text given what he has said here about Christ shutting Judas out. Chrysostom's interpretation is simple, though whether it is scriptural or convincing is open to question. What Christ, meant, he writes, was this, 'I shall not lose anything as far as My part is concerned... He will not be lost through My fault, though I neither force him, nor on the other hand, abandon him. But, if he goes away from me of his own accord, I shall not compel him by force to return' (p382).

3.3 Augustine on Judas as 'not chosen'

A further contrast with Origen is found in the writing of Augustine of Hippo (354-430). His writing on Judas is also discussed here because his importance for the medieval church (in particular for a dispute centred on Rupert of Deutz, as will shortly be seen) and indeed the whole of subsequent tradition. A relatively brief examination will be sufficient to indicate that once again attempts to interpret Judas' participation in the final events of Jesus' life, along with the rest of the apostolic twelve, quickly become problematic.

Augustine's longest treatment of Judas is found in his *Tractates on the Gospel of John*, in particular a discussion of John 13. He argues that what the devil put into the heart of Judas was the 'spiritual suggestion' that 'he hand him over'. Judas did not know this 'thought' came from the devil, though indeed it was at the devil's instigation that he came to the supper as 'a spy on his Shepherd, a plotter against his Saviour, the seller of his Redeemer'.[26] Jesus was not deceived by Judas, for he 'was knowingly using him... this man into [whose] very heart he had looked'.[27] Judas did not know that out of his evil actions good would come, and he was to be humiliated, not least by the fact that Christ 'did not even disdain to wash the feet of that man whose hands he already foresaw in crime'.[28] Augustine does not elaborate as to how the sacramental action might be used to 'humiliate', but in so asserting he has avoided the difficulty perceived by Origen: the fact that it does not cleanse.

Augustine takes John 13.18 ('I am not speaking of you all; I know whom I have chosen. But the scripture will be fulfilled...') to mean that the 'traitor Judas... has not been chosen.' Aware that this raises the question of the meaning of John 6.71 ('Did I not choose you, the twelve, and one of you is a devil?'), Augustine responds, 'Can it be that this man was chosen for something for which he was expressly needed, but not for ...communion of this blessedness.'[29] Neither of Augustine's suggestions is particularly plausible as exegesis of the relevant texts, but each witnesses to the Christological difficulty Augustine perceives in accepting that Jesus could have chosen Judas in the same way as the other disciples.

Unlike Origen, Augustine finds nothing good in Judas, and he therefore needs an alternative way to place Judas within God's providential purposes. He achieves this by suggesting that Judas was 'needed', but never intended for salvation. This immediately raises questions of justice which Augustine does not address. On this reading it appears that the coming of Christ encourages, or even necessitates, tragedy for Judas. Origen accepted that Christ chose Judas in the same way as the other disciples. Given subsequent events, he attempted to solve

---

26 Tractate 55.4,2 *Tractates on the Gospel of John 55-111*, *Fathers of the Church*, Volume 90 (Washington: Catholic University of America Press, 1994) p6.

27 Ibid.

28 Tractate 55.6, p7.

29 Tractate 59.1,3, p25.

the paradox of Christ's apparent limitation in relation to Judas by excluding him from the footwashing. Augustine attempts to solve the same paradox by excluding him either from the original choosing, or from being chosen for the same reasons as the rest of the twelve. So it is their different strategies are responses to what they both perceive as unacceptable: that Christ's relations with Judas could be characterized in terms of human frailty and partiality.

So it is, in Tractate 61, that Augustine continues to argue that Judas was not a member of the twelve in the same way as the others. He writes that when Jesus says 'one of you will *betray* me', he means, ' "one of you" in number, not in merit.' He quotes 1 John 2.19 to back this up: '...if they had been of us, they would surely have remained with us?' He interprets the disciples' uncertainty about whom this refers to as indicating uncertainty about the others, not their individual consciences. The 'beloved disciple' asks Jesus the question that concerns them all, and is told that it is the one about to receive the dipped morsel:

> The traitor has been exposed; the hiding places of darkness laid bare. It is a good thing that he received, but he received it to his own evil because an evil man evilly received a good thing.[30]

In Tractate 62 Augustine considers this further in the light of those who question as follows, 'Did the bread of Christ, proffered from the table of Christ, so deserve this, that after it Satan entered into his disciple?'[31] The point, says Augustine, is the person to whom bread is given. Using the example of Paul's 'thorn in the flesh' (2 Corinthians 12.7), he argues that 'good things hinder and bad things benefit, depending on those to whom they are given.' He refers to the injunction of 1 Corinthians 11.27 not to eat the bread unworthily, and writes that if

> ...the negligence of the one feasting is touched with reprimand, with what punishment is the seller of his host struck? But what was the bread given to the traitor except a manifestation of that grace for which he had been ungrateful?

Augustine comments that after the bread, Satan 'entered into [Judas] not to tempt one who was still another's but to take possession of one who was his own.' He is clear that Judas did receive the sacrament of Christ's body and blood, referring to Luke to emphasise this, and that the morsel was a subsequent event. The morsel served to expose Judas openly, Augustine comments, and perhaps was dipped to signify Judas' pretence, analogous to something dipped in order to be dyed. 'But if the dipping here signifies something good, not undeservedly did damnation follow the one ungrateful for the same good.'[32]

Augustine's verdict of 'deserved damnation' sits uncomfortably with his earlier suggestion that Christ chose Judas for a particular task, presumably the 'handing over', but never intended him to be a recipient of the grace manifested at

---

30 Tractate 61.6,2, p36.

31 Tractate 62.1, p37.

32 Tractate 62.3, 3, p39.

the last supper. Once again, this is reminiscent of Mark 14.21 and parallels. In relation to the sacrament, Augustine implicitly accepts that its power is limited by the moral status of the one receiving it; a limitation that he is never explicitly willing to extend to Christ himself. This theme of the efficacy of the sacrament was central to the medieval dispute mentioned earlier (in which Augustine's name often occurs) and to which the book now turns.

3.4 Rupert of Deutz opposes Alger and Augustine

The years 1113 to 1115 saw an impassioned Eucharistic dispute between Rupert of Deutz and Alger of Liège.[33] It can in some measure be seen as a dispute between the culture of the monasteries, as represented by the Benedictine monk Rupert in his reliance on scripture and the canon of the Mass, and the world of the schools – Alger was a secular cleric who considered Augustine's writings particularly authoritative. Part of the argument concerned the relationship between the manna of the Old Dispensation and the Eucharist of the New. This became a standard question for the schools, and Peter Lombard's Sententiae (Sentences) declared that the former only signified salvation, while the latter actually conferred it.

In his *Commentary on John* Rupert, the purist reformer, argued (despite the established tradition that Christ instituted the Eucharist at the last supper) that the power of the sacrament is derived from the passion of Christ, and that unworthy communicants were effectively slayers of Christ. He was anxious to exclude those considered unfaithful from the sacraments and indeed from the church. For them, he seemed to be saying, the body and blood of Christ simply did not exist. As John van Engen points out, the debate 'came to turn on the question of whether Judas partook of communion at the last supper – Judas having become a symbol of avaricious heretics...'.[34] Alger, wanting to affirm the objective reality of the sacrament, argued that Judas had received the body and blood of Christ. Although Rupert acknowledged this objectivity, he saw such a suggestion as disparaging the sacrament; this despite the fact that Alger could back up his position with reference to Augustine's *Tractates on the Gospel of John.*

Rupert did agree with Augustine against those who argued that Judas must have originally shown some goodness in order to be chosen by Christ. He argued that in the church there were contemporary Judases – those who sought episcopal office from evil motives. In a transparent reference to Otbert, Alger's bishop, Rupert argued that Christ's tolerance of Judas indicated that such bishops are also to be tolerated if their malpractice cannot be put right. If, however, they had been condemned by the church (as Otbert had been, by successive popes in 1095 and 1106) they ought not to be able to receive the sacraments.

---

33 See John H. Van Engen *Rupert of Deutz* (Berkeley: University of California Press, 1983) particularly Chapter IV, 'The Eucharistic Controversy' pp135-180.

34 Ibid. p149.

Rupert argued that Judas had never been 'in communion' with Christ, a conclusion that flowed from his argument that the sacraments were instituted through the passion, death and resurrection of Christ. All that Judas could be said to share with the other disciples was the ability to preach and heal the sick, certainly not to consecrate the elements or forgive sins. Against Alger and Augustine, Rupert asserted that Judas did not receive the sacrament at the last supper. He argued that Augustine's writings, however esteemed, were not part of the sacred canon and therefore could not always be relied on in scriptural matters.

In relation to Judas, therefore, Rupert had something in common both with Origen and Augustine: the exclusion of Judas from full participation in the twelve. Because Judas alone of the twelve dies before the resurrection, he alone is excluded from full communion with Christ. Rupert's motivation, however, is to encourage rigour in access to the sacraments, and so he can point out that the Augustinian position was based on Luke's Gospel, and that in John's Gospel Judas left immediately after receiving the 'morsel' (which, he wrote, no Gospel or patristic writer identified as the body of Christ). In Judas' absence, Rupert argued, Christ ate the paschal meal with the rest of the disciples as a prefiguration of his passion. That the sacred words of this paschal meal are attached to the 'morsel' in Luke he explained as an 'anticipation' of what was to come. Thereby excluded 'from both ordination and communion, Judas had come to symbolize Rupert's indictment of simoniac prelates and immoral priests.'[35] Rupert assumes that the Gospel accounts of Jesus and the apostles offer a providential pattern for the benefit of the contemporary church, and is not alert to the intimations of tragedy, as well as providence, that emerge through close attention to the texts.

Writers such as Peter Damian and Peter Abelard were similarly concerned with simony and clerical dissension. They too discuss this with reference to Judas.[36] Abelard's view has something in common with Rupert's, while Damian argued that the power of God does not 'lose its proper effectiveness because of transactions that flow from human perverseness'.[37] Citing Augustine, he asserts that Judas was part of the Eucharistic meal and indeed was sent out by Christ to preach the kingdom. This he did, argues Damian, so 'that he might show that the gifts of God come to those who receive them through faith, even though he through whom they are received be such as Judas was'.[38]

---

[35] Ibid. p152.

[36] That this is a characteristically medieval theme is emphasized by the similarities in treatment Judas and simonists receive in Dante's *Inferno.* (See *The Divine Comedy* Italian text with translation and comment by John D. Sinclair, Volume I: Inferno, New York: Oxford University Press, 1939, Cantos XIX.22-24 and XXXIV.47-63. Also Chapter 6.2 of this book.

[37] Letter 40.11. Peter Damian, *Letters 31-60*, *The Fathers of the Church – mediaeval continuation* (Washington: The Catholic University of America Press, 1990) p122.

[38] Letter 40.41 ibid. p152. Later in the same letter, Damian writes that 'whatever Judas did as an apostle by reason of the dignity granted him, even though he was a thief and committed sacrilege, the favours given by this unworthy man in no way suffer damage thereby...' (40.69, p177). The crucial thing is not through whom the gift is received, but how it is received. Judas could therefore be a channel of grace, but receive

Peter Abelard was as concerned as Rupert with the kind of bishop he described as having 'neither religion nor discretion', and with using Judas as evidence for his condemnation of the same. In a section of his *Ethics* where he discusses, 'Whether it pertains generally to all prelates to loose and to bind', he argues that Jesus' words to the apostles should be understood as spoken to them personally rather than every bishop. The holiness of the apostles has not been equally granted to their successors, just as Jesus 'did not say to all alike... "But I have called you friends...".'[39] Here Abelard has come up with another strategy to do what Origen, Augustine and Rupert have done – to exclude Judas from full membership of the apostles. He does this by arguing from the *intention* of Jesus, and goes on to point out that Christ's resurrection words 'Receive the Holy Spirit' indicate a gift granted to those 'who were not unworthy of that grace... When neither Judas the traitor now dead nor Thomas still unbelieving was worthy to be present then to obtain this grace.'[40] He cannot accept imperfection and limitation either in the church, the apostles, or in relation to Christ himself.

The difference between Rupert and Abelard on the one hand, and Augustine, Damian and Alger on the other, was that the latter argued the way they did about Judas because they saw that what was at stake was the nature of the church as a body that accepted a measure of sinfulness within it. The boundaries of the cities of 'Babylon' and 'Jerusalem' would not become clear before God's final judgement. This kind of position prevailed at the Council of Sens in 1140 where Abelard was condemned for the kind of writing quoted above.

Rupert only narrowly avoided a similar fate. In 1116 his opponents succeeded in bringing him to court on charges of heresy. He was accused of challenging the authority of St Augustine, and of overweening pride. Rupert was able to provide patristic support for some of his views on the Eucharist, but none for his assertion that Judas had not received communion. Judas, as a symbol of the unworthy, came up for treatment in virtually every Eucharistic treatise as well as in Ivo's *Decretum*,[41] but all followed St Augustine in saying he had indeed received communion and was thus a symbol of the 'mixed' church.[42] It seemed

---

condemnation because of the way he received the sacrament himself. At the last supper, the 'morsel that was offered to Judas was not changed from something good into an evil thing, but for him it became something evil in that he received something good in a wicked, unworthy manner' (Letter 40.59, ibid. p167).

39 Peter Abelard, *Ethics* (or Scito te ipsum – 'Know thyself') An edition with introduction, English translation and notes by D.E. Luscombe (Oxford: Clarendon Press, 1971) p113. Abelard continues as follows: 'But if anyone perhaps objects concerning Judas, who was also one of the apostles when these were being said, he should know that the Lord had not overlooked to whom he had to direct what he was saying, just as when he said: "Father, forgive them, for they know not what they do", it is not thought that this prayer of his should be understood of all his persecutors... the speech is aimed, according to the intention of the speaker, either equally to all present or to some of them whom he has selected' (pp113-115).

40 Ibid. p127.

41 Recently published – c.1095.

42 Op cit. p166

that Rupert was confounded until the Abbot Cuno cited a passage from Hilary's *Commentary on Matthew* agreeing with Rupert's view that Judas had not received Christ's body at the last supper. Rupert was saved from being silenced by a relatively unknown text, but such was clerical hostility towards him that he had to leave for the safety of Abbot Cuno's monastery.[43]

The debate between Rupert and Alger is a dramatic example of what was widely perceived to be the important question of the nature of Judas' participation in the last supper. Even a relatively recent scholar has written that, 'Opinions for and against Judas' participation continue to multiply without end',[44] and the issue was considered significant enough for to be included in Aquinas' *Summa Theologiae*, shortly to be discussed, and argued over in later Eucharistic disputes. For example Caspar Schwenckfeld (1489-1561), a radical German reformer, disputed with Luther about the Mass, arguing for a distinction between an 'inner spiritual eating in faith' (bread which *is* the Lord) and the 'external sacramental eating' (bread which is *of* the Lord). He cannot accept Luther's position that the body and blood of Christ are consumed both spiritually and physically, and he is repulsed by the idea that 'the physical mouth... of the godless communicant, eats the body of Christ physically, yea, that the betrayer, Judas, and his crowd actually ate the glorious body and blood of Christ...'.[45]

Schwenckfeld refers to Augustine, who, as has been seen, is clear that Judas received Christ's body. Aware of the difficulty Augustine and others face – that the sacrament of grace is not salvific for Judas – he attempts to resolve this with his emphasis on the inner faith of the recipient. He does so by implicitly making the very existence of the body and blood of Christ dependent on the faithful. He goes on to deny explicitly that the sacrament is 'a gracious, powerful thing full of

---

43 After the trial, Alger, Rupert's main opponent, wrote *De sacramentis corporis et sanguinis Dominici* in an attempt to set out an authoritative sacramental position. This was completed before he joined the abbey at Cluny in 1121. On the question of Judas' communion he upheld Augustine's arguments, setting out the case for the objectivity of the sacrament. This meant that the good could receive communion alongside, or indeed from, those who were evil. Alger stated that Judas had been included by Christ in order to prevent later schism whereby the proud sought to separate themselves from those considered unworthy by repelling them with kicks (*De sacramentis* 1.21 [Migne, *Patrologiae Latina* 180.803], quoted by van Engen, op cit. p 171).

44 Roman B. Halas, *Judas Iscariot – a scriptural and theological study of his person, his deeds and his eternal lot* (Washington: Catholic University of America Press, 1946) p125. Halas' own conclusion is that Judas did not share in last supper, as (he argues) 'Without this solution, it would seem difficult to understand that Jesus, who knew the hearts of men (Acts 1.24; John 16.30) should have permitted an unworthy Apostle to approach the Holy Eucharist and profane the First Mass with a sacrilege. Holy things are given only to the deserving...'. p135. In this way Halas' argument is similar to that of Rupert of Deutz.

45 'An Answer to Luther's Malediction' (1544), *Spiritual and Anabaptist Writers, The Library of Christian Classics*, Volume XXV, edited by George Williams and Angel Mergal (London: SCM, 1957) p169.

benefit and healing'.[46] Schwenckfeld has simply created another difficulty, however, as he does not say how it could be that for all Judas' proximity to him, Christ could not inspire in him the 'inner faith' as with the other disciples.

Thomas Aquinas (1225-74), in the *Tertia Pars* (3a.79-83) of the *Summa Theologiae*, summarises many of the arguments already encountered. For example, one of the questions is, 'did Christ give his body to Judas?'[47] The first two objections to this are based on the assumption that Judas was wicked. Aquinas quotes Matthew 26.29 to the effect that those to whom Christ gave his body and blood would share in it again 'in the Kingdom of my Father'. As Judas is not among the group who will reach the Kingdom, he cannot have originally received the body and blood of Christ. Moreover, at Matthew 7.6 Jesus said, 'do not give what is holy to dogs', and since 'he knew Judas to be a sinner, it would seem that he did not give him his body and blood.'[48] The third objection cites Augustine (who, confusingly, is quoted in support of opposing conclusions) as saying, in his commentary on John, that Judas did not receive the body of Christ with the dipped morsel mentioned in that Gospel. Judas' actions here show the dangers of coming to the table as an enemy whilst pretending friendship, for after receiving the morsel Satan enters him.

On the other hand, Aquinas continues, Chrysostom argues that Judas did share in the 'mysteries' but was not converted. The argument is similar to Augustine, in that Judas is understood as coming to the mysteries with his own plans in mind, and through them 'did not come to a better heart, neither from awe, nor from gratitude, nor by honour.' In his concluding 'Reply', Aquinas begins by quoting Rupert's rescuer, Hilary of Poitiers, to the effect that Christ did not give his body and blood to Judas. This is acceptable, he writes, only if we focus on the wickedness of Judas. It is not so acceptable when it is considered that Christ is a 'model of justice' to whom it is not right to suggest that he would separate anyone from communion without evidence and proof. The suggestion is wrong both because it would be a precedent for others to unjustly exclude individuals from the sacrament, and 'also lest Judas, turning ugly, should make of it an occasion for sin.' Therefore Judas did receive Christ's body, as Augustine affirmed.[49]

Aquinas argues that the 'wickedness of Judas was evident to Christ as God, yet it was not evident in the manner that men could come to know of it. Accordingly Christ did not expel Judas from Communion, that he might give an example that priests are not able to expel such secret sinners.'[50] Similarly (in relation to Christ's wisdom in perception) in his *Commentary on the Gospel of St John*, Aquinas writes that Peter thought 'that all of [the apostles] would arrive at eternal life. And so our Lord excluded Judas from his community of believers. This trust was commendable in Peter, who did not suspect any evil in his

46 Ibid. p171.

47 3a.81, 2. Volume 59 in the Blackfriars edition of the *Summa Theologiae*, Latin text, English translation (Blackfriars: Eyre & Spottiswoode, 1965) pp91-3.

48 Ibid. p91.

49 Ibid. pp91-3.

50 Ibid. p93.

companions, but we must also admire the wisdom of our Lord, who saw what was hidden.'[51] For Aquinas, consequently, there is no question of any limited perception on Christ's part, even though his emphasis raises the by now familiar question as to why, in that case, Judas was chosen in the first place.

As is characteristic of medieval commentaries, Aquinas explores this question by extensive quotation from the Fathers. He sets out the problem in almost Origenistic terms: 'But if Christ chose Judas, who was later to become evil, it seems that our Lord made a mistake in choosing him'.[52] Rather than mention Origen's conception of Judas as 'holy but changing for the worse', Aquinas begins with Chrysostom's similar but less contentious suggestion that

> ...this choice was not for predestination but for some task, and in reference to a position of present justice. Sometimes a person is chosen this way, not in relation to the future, but according to present realities; for being chosen in this way does not destroy one's free choice or the possibility of sinning... And so our Lord did choose Judas, but not as evil at that time, and being so chosen did not take away his possibility of sinning. Secondly, we could answer with Augustine, who said that our Lord did choose Judas evil. And although he knew that he was evil, because it is characteristic of a good person to use evil for good, God made good use of this evil in allowing himself to be betrayed in order to redeem us.[53]

Having thus briefly set out these contrasting views, which have in common their emphasis on God's providential command of events, Aquinas (echoing Augustine) offers the further comment that 'we could say that the choice of the twelve does not refer here to the persons, but rather to the number... indeed this number did not pass away, because Matthias was substituted for the traitor. Or, according to Ambrose, Jesus chose Judas as evil so that when we read that our Lord and Master was betrayed by his disciple, we might be consoled if sometimes our friends betray us.'[54] He further considers why the disciples do not say 'Is it I?' as in the passion (though this does not occur in John but at Matthew 26.22 and Mark 14.19), arguing that they may have understood Christ to be speaking generally of any act of malice rather than the 'great crime' they later saw his words as referring to.

As in the *Summa Theologiae*, Aquinas gives a range of possibilities with regard to Jesus' choice of Judas; but unlike the *Summa* he declines to arbitrate between them. The key point is that they all emphasize Judas' difference from the other disciples. Aquinas ends not with a judgement on free will as opposed to predestination, but on the easier path of a lesson to be drawn. Nevertheless the possibility that Aquinas attributes to Chrysostom, that Judas was chosen, 'not for predestination but for some task... not in relation to the future, but according to present realities' is at least kept open. This sense of Judas retaining free will, but

---

51 St Thomas Aquinas *Commentary on the Gospel of St John* Part I translated by James A. Weisheipl (New York: Magi Books, 1980) p398. Aquinas is writing about John 6.72.

52 Op cit. p398.

53 Ibid.

54 Ibid. p398.

also chosen to fulfil a particular task in relation to Christ's passion (*not* for the instruction of those in the future), keeps open the question of tragedy. It is not far from the dense text of Mark 14.21 where Judas seemingly has an essential part to play in the fulfilment of scripture, to his own downfall: '...the Son of Man goes as it is written of him, but woe to that man by whom the Son of Man is *betrayed*.'

3.5 Jonathan Edwards and the 'difficulty' of Judas

The theologians considered in this chapter have ranged from Origen, Chrysostom and Augustine, to Aquinas, Rupert of Deutz and Alger of Liege. All have been concerned in different ways with sacramental boundaries and the participation of Judas.[55] Many echoes of earlier disagreements are found in the very different context of New England Congregationalism, and the dismissal of Jonathan Edwards (1703-58) from his post as minister in Northampton. Here again is a theologian struggling with questions of participation and limit. The manner of this struggle illustrates well both the temptation and the danger for the theologian in understanding Judas as excluded from the footwashing and last supper.

The dispute in which Edwards was involved revolved around access to baptism and the Lord's Supper, which Edwards proposed to restrict. Edward's own grandfather, Solomon Stoddard, had written on this issue out of a concern that so few baptized adults were prepared to receive communion because they felt they should only do so in full assurance of their salvation. In three manifestos of 1700, 1708 and 1709 he had argued for an inclusive definition of Church membership on scriptural grounds, including amongst his arguments that 'Judas had participated in the Passover feast and then in the very first administration of the Lord's Supper, therefore Christ had not been concerned to search the hearts of those who were present.'[56]

In his own ministry Edwards was happy to follow this line for a time, and in his turn criticised the leaders of a 1740s revival for considering that certainty could be reached about who was truly part of the Church and who was not. Amongst his arguments were that Christ had accepted Judas as a co-worker. His views changed, however, partly because he perceived a decrease in the religious

---

55 Such contoversies are a recurring feature of the Christian tradition, as this section indicates. One more example is seen in a pamphlet of 1649 by Joseph Henning (London: Printed for Giles Calvert at the Black Spread-Eagle near the West end of Pauls) entitled *Judas Excommunicated, or a Vindication of the Communion of Saints, being A brief Examination and clear Refutation of Mr Peter Lightfoot's Arguments for proof of Judas his receiving the Sacrament of the Lord's Supper (which, could he prove, makes nothing at all for a mixt Communion).* Henning argues that Judas only ate 'the common supper' and did not receive the sacrament. He asserts that Jesus could not have said, 'This is my body, given for you' to Judas 'whom he knew to be a devil, eternally lost' (p15). For Henning, asserting otherwise implies admitting 'brother Drunkard, brother Thief, brother Murderer...' into the Communion of Saints (p20).

56 Introduction, p41, *The Works of Jonathan Edwards*, Volume 12 (New Haven: Yale University Press, 1994) Harry S. Stout, General Editor.

zeal of his own congregation. He became increasingly concerned at hypocrisy and insincere confessions of faith, and in 1749 published *An Humble Inquiry into the rules of God concerning the qualifications requisite to compleat standing and full communion in the visible Christian Church.*[57] In this work he began by setting out his case for the Church achieving as high a degree of probability as possible about the holiness of its members. He then set out eleven reasons for accepting his interpretation of the biblical teaching, and finally gave answers to twenty possible objections to his position on the qualifications for full communion.

Objection seven is as follows: 'Christ himself administered the Lord's Supper to Judas, whom he knew at the time to be graceless; which is a full evidence, that grace is not in itself a requisite qualification in order to coming to the Lord's Supper...'.[58] Edwards' first response to this is to argue that Judas was not present at the Supper. He acknowledges that this does not fit with the Lukan account, and that although Matthew and Mark have the dipping of the sop before the sacrament, they do not mention Judas leaving. He concludes that John's Gospel is the most reliable to chronology, and infers that the 'Lord's Supper' must have occurred after Judas went out (although the Gospel itself does not say so).[59]

Aware that his argument is hardly conclusive, he goes on to say that, 'If Judas was there, I deny the consequence.' The crux of his argument is that Christ dealt with his disciples not 'as the searcher of hearts; but rather as the head of the visible church...'.[60] Because Judas had acted in similar fashion to the other disciples, Christ did not renounce him. Certainly such a reading of the Gospels suits Edwards' argument, but it hardly accords with New Testament texts where Jesus says to his disciples that one of them will *betray* him (cf. Mark 14.18, Matthew 26.23), or John 6.64 which records that 'Jesus knew from the beginning who those were who did not believe, and who it was who would *betray* him.'

Perhaps aware of the unsatisfactoriness of his first two 'answers' to the objection he is attempting to deal with, Edwards then explicitly engages with those who oppose him. He argues that 'there is a remaining difficulty in this matter' which counts as much against his opponent's position as his. They have argued that moral seriousness, rather than saving grace, is required for attending the Lord's Supper. To this Edwards rejoins (in a passage that undercuts his previous argument that Christ was not a searcher of hearts) that Christ knew Satan had entered Judas, 'that he had a malignant malicious spirit against his master', that 'he had already formed a traitorous murderous design against him... and knew Judas

---

57 Ibid pp165-348.

58 Ibid. p288.

59 Edwards argues that 'many of the best expositors are of this opinion, such as van Mastricht, Dr. Doddridge, and others' (ibid. p289). Peter van Mastricht (1630-1706) was a Reformed theologian, and his work *Theoretica-Practica Theologia* (Amsterdam, 1705) contains his views on this issue. Philip Doddridge (1702-51) was an English Nonconformist minister, and here Edwards alludes to his work *The Family Expositor; or, a Paraphrase and Version of the New Testament: with Critical Notes* (London, 1760, two volumes).

60 Ibid. p289.

was utterly unqualified for the holy sacrament of the Lord's Supper; though it had not yet been made known to the church, or the disciples.'[61] This applies both to Judas receiving the Passover sop and/or the sacrament. Therefore, writes Edwards, it should concern his opponents to 'find out some solution of this difficulty, as much as it does me...'.[62]

In 1752 Edwards responded to criticism of his position by Solomon Williams[63] in *Misrepresentations Corrected, and Truth Vindicated.*[64] Here he returns to the 'difficulty' discussed above – the question of Judas sharing in the Passover and Lord's Supper. He correctly points out once more that Judas' apparent participation does not support Williams' argument any more that it does his own; for Judas was understood by both men to be unregenerate and without moral sincerity. Edwards points out that the argument that might gain credence here, with the additional support of the commands to Israel in the Old Testament that *all* should be circumcised and partake of the Passover, is for the unconditional inclusivity mentioned above:

> ...that all persons, of all sorts, throughout all Christendom, might lawfully come to baptism and the Lord's Supper; godly and ungodly, the knowing and the ignorant, the moral and the vicious, orthodox and heretical, Protestants and papists alike. But this don't agree with Mr Williams' principles, any better than with mine.[65]

Edwards has at least seen the logic of his own methodology, but he cannot accept the outcome of this particular 'argument from scripture'. This 'difficulty' in fact undercuts his entire project. If he wants to base his position on 'biblical teaching', the most central texts must be the narrative of the 'Lord's Supper' as found in the Gospels. However, any attempt to draw Eucharistic boundaries on the basis of an interpretation of those narratives will either founder on the difficult case of Judas,

---

61 Ibid. p290.

62 Ibid.

63 The people of Northampton encouraged criticism of the position taken by their minister. So it was that in May 1751 that the minister of Lebanon, Solomon Williams, published (with the costs paid by local townspeople) *The True State of the Question Concerning the Qualifications Necessary to lawful Communion in the Christian Sacraments*, arguing for the sufficiency of moral sincerity (rather than assuredness of salvation) in receiving the sacrament. He argued that barring people who lacked such assurance from the sacrament could only worsen the situation, in that this would deprive them of the means of grace. While Williams thus criticised Edwards, the two of them were actually engaged in a similar task: to steer a course between the extremes of admitting all comers to communion, and the claims of the so-called 'separates' who argued that the spiritually enlightened could discern who was a 'saint' and who was not. Edwards agreed with Williams against the 'separates' that the church could not know for certain who was saved and who was not.

64 *The Works of Jonathan Edwards*, Volume 12 (New Haven: Yale University Press, 1994) Harry S. Stout, General Editor, pp349-503.

65 Ibid. p478.

or resort to ignoring it. While his statement of this 'difficulty' only deepens the force of the objection under consideration, Edwards' point is well made. It shows yet again the difficulty of interpreting the New Testament texts concerning Judas. If the accounts of the last supper are looked to for help in setting Eucharistic boundaries, the presence of Judas Iscariot offers little help unless the argument is the absence of preconditions. Trying to argue otherwise will, in fact, inevitably lead to incoherence, as writers as diverse as Rupert of Deutz and Jonathan Edwards both witness.

Edwards attempts to have it both ways, however. He discusses Judas, and within the context of his debate with Williams and others, highlights the difficulties so raised. He then proceeds by ignoring the argument that 'all persons, of all sorts... might lawfully come to baptism and the Lord's Supper', because within the parameters of the debate this is simply not credible. He wants to assert that Judas was not present at the last supper. Fidelity to scripture keeps him from such an Origenistic argument, however, a position that lands him with all manner of difficulties. He does not have to grapple, as Origen did, with a holy Judas who changed for the worse; rather he struggles with the sacramental participation of a disciple he characterizes as 'malignant' and 'malicious'. Like Rupert of Deutz before him, Edwards assumes that the New Testament account offers a providential pattern offering an exemplar to the Church, and finds it difficult to respond to the tension between providence and tragedy that characterizes the texts. This, in conjunction with his crude characterisation of Judas, leads him into the kinds of difficulty identified above.

3.6 Conclusion

The argument of this book is that attending to the tension between providence and tragedy is the best way to explicate texts relating to Judas and Jesus, from the New Testament onwards. It has been seen that the writers discussed in this chapter have perceived this tension, but nearly always attempted to avoid or deny it. This has only resulted in the emergence of fresh difficulties and incoherence. Without a Christology able to accept limitation of some kind, writer after writer has argued for the essential *difference* between Judas and the other disciples. While Origen, Rupert and Edwards share a strategy of direct exclusion from the footwashing or last supper, Augustine argues Judas was not chosen in the same way as the rest of the twelve, Chrysostom that Jesus finally 'cut Judas off', and Abelard that the 'intention' of Jesus was different with regard to Judas. The implications of limit in relation to Christ, if Judas was understood to have participated in the same way as the rest of the 'twelve', are found to be unacceptable. This issue not only involves Christological questions, but questions of practice of the most sensitive kind – who is included and who excluded from the community of faith.

It seems that one of the results of attending to the tension between providence and tragedy in the New Testament and subsequent debates is the emergence of the category of *limit* in relation to Christ. This does not happen in any straightforward way, and exploring the implication that not only does Christ encounter human intractability, but indeed plays a part in bringing such intractability into the world, is a strategy many theologians find uncomfortable. But that does not invalidate the strategy; indeed it may indirectly commend it. Attending to difficulty, and the tension between opposing interpretative approaches, is likely to be fruitful as well as demanding. Such will be seen in the succeeding chapters, examining further themes that emerged from the examination of the New Testament texts concerning Judas in Chapter 1 in the light of the paradigm identified in the opening chapters of this book. Next to be discussed is a key issue identified in Chapter 1 and given particular significance by Barth in Chapter 2 – the New Testament use of παραδίδωμι, particularly in relation to the parallelism between the actions of Judas, other participants in the drama of the passion, and indeed the purposes of God.

Chapter 4

Judas' Place in the 'Handing Over' of the Son

Delivering up was done by the Father, delivering up was done by the Son, delivering up was done by Judas; one thing was done.[1]
Augustine

One of the key issues that emerged in Chapter 1 was the significance of the New Testament usage of παραδίδωμι, and in particular the way this verb and its various uses indicate the workings of divine providence. In Chapter 2 we examined Barth's suggestion, following his analysis of the uses of παραδίδωμι, that Paul 'took over Judas' place and the role abandoned by him'.[2] Barth's unusual argument contrasted Paul's *faithful* 'handing over' of Jesus to the Gentiles, with Judas' evil handing over of Christ into the hands of sinners. He considered that the parallelism between the 'handing over' of the apostles, Judas, and God, was no semantic accident, but evidence of the providential ordering of the narrative. MacKinnon, on the other hand, focused on Mark 14.21 ('For the Son of Man goes as it is written of him, but woe to that man by whom the Son of Man is *betrayed*'). In this can be seen both agreement with Barth – that Judas was understood to have had a providential role – and disagreement, with MacKinnon's emphasis on the bitter finality and tragedy of Judas' death indicating a defeat for Jesus.

This chapter will explore the theological implications of the linguistic parallelism found in the New Testament and made so much of by Barth. This will be achieved by examining the arguments deployed in the tradition by those writers perceptive enough to spot that there is an issue to discuss. In fact few writers do so, with the result that this is the shortest of the thematic chapters in this book. The issue at its heart is crucial, however, for failure to attend to the language of 'handing over' will inevitably distort interpretation of Judas. The parallelism of Judas' actions with others and indeed with God is likely to be missed, commonly with the result that providence is played down and the badness of the 'betrayer' is emphasized. And as soon as the New Testament emphasis on providence is missed or reduced, the tension with the tragic aspect of Judas' membership of the

---

1 Augustine, *Tractates on the First Epistle of John, Fathers of the Church* Volume 92, (Washington: Catholic University of America Press, 1995) Tractate 7.7 p222.

2 Op cit. p478.

twelve is reduced also. This chapter, therefore, explores a theme that demands attention if a proper explication of the theological issues relevant to the place of Judas in the economy of salvation is to be achieved.

Discussions of the possible implications of New Testament vocabulary in relation to Judas are found most substantively in major writers such as Origen, Augustine and Aquinas, and it is on them that this chapter focuses. It is perhaps surprising that this list is not longer, as Jerome's Vulgate translation of the New Testament meant that exegetes did not have to be familiar with Greek to discern links between the various 'handings over' found within it. This is because the Vulgate offers a Latin equivalent to the παραδίδωμι / προδίδωμι distinction, namely that between 'trado' and 'prodo'.[3] Prodo is a new Latin word formed from the Greek, significantly one destined to be used far more in commentaries on the Gospels than in the Vulgate New Testament itself.

The occurrence of παραδίδωμι / προδίδωμι and trado/prodo in the Greek and Latin fathers respectively can be a helpful indicator both of their faithfulness to the language of scripture, where the figure of Judas Iscariot is concerned, and of the overall tone and direction of their writing. While it is certainly not the case that using trado/ παραδίδωμι necessarily indicates a sympathetic consideration of Judas, it can be said that when prodo/ προδίδωμι are freely used the portrayal will be at variance with the Gospels in its overt negativity. In this respect the Vulgate is *nearly* always exemplary. Jerome faithfully renders 'proditor' for the προδότης of Luke 6.16 and 'proditores' for the προδόται of Acts 7.52 and 2 Timothy 3.4. Various forms of 'trado' are used throughout to translate παραδίδωμι, with the one exception of Mark 14.10 (Judas going to the chief priests 'in order to παραδοῖ him to them'), where *proderet* is found.[4] It is impossible to know whether or not Jerome was reflecting an underlying Greek manuscript or Old Latin text, or innovating at this point. Either way this small shift in the text is worth noting, as it effectively doubles the application in Scripture of the more overtly negative word to Judas.

The New Testament, with the one exception of Luke 6.16, describes Judas in terms of what he does, the action he performs, rather than labelling him in this way. Writing from the first Christian centuries onwards indicates a tendency increasingly to 'label' Judas, and in this shift to begin to lose the implication of

---

[3] According to the *Oxford Latin Dictionary* (edited by P.G.W. Glare, Oxford: Clarendon Press, 1982) a 'traditor' is 'one who hands over' and 'trado' means 'to hand or pass over', 'to hand over, deliver into the keeping of another', 'to hand over to an enemy or opponent' or 'hand down/bequeath' (p1956). 'Proditor' means 'a betrayer, traitor', whilst 'prodo' has a range of meaning from 'to thrust forward or out' to 'to hand down or transmit' to 'give up or abandon (to the power of an enemy, hostile influence, etc) betray, forsake'.

[4] *Biblia Sacra Latina – Ex Biblia Sacra Vulgatæ Editiones* (London: Samuel Bagster & Sons, 1977).

παραδίδωμι, that Judas is part of the 'handing over' of Jesus by God.[5] This process was accelerated once the Bible began to be translated into languages other than Latin, for almost invariably different words were used to render the handing over of God and Judas respectively. For example Luther translates Romans 8.32 using the word 'gegeben' (given) and John 6.71 using a form of 'verraten' (betray).[6]

English translations of the Bible never reproduce the semantic parallelism of the New Testament – with one early exception. John Wycliffe (1325-84) initiated a translation of the Bible into English (from the Vulgate) which retains a verbal link between the different uses of the Latin verb 'trado'. This is achieved by the use of 'bitook' and 'bitraye'. So, for example, in Romans 8.32 the text records that God 'sparide not his owne sone, but for vs alle bitook hym...' and John 6.71 tells the reader that Jesus 'seide this of Judas of Symount Scarioth, for this was to bitraye him...'.[7] Here, at least, there is the possibility of discerning a parallelism between the action of God and Judas, even if the words used are not identical.

Already by Tyndale's translation, half a century later, this linguistic connection is hidden from those not working from the Latin or Greek. Romans 8.32 has become '...which spared not his own son, but gave him for us all...', and John 6.71, 'For it was [Judas] that should *betray* him...'.[8] From Tyndale onwards this kind of rendering has become standard in English. Whilst some may argue,

---

5 One way of showing the shift in emphasis from the New Testament itself is the linguistic evidence. It has been stated several times that Judas is referred to as 'traitor' only once in the Gospels (at Luke 6.16). At the beginning of this Chapter Jerome's doubling of this in the Vulgate (to include Mark 14.10) was noted. And if the printout of texts containing 'Ioudas' from the CETEDOC CD Rom of the Latin Fathers (Brepols-Turnhout: Universitas Catholica Lovaniensis, 1994) is examined, 63 forms of 'prodo' can be counted as compared with 135 forms of 'trado'. The significance of this is emphasized by the fact that Augustine, for example, is highly negative in his portrayal of Judas whilst almost always using 'trado'. It is relevant also, that the 63 include 42 uses of 'proditor', 'traitor' (needless to say English scholars usually also translate 'traditor' as traitor).

6 *The Oxford-Duden German Dictionary* (revised edition, Oxford 1997). For Luther's text compared with other translations, see *Biblia Sacra Polyglotta* (Londini: Sumptibus Samuelis Bagster M.DCCC.XXXI) which gives not only the Greek and Vulgate texts of the New Testament, but also Luther's Bible and translations into German, French, Italian and Spanish. At John 6.71 Luther has 'verrieth'. Interestingly, the Spanish does preserve the lingustic parallelism of the New Testament by the use of 'entrego' (Romans 8.32) and 'entregar' (John 6.71). The meaning is 'to deliver' – sometimes with the connotation of handing over to the authorities (*The Oxford Spanish Dictionary*, New York: Oxford University Press, second edition, 1994) p301.

7 *The New Testament in English* according to the version by John Wycliffe about A.D. 1380 and revised by John Purvey about A.D. 1388. Edited by Josiah Forshall and Frederic Madden (Oxford: Clarendon Press, 1879).

8 *Tyndale's New Testament* translated from the Greek by William Tyndale in 1534. In a modern spelling edition by David Daniell (New Haven: Yale University Press, 1989). Tyndale worked from an edition of the Greek New Testament prepared by the Dutch humanist Desiderius Erasmus (c.1469-1536).

along with John P. Meier,[9] for continuing to use betray 'for the sake of convenience and convention', a strong case can surely be made for biblical translators to return to Wycliffe in faithfulness to New Testament vocabulary by restoring the linguistic parallelism between texts such as the two mentioned above. Such a step would clearly be theologically as well as semantically significant, as awareness of the parallelism increases the likelihood of questions arising about the place of Judas in the purposes of God. So it was with such as Origen and Augustine, to whose writing on the subject we now turn.

4.1 Origen, Augustine and the Cainites on the intention of Judas

In the previous chapter, it was seen that at one point Origen argues that John 13.27 ('what you are going to do, do quickly') refers either to 'summoning the opponent to the battle, or summoning the betrayer to render his service to the economy [of suffering] that was to bring salvation to the world'.[10] It was noted that Origen is prepared to countenance the idea that Judas has some role to play in the divine economy, even if he does not develop this idea at this point his *Commentary*. Here Origen comes closest to the range of meaning opened up by the use of παραδίδωμι in the New Testament and (for the most part) in his own writings; for as both Judas and God 'hand over' it may be that there is a relationship between the two. While Origen does not examine Judas' possible place in the divine economy in any detail, Laeuchli mentions two intriguing texts that do keep this possibility alive. The first is a not entirely trustworthy Latin text that nevertheless is clear in outline: it relates Matthew 26.2 ('the Son of Man will be *delivered up* to be crucified') to Romans 8.32 ('He who did not spare his own Son but *gave him up* for us all'). It stresses the insight that in Chapter 1 was attributed to scholars such as Popkes and Büchsel – that God, Judas, Satan, and the High Priests all deliver or hand over Christ. Origen states that the passive 'will be delivered up' is used so it can be related to these different agencies.[11]

Backing up this text is a fragment of Origen's lost commentary on Luke which also refers to Romans 8.32. In discussing Luke 9.44, where Jesus declares that 'The Son of Man is to be *delivered* into the hands of men', Origen argues that there is no clear answer to the question 'by whom?' Some, he writes, will say 'Judas', others 'the people'. Given that both possibilities are human beings, Origen prefers to follow Paul, as in the Romans text, in seeing God as the

---

9 See *A Marginal Jew – Rethinking the Historical Jesus* Volume Three, 'Companions and Competitors' (New York: Doubleday, 2001) p178. Meier is aware both that 'betray' is an inaccurate translation, and of the parallelism with the actions of others revealed by παραδίδωμι, which makes his position all the more surprising.

10 *Commentary on the Gospel according to John*, Books 13-32. *Fathers of the Church*, Volume 89 (Washington: Catholic University of America Press, 1993) 32.295, p397.

11 Laeuchli, op cit. p265. He gives the reference as *Matth. Comm. Ser* 75.

'deliverer'. The question then arises as whether the meaning of the words is the same when applied to Judas and to God. Origen's answer is as follows:

> Anyone who says that they are the same as regards their end will grant this difference: Judas betrayed him for the sake of money and handed him over as an act of treachery, whereas the Father did it out of beneficence.[12]

The 'end' is the same for Judas and God, and the implication is therefore that Judas (and 'the people') played a part in God's purposes. Origen has previously written of the possibility that Judas renders a service in the economy of salvation, but shies away from exploring this here. He prefers to play down the relation between the actions of God and Judas by contrasting a difference in intention. God, he argues, acted out of 'beneficence' while Judas had a double motivation of evil provenance; avarice and treachery. What is not examined, however, is the possibility that God has acted through the agency of Judas, even that he is called to be one of the twelve in order to play a particular role in the economy of salvation. Theologically this is the heart of the matter, but it raises difficult questions, particularly about the fate of Judas if his actions are understood as part of the providential purposes of God.

A version of the Origenistic argument which does take this line is developed by Augustine. The starting point is the same as Origen's, that is a consideration of John 13.27. Augustine writes that Christ 'hands over' bread to the 'hander over' of the Bread, before saying, 'What you do, do quickly'. Aware that this could be understood to mean that Judas is acting according to Christ's instructions, he writes (in a passage worth quoting at length) that Christ

> ...did not foreordain a crime, but foretold an evil for Judas, a good for us. For what is worse for Judas, and what is better for us, than Christ handed over, by him to his disadvantage, on our behalf to his exclusion? 'What you do, do quickly.' Oh, word of one willingly ready rather than angered! Oh, word not so much expressing the punishment of the traitor as signifying the reward of the Redeemer! For he said, 'What you do, do quickly,' not so much in rage for the destruction of the scoundrel as in haste for the salvation of the faithful; for he was handed over for our sins, and he loved the Church, and he handed himself over for it... unless Christ handed himself over, no one would hand Christ over. What does Judas have except sin? For in handing Christ over he did not think of our salvation, for which Christ was handed over, but he thought of the monetary gain and he found the loss of his soul. He received the payment that he wanted, but there was given to him [the payment] that he did not want. Judas handed over Christ; Christ handed over himself. The former was conducting the business of his sale; the latter, that of our redemption.[13]

---

[12] Origen, *Homilies on Luke, Fragments on Luke, The Fathers of the Church*, Volume 94 (Washington, Catholic University of America Press, 1996) pp185-6. Reference given in Laeuchli as *Luke Fragment* 26 (Greek) [GCS IX 245, 18-25] , op cit. p268.

[13] Tractate 62.4,2 *Tractates on the Gospel of John 55-111, Fathers of the Church*, Volume 90 (Washington: Catholic University of America Press, 1994).

Throughout this passage Augustine indicates his awareness that the New Testament terminology for Judas' action makes possible parallels with the 'handing over' of others, in this case Christ. It seems that Christ hands himself over through Judas' action (perhaps this is why Judas was 'expressly needed' as Tractate 59 puts it). Here, however, the whole explanation for Judas' actions, in language reminiscent of Origen but expressed more strongly, is found in 'thought of monetary gain'. Throughout the quotation runs Augustine's insistence that Jesus was not sanctioning a 'crime' but had in mind the salvation of the faithful. His words struggle with the proximity of destruction and salvation, loss and redemption, and the respective handings over of Judas and Christ. This is also the case in Tractate 7 on the First Epistle of John, this time in relation to Romans 8.32. Augustine writes that:

> If the Father delivered up the Son and the Son delivered up himself, what did Judas do? Delivering up was done by the Father, delivering up was done by the Son, delivering up was done by Judas; one thing was done. But what thing distinguishes the Father delivering up the Son, the Son delivering up himself, and the disciple Judas delivering up his Teacher? That the Father and the Son did it in love, but Judas did this in betrayal [proditione]. You see that it is not what a man does that must be considered but with what intention and will he does it. We find God the Father in the same act in which we find Judas; we bless the Father, we detest Judas. Why do we bless the Father and detest Judas? We bless love, we detest iniquity. For how great a benefit was bestowed upon the human race from the delivering up of Christ! Did Judas think this, that he might deliver him up? God thought of our salvation because of which we were redeemed; Judas thought of the price at which he sold the Lord. The Son himself thought of the price that he gave for us, Judas thought of the price that he received to sell him. Therefore, a different intention effected different acts. Although there is one thing, if we should appraise it from different intentions, we find that one act should be loved, the other condemned; one should be glorified, the other detested.[14]

The rare use of 'proditione' is necessary in the context; since Augustine's argument depends on his understanding of Judas' 'intentions', he could hardly have used 'traditione' to the same effect. Again, there is a sense of struggle about this text, as Augustine attempts to argue that although the actions of God, Jesus and Judas are 'one', we are nevertheless right to despise Judas. The resultant emphasis on intention can be seen in a section of the same Tractate where Augustine calls Judas 'traditor' and asks if God can be so called also (traditor iudas, ergo traditor et deus pater?). John Rettig, in his translation for the *Fathers of the Church* series, does not help by rendering 'traitor' for both. For although Augustine has his imagined audience saying 'far from it', he then comments, 'I do

---

[14] Tractate 7.7 *Tractates on the First Epistle of John, Fathers of the Church*, Volume 92, (Washington: Catholic University of America Press, 1995) pp222-3. This is reminiscent of Origen's comment that God handed over Christ in a 'beneficent' way, Judas in a 'treacherous' way.

not say it, but the Apostle says it...', and then quotes Romans 8.32 ('Who spared not his Son but delivered him up for us all'). Augustine recognizes that God *can* be called 'traditor', a conclusion obscured by Rettig's translation, for God could hardly be labelled 'traitor'.

Augustine goes on to offer the general, psychologically acute, comment that 'many things have a good appearance on the exterior and do not proceed from the root of love.... Let the root of love be within; from this root only good can emerge.'[15] With regard to Judas it seems that his action has at least the appearance of co-operation with the purposes of God. As has been seen, for Augustine the vital distinction between the Father and the Son and Judas lies in intention, specifically with reference to the 'price that [Judas] received to sell him.' Given that the intention of a disciple is hard to discern beyond a few brief references in the Gospels (mainly John) to go on, this is problematic. As was seen in Chapter 1, in Mark and Luke money is not the motivation for Judas' actions in the way it is in Matthew, and in Matthew this is seen not simply in terms of individual agency but in relation to the fulfilment of Old Testament prophecies. The significant role of Satan in Luke and John, as reflected in Augustine's account only adds to the difficulties in this focus. The implicit limiting of Judas' ability to act as a free agent is not discussed here, although to be fair Tractate 62.4.1 on John does state that the entry of the devil following the morsel indicates that 'the full effect of so great an evil already conceived in the heart awaited completion, the damnable affective intention to do it had already been effected.' Augustine never accounts for this initial intention, as in his portrayal Judas is evil from the start. That he cannot explain Judas' intentions is unsurprising given that the New Testament does not elaborate on this point beyond the kind of brief references indicated above.

What Augustine has done is make assumptions based on the already extensive traditions, both oral and written, which are uniformly negative about Judas. So it is that Augustine writes in Tractate 63 on John's gospel that, 'When the most wicked one has been separated from [the disciples] and his holy ones remain with him, his glorification has been signified when, after the separation of the wicked, he will remain forever with the saints.'[16] So it is that when 'the son of perdition went out and the Son of Man is glorified'[17] the last judgement is prefigured, for here Judas 'was separated from even that physical association with the saints'.[18]

In Tractate 107 Augustine comments that the one handing over Christ, 'predestined to perdition, was called the son of perdition, according to the Scripture that in the one hundred and eighth psalm especially prophesied about

---

15 Ibid. Tractate 7.8.

16 *Tractates on the Gospel of John 55-111*, op cit. Tractate 63.2,3.

17 Tractate 63.2,2.

18 Tractate 64.1.

him'.[19] Augustine has written earlier, in Tractate 59, that perhaps Judas was 'chosen for something for which he was expressly needed, but not for... blessedness.' Neither was Judas ever a genuine disciple, being one of the twelve only in 'number, not merit' (Tractate 51). It does seem that Augustine's understanding of Judas (always comprehensively negative, and describing him as evil from the start) can be summarised as 'predestined to evil'. Judas is a lesson to the church, particularly showing the necessity of judging people by their intentions. This is a challenging lesson as such judgements are hard to make with a high degree of confidence; certainly difficult in the case with Judas. The implied picture of Jesus, choosing a disciple for the furthering of God's purposes but expressly not for 'blessedness', and having Judas share in his salvific work without any apparent effect on his 'wickedness', has difficulties of its own. Not the least of these is that the focus has shifted from Judas' intention to the providential intentionality of God, which on this account purposes to achieve the salvation of the world by means of a disciple who is always destined to be excluded from the blessed.

For all the difficulties in their handling of the issue, it can at least be said that both Augustine and Origen are perceptive enough to notice the linguistic linkage of the 'handing over' of God and of Judas. Both agree that God handed over Christ in a 'beneficent' way, while Judas acted out of hostility and avarice. Where they differ is that Origen has less of the Augustinian notion of Judas' actions as providentially ordered, indeed predestined by God.

On the basis of scripture alone there must be an ambiguity or lack of clarity about Judas' intentions, but Augustine and Origen both describe it in terms of evil. It seems that where there is ambiguity or uncertainty about Judas, negative aspects of the New Testament portrayal of Judas are amplified and added to without respect for the distinctive pictures of each Gospel (such as the absence of Satanic influence on Judas in Matthew and Mark). Nowhere, with the exception of a Cainite text, is Judas' participation in the divine 'handing over' ever seen in an explicitly positive light.

Unfortunately the text of the gnostic group known as the Cainites has not survived bar its title, the *Gospel of Judas*.[20] It must have been written before 180 A.D., this being the date it is first referred to by the Fathers. While the precise nature of the gnostic understanding of Judas cannot be known, it can be said that

---

19 Tractate 107.7. In Tractate 106.2 Augustine comments that the phrase 'son of perdition' (or 'son of destruction') signifies Judas, 'for indeed from that number of twelve Apostles he alone was lost.'

20 The number of novelists apparently seeking to make up for the loss of this text is intriguing. Examples include Aaron Dwight Baldwin's *The Gospel of Judas Iscariot* (Chicago: Jamiesin-Higgins, 1902), Henryk Panas' *The Gospel according to Judas* (London: Hutchinson, 1977) and Michael Dickinson's *The Lost Testament of Judas Iscariot* (Dingle, Co Kerry: Brandon, 1994). The theologian Ray S. Anderson uses fictional techniques in his *The Gospel According to Judas – Is There a Limit to God's Forgiveness?* (Colorado Springs: Navpress, 1991).

his role in the economy of salvation was recognized even to the extent of his having a particular share in the divine. Irenaeus (c.130-c.200), who thought the Cainites amoral, writes as follows:

> Others, again, say that Cain comes from the Supreme Authority on high. They confess that Esau, Core, the Sodomites, and all such persons are their relatives. And so they indeed were attacked by the Maker; but none of them were injured; for Wisdom snatched to herself from them whatever they possessed that was proper to herself. Also Judas, the traitor, they say, had exact knowledge of these things, and since he alone knew the truth better than the other apostles, he accomplished the mystery of the betrayal. Through him all things in heaven and on earth were destroyed. This fiction they adduce, and call it the *Gospel of Judas*.[21]

Epiphanius gives a similar account, also mentioning what he describes as a 'short writing' called the *Gospel of Judas*. He goes on to describe the Cainites as having two opinions about Judas' role in Christ's crucifixion:

> Some of them say that it was because Christ was wicked that he was betrayed by Judas, because he, Christ, wanted to distort what pertains to the law. They admire Cain and Judas, as I said, and they say: For this reason he betrayed him, because he wanted to destroy sound teachings. But others of them say: Not at all; he betrayed him, although he was good, because of his [Judas's] knowledge of heavenly things. For, they say, the archons knew that if Christ were given over to the cross, their weak power would be drained. Judas, knowing this, bent every effort to betray him, thereby accomplishing a good work for our salvation. We ought to admire and praise him, because through him the salvation of the cross was prepared for us and the revelation of things above occasioned by it....[22]

Here is a rather different account of Judas' intentions, which does at least recognize one aspect of the New Testament portrayal of Judas: that he has a necessary part to play if Christ is to go 'as it is written of him'. The fact that this recognition comes from a gnostic group which admired Adam's actions in the Garden of Eden as a blow against the evil Demiurge whose false values imbued the Bible, was hardly likely to help, however, in encouraging a theologically nuanced portrayal of Judas in mainstream Christianity. Quite the contrary, as is indicated by Epiphanius' firm statement that 'Judas perished utterly'.[23] The closest patristic writers ever come to making a link between Judas and the economy of salvation, other than Origen's 'summoning the betrayer to render his service' or Augustine's 'chosen for something for which he was expressly needed, but not for... blessedness', is indicated by the approach of Hilary of Poitiers. In his work on *The Trinity* Hilary three times links the glorification of Christ with the going

---

21 St Irenaeus of Lyons *Against the Heresies* 1. 31,1. Ancient Christian Writers – the works of the Fathers in translation No.55 (New York: Paulist Press, 1992) pp102-3.

22 The *Panarion* of St Epiphanius, Bishop of Salamis – selected passages translated by Philip R. Amidon, S.J. (New York, Oxford: Oxford University Press, 1990) 38.3, 3-5.

23 Ibid. 31.35.4.

on *The Trinity* Hilary three times links the glorification of Christ with the going forth from the last supper to raise the arresting party. The clearest example is as follows:

> ...after Judas had gone forth to the betrayal, [The Lord] expressed His happiness at the consummation of the plan of salvation in these words: 'Now is the Son of Man glorified...'.[24]

In this kind of indirect way the role of Judas in that consummation is implied but not examined. Hilary thereby avoids struggling with the 'handing over' in the way that Origen and Augustine do, but (no doubt unintentionally) implies that Jesus is 'happy' at the prospect of 'plan of salvation' coming to fruition even though this will involve the destruction of 'one of the twelve'. The blame that rests on Judas, for all that his actions share in the divine 'handing over', is a theme that Aquinas addresses in a way that owes much to Augustine, but brings out one fruitful aspect of the theme: its trinitarian nature.

4.2 The Trinitarian insight of Aquinas, Augustine and Donne

The *Summa Theologiae* has little to say about Judas except at two points. Both, however, discuss significant questions for this book. Aquinas examines the nature of Judas' participation in the last supper, as discussed in the previous chapter, and also the relationship between the respective 'handing over' of Christ by God and Judas, the concern of this one. His analysis of the latter comes in the context of his attempt to attribute responsibility and guilt for the crucifixion.

The *Tertia Pars* has a section on the passion of Christ (3a.46-52) which includes a question on the cause of Christ's passion. Within this comes a consideration of the question 'did God the Father give Christ over to his passion'.[25] The first two objections Aquinas gives are that to do so would be wicked and cruel, given Christ's innocence; and that someone cannot be handed over both by himself (as Christ did) and another. Aquinas then notes that Judas, the Jews, and Pilate all handed over Christ, as follows:

> Judas is blamed for handing over Christ to the Jews, for in John we read, *one of you is a devil.* Now he said this of Judas who was to hand him over. The Jews who handed Christ over to Pilate are likewise censured, *Your own people and the chief priests have delivered you to me.* Pilate however *handed him over to be crucified.*

---

[24] Book 9.40, *The Trinity*, St Hilary of Poitiers, *Fathers of the Church*, Volume 25 (Washington: Catholic University of America, 1954) p360. See also Book 10.28 and Book 11.42.

[25] 3a.47,3 Volume 54 in the Blackfriars edition of the *Summa Theologiae*, Latin text, English translation (Blackfriars: Eyre & Spottiswoode, 1965) pp61-65.

> Paul notes, however, that *there is nothing in common between justice and iniquity.* It seems therefore that God the Father did not deliver Christ over to his passion.[26]

On the other hand, Aquinas goes on, Paul did write that God did not spare his Son but delivered him up for us all. He asserts (at 3a.47.2) that God the Father indeed 'delivered Christ to his passion' in three ways:

1. 'He ordained our Lord's sufferings in advance, for the liberation of the human race.' Aquinas argues that the objection that this is cruel, noted above, only holds if the innocent Christ is handed over against his will. Here is shown both God's severity (for there can be no sin without punishment) and goodness (for only by not sparing his Son can satisfaction be made).
2. 'He inspired in him the will to suffer for us... Christ as God delivered himself into death by the same will and act as that by which the Father delivered him up.' Here, as in the previous point, Aquinas protects himself against one of the most powerful criticisms of an Anselmian doctrine of the atonement (that it is cruel and unjust) by a trinitarian emphasis. In the following point he goes on to argue that not only is God not motivated by cruelty, he positively acts out of love.
3. 'He did not shield him from suffering, but abandoned him to his persecutors.' Here Aquinas uses the argument already encountered in Augustine, that one and the same act can be judged entirely differently depending on its source or motivation. 'It was from love that the Father delivered Christ, and Christ gave himself up to death; it is for that reason both are praised. Judas however delivered him out of avarice, the Jews out of envy, and Pilate because of the worldly fear he felt towards Caesar, which is why they all have such bad names.'[27]

Aquinas' view of Judas' intention, as indicated in the third point above, is also found in Peter Abelard's *Ethics*, where he writes that

> ...the betrayer (proditor) did what God also did, but surely he did not do it well. For although what was done was good, it certainly was not well done nor should it have benefited him. For God thinks not of what is done but in what mind it may be done, and the merit or glory of the doer lies in the intention, not in the deed.[28]

Here Augustine, Origen, Aquinas and Abelard unite in an argument that highlights the difficulty of adequately portraying Judas. They recognise the linguistic connection between the 'handing over' of God and Judas in the New Testament.

---

26 Ibid. p63. I have used 'hand over' in relation to Judas, whereas the Blackfriars translation has 'betray' for both *tradidit* and *traditurus*.

27 Ibid. p65. Once again the English translation has 'betray' instead of 'deliver'.

28 *Ethics* (or *Scito te ipsum* – 'Know thyself'), An edition with introduction, English translation and notes by D.E. Luscombe (Oxford: Clarendon Press, 1971) p29.

This connection is then broken by emphasizing motivation and intention, of which the Gospels say little. What is said by way of Gospel 'explanation' relates to avarice and Satan. Yet money cannot be a complete explanation, as Matthew records Judas returning it and repenting of his actions. It is also the case that the role of Satan in Luke and John tends to place Judas' actions in the context of a battle with evil, rather than the intention of an individual disciple alone. The weight each of the above writers place on Judas' intentions is too great to bear, therefore, for the reasons cited and because these intentions cannot be known with sufficient certainty to be the sole basis on which Judas' actions are distinguished from the actions of God. It is this very lack of certainty that has made the character and intention of Judas such fertile ground for novelistic treatment.

Aquinas, however, does judge Judas solely on the grounds of intention. For the sake of his argument he wisely avoids any reference to Satan, simply referring to Judas' 'love of money'. This occurs in his consideration of a subsidiary question, 'did those who crucified Christ commit the most grievous of sins?' Aquinas cites John 19.11, where Jesus says to Pilate that 'he who *delivered* me over to you has the greater sin.' Pilate, indeed, had Christ crucified by his soldiers. 'It seems then that the sin of the traitor [proditoris] Judas was greater than the sin of those who crucified Christ.'[29] This sin Judas shares with the chief priests, for it was they to whom Christ was 'handed over' before they in their turn delivered him to Pilate. For Aquinas 'these men were all guilty of a sin greater than Pilate's, for he put Jesus to death out of a fear of Caesar; and greater also than the soldier's sin, for they crucified Christ, not out of love for money (as Judas did), nor out of envy and hate (as did the priestly leaders), but on orders from their commanding officer.'

What needs to be brought out at this point is the trinitarian emphasis that Aquinas shares with Augustine (although this is not evident in Origen). On their account the handing over of God the Father and God the Son coincide. The role Judas plays is seen as bound up with this trinitarian action of 'handing over', even if in a wholly negative sense. This is an insight also found in a sermon by John Donne, although the way it is articulated is unusual, as will shortly be seen.

Donne is not usually the person to read in search of answers to the puzzles arising from the particularities of the New Testament texts.[30] His portrayal of

---

29 Op cit. p71.

30 For example, he does not distinguish very clearly between the Sacrament and the sop given to Judas. In one place he writes that there are 'often snares to corrupt, as well as arguments of love... for even [at Christ's table] the Devil entered into Judas with a sop...' (*The Sermons of John Donne* edited, with introductions and critical apparatus by George R. Potter and Evelyn M. Simpson, Berkeley and Los Angeles: University of California Press, 1962, Volume I, Sermon No 5, p240). In the same volume, Sermon No 6, Donne writes that 'the Devil entred into him when Christ gave him the sop...' (p255) However he also describes how his listeners must crucify themselves to the world, or they will 'make that day of Christ's triumph, the triumph of Satan, and... make even the body and bloud of Christ, *Vehiculum Satanae*, his chariot to enter into you, as he did into Iudas.' (Volume II, No 18, p362) In yet another place he writes of the sop and Sacrament as though they are the same thing. The context is an exhortation to test

Judas tends to mix together the most potent elements from the mainstream 'Judas tradition' in a fairly uncritical way. Given such a conclusion, there is a perhaps surprising discussion of Judas in a sermon (unfortunately undated) Donne composed for a Christening.[31] There he refers to a sect called the 'Judaists' (presumably the Cainites discussed earlier in this chapter) who magnify Judas' actions by arguing that he is owed gratitude for hastening the economy of salvation.

Donne, in common with almost the entire tradition, cannot accept that Judas had any good purpose or compassion for humankind in what he did. He does acknowledge that Jesus permitted Judas to act thus; and argues, citing Augustine, that Judas could not have 'given' Christ, if Christ had not freely given himself motivated solely by his own goodness. Donne goes on to argue that Christ not only *gave* himself, but also *delivered* himself. In the following passage he shows that he is aware of the parallelism in the New Testament between the actions of God and Judas:

> Yea the word [tradidit] implies a further operativeness, and working upon himself, than all this; for the word which the *Apostle* uses here, for Christ giving of himselfe, is the same word, which the *Evangelists* use still, for Judas betraying him: so that Christ did not onely give himselfe to the will of the Father, in the eternall Decree; nor onely deliver himselfe to the power of death in his Incarnation, but he offered, he exhibited, he *exposed* (we may say) he *betrayed* himselfe to his enemies... .[32]

The notion that Jesus 'betrayed himself' is an unusual one. It might have been more accurate if Donne, having noticed the linguistic parallelism in the New Testament, had chosen to speak of Judas 'delivering' rather than Jesus 'betraying'. However he does at least imply a closer relationship between the actions of Jesus and Judas than is commonly found in the tradition. The strange notion of Jesus 'betraying' himself gives a sense of how both he and Judas might be bound together within the 'eternall Decree' of the Father. If the Father and the Son are united in self-giving, so Judas and Christ are united in 'handing over', and all is within the providence of God. Here is articulated something of the impression given by much of the argumentation discussed in this chapter; that it is rather harder to separate the actions of Judas, Jesus and God in 'handing over' than most writers who have spotted the parallelism are prepared to credit.

---

one's conscience before receiving communion, for otherwise your case 'shall be like the case of Judas, if the devill have put in his heart, to betray Christ, to make the body and bloud of Christ Jesus false witnesses to the congregation of his hypocriticall sanctity, Satan shall enter into him, with this sop, and seal his condemnation' (Volume II, No 10, p224).

31 Ibid. Volume V (1959) No 5, 'Preached at a Christening', pp113-129.

32 Ibid. p123.

4.3 Conclusion

Through the preceding discussion, a strong general pattern has emerged for interpreting the role of Judas in relation to the New Testament and Vulgate vocabulary of 'handing over'. The repetition of a broadly similar approach based largely on focussing on intention has been seen to be inadequate. Not only does it go beyond what it is possible to know of Judas' motivation, it does not do justice to the complex of providence, the demonic, calling, fulfilment and freedom found in the biblical texts relating to Judas that MacKinnon has characterized as pointing to tragedy. Those theologians who have discussed the implications of the parallel uses of παραδίδωμι cannot satisfactorily show how the actions of God, Jesus and Judas are one, whilst simultaneously understanding Judas in entirely negative terms.

A clear case can be made that future translations of the Bible should ensure that the parallelism between the different usages of παραδίδωμι in the New Testament is not obscured. This is more than a semantic issue. The word is used again and again in defining Judas' role in the Gospel accounts of the economy of salvation, and while an unassailable case can be made that it does not mean 'betray' (as was seen in Chapter 1) commentaries and books continue to be written, sermons preached and liturgies conducted, as though it did. It is not simply a matter of misunderstanding the character of Judas, but of misunderstanding aspects of the formative events of the Christian faith; indeed the very nature of Christ and the providence of God. Discussions of the place of Judas in Christology must take account of the issue that this chapter has focused on if they are to explicate the theological issues with any adequacy.

For all the contrast between the 'handing over' by God and the action of Judas, Aquinas, Augustine and Donne emphasize the unity of will and purpose between the Father and the Son in relation to what Judas does. Even though their emphasis on intention cannot be justified, the explicitly trinitarian aspect to their discussion deepens the argument in a way that potentially enables the kind of misunderstandings mentioned in the previous paragraph to be overcome. This theme will be taken up and discussed further in Chapter 7. Before then, however, it is necessary to discuss the repentance and death of Judas. This chapter has examined the implications of the parallelism between the deeds of Judas and the purposes of God; it is in consideration of the events of Matthew 27.3-10 and Acts 1.15-26 that the question of what the will of God is for Judas comes to the fore.

Chapter 5

Judas' Repentance and Death

If only you had waited for the completion of your crime
until the blood of Christ had been poured out for all sinners,
you would have put off the gruesome death by hanging.[1]

Leo the Great

One of the issues identified in Chapter 1 was the nature of Judas' repentance and death, and whether or not eschatological damnation is the implication of the relevant texts. In Chapter 2 we encountered Barth's contention that Judas' suicide occurred the 'wrong side' of the salvific event of the cross; that is before the saving triduum of Good Friday, Holy Saturday and Easter Sunday are completed. This 'incompleteness', he asserts, corresponds to the incompleteness of Judas' surrender to Christ. As Judas has rejected grace, argues Barth, so there cannot be grace for him in repentance. In summary, therefore, 'no promise of grace could be held out for Judas, and no genuine penitence was possible.'[2]

It would be a mistake, however, to understand Barth as arguing for the final damnation of Judas (which MacKinnon sees as the unambiguous implication of the New Testament texts). There may be no *promise* of grace, but the status of Judas' repentance remains, according to him, an 'open question'.[3] What Barth means by this is that Judas' situation is a heightened form of the status of humanity as a whole – in which the 'reality of human wickedness' is in tension with the 'overwhelming power of grace'.[4] Having identified this tension, Barth struggles to articulate its nature, particularly in relation to the grace of God. About the wickedness, he is clearer: Judas' suicide belongs to the night and to Satan; it deserves the full horror of the New Testament. Judas shows the guilt of the apostles and of Israel, and his repentance cannot make restitution for this or the process he has begun, nor alter Jesus', 'woe to that man....' saying. Judas has taken the consequence of free will to its uttermost point in disobedience to God.

About Judas' wickedness, it can be seen, Barth makes *statements.* About God's grace, in contrast, Barth raises *questions*: 'What is the will of God for him?

---

1 *St Leo the Great – Sermons,* Sermon 54.2-3, Palm Sunday, 5 April 442, *Fathers of the Church,* Volume 93 (Washington: Catholic University of America Press, 1996) p234.

2 Karl Barth, *Church Dogmatics* II.2 'The Doctrine of God' (Edinburgh: T&T Clark, 1957) p467.

3 Ibid. p466.

4 Ibid. p476.

What has God determined concerning him?'[5] He explores these questions through typology, in particular his triumvirate of Judas, Jesus and Paul, in which Judas is seen to have a providential role within the task of the apostolate and the Church. An analysis of this exegesis in Chapter 2 highlighted its problematic aspects, with particular reference to MacKinnon's emphasis on the finality of the texts concerning Judas' fate in the New Testament.

It is not only Barth's exploration of grace that is problematic, however. Questions relating to the validity of his providential typology also extend to his statements about Judas' wickedness. He seems aware that the New Testament is not explicit about the supposed inadequacy of Judas' repentance (Matthew 27.3ff does not overtly suggest that it falls short), and relates this to Judas' representative function as embodying the guilt of the apostles and the whole nation of Israel. Barth also writes that Satan is at work, and yet that Judas shows the consequences of misusing free will. The interweaving of providence, the demonic and freedom is hardly straightforward, especially as Judas is portrayed as bound up with the wickedness of both humanity and Satan – while it is seemingly him alone who bears the consequences indicated by Jesus' 'woe to that man... it would have been better... if he had not been born' (Mark 14.21 and parallels).

The tension between wickedness and grace, despite Barth's exegetical labours, remains unresolved and arguably unresolvable by him as Barth cannot accept any suggestion of tragedy. Barth struggles with intimations of tragedy, referring to the 'expressions of horror with which the New Testament surrounds his figure....',[6] but in the end he denies these within his overall providential argument. The biggest difficulty in Barth's account is that he does not adequately show how Judas' fate remains an 'open question', or how God's grace might prevail. His typological approach is vulnerable to MacKinnon's remorseless emphasis on particularity and the 'hard sayings' about Judas found in the New Testament. MacKinnon, in contrast, cannot be said to have conclusively shown that there is nothing more to be said about Judas than that he is eternally condemned.

The work of Barth and MacKinnon can in this sense be said to indicate a kind of theological and Christological impasse that reveals itself again and again in the Christian tradition, as writers struggle with the issues that arise from considering Judas in relation to Jesus: wickedness and grace; repentance, forgiveness and condemnation; individual and corporate responsibility; tragedy and providence. Something of this will shortly be seen in the writing of three patristic writers, Augustine, Jerome and Leo the Great, as they seek to explore the repentance and death of Judas and whether or not there is any hope of forgiveness for him.

Leo, like Barth, argues for the significance of the *timing* of Judas' death, just prior to the salvific events of the cross. He also agrees with Augustine in attributing despair to Judas, as do Luther and many other writers. Why this

---

[5] Ibid. p471.

[6] Ibid.

unscriptural assertion is so commonly made, and why Judas' repentance is routinely portrayed as flawed and unacceptable to God, are important issues for this chapter.

There is an alternative minority view in the tradition that articulates a view of Judas as one who has not given up hope, and whose redemption is still possible. There are hints of this in Origen which are filled out in an apocryphal Coptic text, and then taken up in different ways by lesser known figures such as Thomas Gent, Robert Buchanan and Ruth Etchells. The theological issues raised by such writers, in particular the significance of Christ's descent into hell, will receive some consideration in this chapter before receiving more substantial treatment in the next.

5.1 Augustine, Jerome and Leo on the absence of hope

As so often in this book, it is Augustine who articulates key aspects of the tradition even where he is not entirely consistent in his approach. On the issue of Judas' repentance, he argues in one place that Judas might have found absolution if he had sought it in the right way, and in another that his actions were sufficiently serious as to make pardon impossible. Consider his exegesis of Psalm 109,[7] where his struggles with this question result in his arguments working in contradictory directions. For example Augustine writes, with reference to verse 7 of the Psalm, that Judas' prayer was turned into sin when he was considering betraying Christ,

> ...for he could no longer pray through Christ. For after he betrayed Him, and repented of it, if he prayed through Christ, he would ask for pardon; if he asked for pardon, he would have hope; if he had hope, he would hope for mercy; if he hoped for mercy, he would not have hanged himself in despair... . (109.9)

Here Augustine places the fault not only of betrayal but of incomplete repentance firmly on Judas' shoulders, implying that mercy might have been forthcoming. There was still hope for Judas, even if (on this account) he did not grasp the opportunity. Yet later he states unequivocally that 'this great crime should be without pardon, both here, and in a future life' (109.15). This is the punishment, he argues, that God delivers – but not with delight in misery, but a 'love of justice, which is good for evil' (109.7). Nothing of what Judas has done, he writes, should be passed down the generations, and so it was that the whole of Judas' family 'were consumed in the short space of one generation...'. (109.15) It seems that any lack in Judas' repentance is inconsequential, as he had no grounds for hope anyway.

---

7 *Expositions on the Book of Psalms, A select library of the Nicene and post-Nicene Fathers of the Christian Church*, Volume VIII (Edinburgh: T.&T. Clark/Grand Rapids, Michigan: Eerdmans, 1989 reprint of the 1888 edition) pp536ff. This Psalm was commonly thought to refer to Judas.

Augustine does not seek to resolve the contradictions in his exegesis. It is worth contrasting his exposition of Psalm 109 with a homily by his contemporary Jerome (340-420) on the same text, which exhibits a different problematic. In it Jerome dramatizes the tension between wickedness and grace identified by Barth, and like Barth emphasizes the representative nature of Judas. Jerome tries to resolve this tension in concentrating on Christ's compassion for Judas, but this results in an unintended portrait of Christological failure.

In relation to the opening words of Psalm 109 ('O God, be not silent in my praise...') Jerome argues that God should not be silent because 'Judas betrayed Me, the Jews persecuted and crucified Me...'. He goes on to speak for Christ about Judas and the Jews, as follows:

> Let us reflect upon the traitor Judas and his treacherous malice against the Lord. He comes to the Lord deliberately to betray Him, and calls Him Rabbi, Master. Here, we have a perfect example of the malicious mouth of a sinner, the lips of a treacherous man. In My compassion I want to save him, and I respond to his kiss of greeting, so great is My longing to overcome his malice, but he persists in his treachery and betrays Me. In particular, this is the story of Judas; in general, it is that of the Jews... .[8]

Throughout Jerome's homily the desire of Christ to save even his enemies is emphasized. He underlines Christ's generous love, and starkly contrasts this with Judas and the Jews. He nevertheless states that persecutors should be prayed for in the spirit of the Christ who prayed 'Father, forgive them...', and 'received His deadly conspirator with a kiss'.[9] It seems that for Jerome, however, failure to respond to this kind of love leads ultimately to condemnation. In this sense wickedness can be said to have triumphed over grace, as for Jerome there is no 'open question' about Judas' fate. Jerome emphasizes Jesus' wish to save, in attempting to absolve Jesus of any responsibility for the fate of Judas and the Jews. The result is hardly what he intended – to give a picture of ineffective grace that turns to condemnation when the result it seeks is not forthcoming. For this is the implication of Jerome's argument that Judas' betrayal was bad enough, but his actions following Christ's continued wish to 'save' him were even worse. He writes that the

> ...repentance of Judas became worse than his sin. How so? He went out and committed suicide by hanging himself; he who became the betrayer of God became his own hangman. In regard to the clemency of the Lord, I say this, that Judas offended the Lord more by hanging himself than by betraying Him. His prayer should have been repentance, but it turned into sin.[10]

---

8 Jerome, Homily 35, in *Homilies*, volume 1, 1-59, *Fathers of the Church*, Volume 48 (Washington: Catholic University of America, 1964) p255.

9 Ibid. p257.

10 Ibid. p259.

Jerome is aware that Matthew 27.3 records that Judas did repent, but considers his subsequent actions to demonstrate this was not the kind of repentance Christ wanted. In a way that he does not elucidate any further, this is true of the prayer of the Jew and heretic also – 'it turned to sin'. While it is not clear what was at fault in Judas' repentance, the end result – condemnation – is not at issue. On this there is widespread consensus amongst patristic writers.[11]

Augustine and Jerome are clear in their own minds that Judas' repentance and manner of death found no favour with God, and that he had lost hope. In this they fill out the terseness of Matthew 27.3 with theological interpretation that for most of the tradition is uncontentious. By contrast Origen suggests that it was Judas' intention to die before Jesus so that he might receive mercy from him.[12] This theme is picked up in a later Coptic apocryphal text that portrays Judas hanging himself so that he can meet Jesus in Hell.[13] Origen does not give the outcome, leaving open the possibility of damnation or reconciliation – as Barth seeks to do. His argument could be accused of being unduly speculative, but it is hardly more so than Augustine or Jerome, and it avoids the difficulties in their writing identified above.

Barth does not discuss the 'open question' of Judas' fate in relation to the descent of both Judas and Jesus into Hell, and the briefness of Origen's remarks and the Coptic text cannot provide an adequate exploration. Their suggestion does seem worthy of further exploration, however, which it will receive later in this chapter and particularly in the next. For the moment, however, the writing of Leo the Great (c395-461) remains to be discussed, indicating as it does an awareness of an aspect of Barth's exegesis – that Judas' death occurs the 'wrong side' of Good Friday.

In a Palm Sunday Sermon of 442, Leo attributes yet another state of mind to Judas when near to death. A year earlier, on the same festival, he had offered the unusual suggestion that Judas was guilty of heresy, arguing that Christ's healing, as represented by his words 'Father, forgive them...',

---

11 For example, although Maximus of Turin sees a measure of appropriateness in Judas' actions following his 'handing over', there is no hint of even the possibility of salvation: '...knowing what a great crime he committed, it was not enough for him to deprive himself of the price of his sacrilege unless he deprived himself of his life as well. He judged himself worthy of death because he had betrayed Christ, the life of all. Judas is his own most severe judge, therefore, and in his punishment he confesses the one whom he had denied by betraying him.' Sermon 59, *The Sermons of St Maximus of Turin* (*Ancient Christian Writers*, Westminster, Maryland: Newman Press, 1989) p140.

12 Described in Samuel Laeuchli's article 'Origen's Interpretation of Judas Iscariot' (*Church History* Volume XXII, No. 4, December 1953, pp253-268) p259. He gives the reference as Origen's *Matthew Commentary*, Sermon 117, which exists only in a late Latin text.

13 'Acts of Andrew and Paul', pp301-2 in *The Apocryphal New Testament – A Collection of Apocryphal Christian literature in an English Translation* edited by J.K Elliott (Oxford: Clarendon Press, 1993). This text will be discussed in greater detail later in the chapter.

> ...would not have passed you by, Judas, if you had fled to that penitence which would recall you to Christ – and not to that which would urge you on to the noose. But, though saying, 'I have sinned, handing over innocent blood,' you persisted in the wickedness of your disloyalty. Even in the ultimate danger of your own death, you believed Jesus to be not God the Son of God, but only a man of our own race. You would have drawn his mercy to you if you had not denied his omnipotence.[14]

On this account Judas does not offer appropriate repentance, and it is not his actions that are central to his condemnation, but his beliefs. In the sermon of 442 Leo returns to the theme, but qualifies it. He says that Christ

> ...used the malice of his persecutors for the redemption of all, so that even his murderers could be saved if only they would believe in the mystery of his Death and Resurrection. You stand out, Judas, as more wicked than all the rest, and more unhappy, for penitence did not call you back to the Lord, but despair drew you to the noose. If only you had waited for the completion of your crime until the blood of Christ had been poured out for all sinners, you would have put off the gruesome death by hanging. When so many miracles of the Lord and so many of his gifts tortured your conscience, these mysteries at least would have called you back from your rash deed, the ones you had accepted when already at the Paschal meal you were detected in your treachery by the sign of divine knowledge.[15]

In this portrayal Leo makes of Judas something uniquely tragic, unfortunate enough to die just before Christ's redeeming death that would have changed things for him. His heresy, it seems, might have found forgiveness but for the timing of his suicide. Leo writes of Judas as simultaneously wicked, unhappy and in despair. This state of mind, which Leo call a 'madness of the heart', along with the presence of Satan, leads Judas to 'distrust [Christ's] forgiveness' even though he 'did not refuse you the communion of his body and blood', and hang himself. The implication, explicitly spelled out by Ambrose, is that, 'The Lord Jesus is so loving that He would have given [Judas] pardon had he awaited Christ's mercy.'[16] Leaving the question as to why that first communion did not 'call back' Judas, Leo

---

14 Sermon 52.5 (Palm Sunday, 16 March 441) *St Leo the Great – Sermons* (*Fathers of the Church*, Volume 93, Washington: Catholic University of America, 1996) ibid. pp229-230.

15 Sermon 54.2-3 (Palm Sunday, 5 April 442) ibid. p234. Leo continues in vituperative fashion: 'Why do you distrust [Christ's] forgiveness, who did not refuse you the communion of his body and blood... you are an incorrigible man... you followed the madness of your own heart... the wickedness that you had armed against the chief of all the saints you have now turned against your own head. Since your crime has surpassed all measure of punishment, your wickedness makes you the judge, and your punishment allows you to be your own executioner.' Sermon 54.3 p234 This is the verdict of one labelled the 'wisest of Popes' by Pope Benedict XIV in 1754 on the occasion of naming Leo a 'Doctor of the Church.' (*Militantis Ecclesiae*, 12 October 1754, Pope Benedict XIV. Quoted in *Fathers of the Church*, Volume 93, ibid. p6).

16 Ambrose, 'Letter to Simplicianus', in *Letters 1-91*, *Fathers of the Church*, Volume 26 (Washington: Catholic University of America, 1954) letter 57, p315.

has offered an interpretation in which the salvation or damnation of Judas becomes a matter of timing. This is the implication for Leo of the 'wrong side' of salvation, and with no hint of the 'open question' affirmed by Barth, the consequences for Judas could not be more serious or final.

Here Leo's argument demonstrates something of why Barth argues as he does, because if the *timing* of Judas' death was the crucial factor in eternal damnation, that would certainly make him the tragic figure that MacKinnon asserts and Barth denies. For on this account Judas alone of the apostles cannot find redemption, not because his 'betrayal' deserves condemnation but as consequence of his death taking place just before the consummation of the salvific process.

5.2 Luther on Judas' despair

It has been seen that Augustine and Leo assert that Judas' death was motivated by despair. The validity of this conclusion, and the way it is utilized in relation to Judas, needs further exploration. This will now be done with reference to Luther, who returns to the motif of despair many times.

In *De servo arbitrio*, for example, Luther alludes to the distinction between the ordained and absolute will of God; a distinction he was familiar with from the Occamist theology he encountered in the monastery. By 'ordained will' was meant that by which God upholds both 'the world of nature and the realm of grace'.[17] By 'absolute will' was meant God's ability to interrupt the order of nature by miracles, and limit the realm of grace through predestination. This limit opened 'the frightening uncertainty as to whether one had been predestined to salvation or was not one of the chosen'.[18] Luther came to argue, however, that the despair he had himself experienced was only partly a justified reaction to the wrath of God. In his *Lectures on Genesis* he explains what he means, first writing that the law drives people to despair:

> ...it shakes your heart, because it is the eternal and immutable judgement of God, whose accusation and assault you will not easily endure. Thus Judas and others who were smitten by it perished, since they were not able to overcome the horrible torments of the heart and that fury of conscience which drives and pursues it by means of the law of God... The only remedy is confession and repentance.[19]

Here the 'your' and 'you' in the first sentence of the quotation indicate that Luther's writing reflects personal experience, and that he expects recognition from his readers. His comments on Judas are not simply objective exegesis, but have a

---

17 Op cit. p190.

18 *Martin Luther – An Introduction to his life and work* Bernhard Lohse (Edinburgh: T.&T. Clark, 1987) p24.

19 *Luther's Works* edited by Jaroslav Pelikan, Volume 7 'Lectures on Genesis' Chapters 38-44 (Saint Louis, Missouri: Concordia Publishing House, 1965) p275. See also Volume 3, p62 (0n 16.9); Volume 5, p154 (on 27.36); Volume 6, p370, etc.

purpose: to demonstrate to Christians how they may overcome spiritual torment through confession and repentance. In this respect Judas is often mentioned together with Saul; the two being exemplars for Luther of those who ended their lives in grief and sorrow at their sins. They bring their death upon themselves, because they respond wrongly to their consciousness of sin. For God does not promise 'that you will be sure to return after a fall... He hates both presumption and despair.'[20] While Luther does not spell this out, presumably what is wrong both with presumption and despair is that they are premature and do not keep open the question of salvation. They make assumptions about God, leaving no room for hope. Indeed, Luther's characterization of Judas could be summed up in terms of *hopelessness.*

Judas, to Luther, has given up any hope of mercy from God. In his portrayal the theme of premature closure, of failing to keep possibilities open, is found again and again. Many times Luther makes reference to the despair of Judas, often also with reference to Saul, and the manner or lack of his repentance. In the *Lectures on Genesis* Judas and Saul are described as 'making conclusions out of thoughts'; that is constructing, out of a feeling of wretchedness, a definite opinion as to their eternal punishment. So doing they throw out 'the Word, faith and prayer'.[21] On Luther's account both were 'tired, vexed and purged, but only by the feeling of contrition... [and] this is not repentance to salvation'.[22] It could be argued that what is wrong with Judas' contrition is simply that, on Luther's account, Judas cannot believe salvation is for him – and that therefore Luther ought to account for how Judas (or the contemporary reader he is addressing) has come to such a conviction, having experienced the company and teaching of Jesus for a considerable period. The possibility raised by Origen, that Judas has not given up hope, is not even a possibility as far as Luther is concerned.

Luther, having said that God dislikes closure, that is the assumption of either salvation or damnation, cannot avoid falling into this himself. Further on in the same lectures he argues that not even contrition was present in Judas' repentance, for Judas was not truly sorry: 'No, he hated the punishment more than the guilt, he was sorry that he had been rejected, and he did not take hold of the mercy of God.'[23] Luther does not write that Judas *thought* he had been rejected, but that he had been. This makes the end of the sentence incoherent, as Judas could not 'take hold' of God's mercy as it was apparently not open to him.

It is more common for Luther to argue that Judas' repentance was incomplete (as indicated above) rather than entirely without merit, although there are further examples of this starker view (which goes beyond the scriptural account). In his *Sermons on the Gospel of St John*, Luther writes of 'Pharaoh,

---

20 *Luther's Works* Volume 8 'Lectures on Genesis' Chapters 45-50 (Saint Louis, Missouri: Concordia Publishing House, 1966) p329.

21 *Luther's Works* Volume 6 'Lectures on Genesis' Chapters 31-37 (Saint Louis, Missouri: Concordia Publishing House, 1970). See the commentary on 32.24.

22 *Luther's Works* Volume 7 'Lectures on Genesis' Chapters 38-44 (Saint Louis, Missouri: Concordia Publishing House, 1965) p229.

23 Ibid. p237.

Judas and others who do not want to repent and cannot repent.'[24] Judas is also described as sinning 'stubbornly and defiantly... because of his stubborn wickedness, [he] could not be corrected'.[25] It seems that Luther cannot decide whether or not Judas did offer at least 'incomplete repentance'. The view that he did not, as just cited, is opposed by the instances given in previous paragraphs and several others. For example Judas and all the despairing are criticized because they 'confess that they have sinned, but they do not offer the confession of praise... or hope in His mercy'.[26] Luther describes all the enemies of Christ as 'Judas' kin, who see nothing but God's anger in their misery. They remain in their distress eternally; they descend into the abyss of hell.'[27] This contemplation of one's own sin is described by Luther as 'Judas contrition' or 'gallows contrition', lacking as it does the grace of the Holy Spirit. Once again, the manner of expression indicates that Luther expects his reader to recognize this spiritual phenomenon. It is not clear, however, what encouragement the reader can take from Luther's diagnosis of the crucial lack of grace. This lack is crucial, for otherwise 'Judas' contrition would have been the best, for he thought of his sin with great sorrow.'[28] No explanation is given for the absence of grace, nor for Judas' inability to understand the mercy of God despite his close association with Jesus.

Some comments by John Calvin on Jesus' words, 'I lost not one', spoken at his arrest (John 19.9), emphasize the point. He writes that Jesus had not promised to keep his disciples from danger, but that 'He kept safe their eternal salvation.' The crucial exception of Judas is not mentioned, but Calvin does write that Jesus 'never brings His people to the battle unless they have been well trained; so that even in perishing they do not perish...'.[29] He means that physical death will not affect eternal salvation, and yet the first of his disciples to die physically is in fact eternally damned. Judas had seemingly not been 'well trained' for the battle with himself or Satan. For this, it seems, Christ must bear some responsibility. It is such disturbing thoughts, perhaps, that led Calvin to write that, '...the memory of Judas might even today harm us grievously.'[30]

---

[24] *Luther's Works* Volume 24 'Sermons on the Gospel of John' Chapters 14-16 (Saint Louis, Missouri: Concordia Publishing House, 1961). On 15.6, p237.

[25] *Luther's Works* Volume 30 'The Catholic Epistles' (Saint Louis, Missouri: Concordia Publishing House, 1967). On 1 John 5.16 p325.

[26] *Luther's Works* Volume 11 'First lectures on the Psalms' Psalms 76-126 (Saint Louis, Missouri: Concordia Publishing House, 1976). Lecture on Psalm 111, p371.

[27] *Luther's Works* Volume 22 'Sermons on the Gospel of John' Chapters 1-4 (Saint Louis, Missouri: Concordia Publishing House, 1957). On 1.11, p86.

[28] *Luther's Works* Volume 32 'Career of the Reformer II' (Saint Louis, Missouri: Concordia Publishing House, 1958). In 'Defense and Explanation of the Articles' (1521), p36.

[29] John Calvin, *The Gospel according to St John 11-21* translated by T.H.L. Parker. One of a series of Calvin's Commentaries issued under the general editorship of David W. Torrance and Thomas F. Torrance (Edinburgh: Oliver and Boyd Ltd, 1961) p156.

[30] Ibid. p64.

The closest Luther's readers come to an explanation of Judas' actions following the 'handing over' is the occasion on which his 'partial repentance' is ascribed to the devil, who is described as bringing home to

> ...Judas' heart that he had betrayed innocent blood; Judas could not deny that. But it was an invented lie when he told him to despair of God. Nevertheless, he increased this despair by means of the truth so mightily that as a result Judas felt obliged to go and hang himself... .[31]

Here Luther states clearly that Judas should not have despaired of God, despite what he had done. However, attributing even Judas' sorrow at his deeds to the devil[32] implies that there was little or no possibility of the 'confession of sin' turning to the 'confession of praise.' Since the repentance of Judas occurs in Matthew's gospel (27.3), a Gospel that does not describe Judas as influenced by the devil, this is unscriptural. But it does give the impression that for Luther there was an inevitability about both Judas' actions and his fate. This impression is only heightened by statements such as, 'Before Christ could be crucified by Pilate, it was necessary that there be a Judas',[33] and that:

> Every Abel has his Cain... every Jacob, his Esau; and Christ, His Judas, who was against his soul, especially in those things which pertain to the soul, namely faith and righteousness.[34]

Moreover Luther explains that Joseph's brother Simeon is seen by some as the ancestor of Judas Iscariot, which is why 'Simeon is not counted in the blessing of Moses'[35] (and so by implication excluded from salvation). If this is true of an ancestor, it indicates that for Luther Judas is of a 'line' that opposes the will of God, for, 'It is necessary that the Word of God should have gainsayers.'[36] It may be that some, even most, of these 'gainsayers' will be forgiven, but it seems not all. The sin of Joseph's brothers in delivering him up into slavery with Judas can be seen (as was discussed in Chapter 1) as prefiguring Judas' actions. On Luther's understanding, this offers encouragement to the majority – but not to all:

---

31 *Luther's Works* Volume 38 'Word and Sacrament IV' (Saint Louis, Missouri: Concordia Publishing House, 1971). In 'The Private Mass and Consecration of Priests' (1533) p157.

32 Perhaps because at the last supper Judas 'fills himself up, not with wine, but with the devil...' *Luther's Works* Volume 41 'Church and Ministry III' (Saint Louis, Missouri: Concordia Publishing House, 1966), 'Against Hanswurst' (1541), p239.

33 *Luther's Works* Volume 29 'Lectures on Titus, Philemon and Hebrews' (Saint Louis, Missouri: Concordia Publishing House, 1968). On Titus 1.9, p33.

34 *Luther's Works* Volume 14 'Selected Psalms III' (Saint Louis, Missouri: Concordia Publishing House, 1958). On Psalm 142.3, p197.

35 *Luther's Works* Volume 8 'Lectures on Genesis' Chapters 45-50 (Saint Louis, Missouri: Concordia Publishing House, 1966). On 49.5, p216.

36 *Luther's Works* Volume 29 'Lectures on Titus, Philemon and Hebrews' (Saint Louis, Missouri: Concordia Publishing House, 1968). On Titus 1.9, p33.

> For since they obtained their pardon and remission, there is no need at all to despair on account of our sins. But see you do not tempt God, for Judas in despair ended his life with a noose![37]

Here Luther admonishes his readers with the example of Judas, but the notion of Judas 'tempting God' is harsh considering what he has written about Judas' despair, and the influence of the devil. But as has been seen, Luther's writing on Judas does contain this harsher side to it, such as when Judas, Saul, Ahitophel and Absalom are seen as obstinately sinning against the mercy and grace of God and so 'not able to sigh for forgiveness'.[38] Moreover, in his introduction to the seventh chapter of Amos, Luther writes that while God always wishes the conversion of a sinner, the invitation to repentance is not unlimited. For when God

> ...sees that He is moving things forward neither with threats nor with blandishments, He becomes very angry and takes to blows. This is the way He always acted with the Jews, with Pharaoh, with Judas, the betrayer.[39]

The message to his readers is clear, but to infer an image of God as 'taking to blows' with reference to Judas is highly questionable. For throughout his writing on this theme there is a tendency to assume both Judas' 'badness' and his rejection by God rather than to attempt a convincing account of it, and to include Judas in *any* list of sinners or opponents of the faith. While this is true of Luther throughout his career, the passing years seem to have intensified it. For example, in his earliest lectures on the Psalms (1513-16) his exegesis of Psalm 109 makes no reference to Judas. This is despite the fact that he constantly quotes Augustine and Jerome, both of whom (as was seen earlier in the chapter) understand that Psalm to be particularly concerned with Judas. By 1526 this has changed to the extent that Luther's exegesis begins as follows:

> David composed this psalm about Christ, who speaks the entire psalm in the first person against Judas, His betrayer, and against Judaism as a whole, describing their ultimate fate.[40]

Luther now sees the entire psalm as a denunciation of Judas and those who act in related ways, particularly the Jews. Because they show hatred in response to Christ's love, they are accursed. Of 109.6 ('Appoint a wicked man against him; let an accuser stand at his right hand') Luther writes, 'Nowhere in all the Scriptures have I read a more horrible curse or a more terrible misfortune...'. The recipients of this curse are so dazzled by the devil that even their good intentions come to nothing and they become incapable of hearing the truth, however clearly

---

37 Ibid. p404.

38 Ibid. p330.

39 *Luther's Works* Volume 18 'Minor Prophets I' (Saint Louis, Missouri: Concordia Publishing House, 1975) p173.

40 *Luther's Works* Volume 14 'Selected Psalms III' (Saint Louis, Missouri: Concordia Publishing House, 1958) p257.

presented. While this relates to the Jews, writes Luther, here Christ is particularly speaking about Judas:

> When he refused to listen to Christ, he had to listen to the wicked high priests; and although he was sorry afterwards and acted as though he wanted to do right, he did not return to the right path but fell into despair. For Satan was standing directly at his right hand and holding on to him. Paul speaks of such punishment in 2 Thessalonians 2-11 when he says that God sends strong delusions upon those who did not accept the truth and insisted on believing lies.[41]

Therefore, Luther argues, although Judas and the Jews had been entitled to hold apostolic office and preach the gospel, they had been replaced by Matthias and the Gentiles respectively. He continues in vilificatory language, seeing the hanging of Judas and the destruction of Jerusalem by the Romans as fulfilling the words of 109.8: 'May his days be few; may another take his office!' Both Judas and the Jews have rightly been 'reviled continually' ever since these events.[42] Through all this it seems that Judas' despair has a particular quality to it. As argued earlier, despair implies both a knowledge of hope and a feeling that there is no way to achieve it. It seems that through Luther's inconsistent writings on Judas runs a sense that indeed Judas' despair is justified. It is not an inaccurate personal apprehension, but a reflection of the true state of affairs. Judas, apparently has been given up to the devil and objectively has 'no hope'; and yet paradoxically is found at fault for sensing this subjectively.

The kind of approach Luther takes in his writing on Psalm 109 is a graphic illustration of the fact that the way Judas (and the Jews) are understood has implications for practice. If it is particularly clear with Luther that he is writing with a pastoral function in mind, it is also clear that the reader can take from his writings a mixed message about personal despair, and a straightforward message about reviling Jews. With regard to the former, Luther's reflections on Judas indicate the strong need for repentance, but also an uneasy sense that this may be inadequate as one is already condemned. This is hardly likely to encourage an unreserved grasping of the mercy of God, although it certainly precludes presumption. The difficulty is not so much with his criticism of such supposition, but that the grounds for it are shaky. On Luther's account, God's treatment of Judas and others is not self-evidently just, or even comprehensible.

On just one occasion in his collected works does Luther offer the contrary view that Judas might have been saved. It is startling in its singularity, and occurs during a discussion of God's election. Luther states that this election cannot be hindered by any creature (cf the earlier section on *De servo arbitrio*), as is indicated by the fact that many who have great good deeds to their name are not saved. Luther continues as follows:

---

[41] Ibid. p261.

[42] Ibid. p266. These words are found in Luther's comments on 109.15, 'their memory is cut off even on earth.'

> He permits many people to do great evil, and yet they are suddenly converted and saved. Examples of this are Saul and Manasseh. Likewise Judas the betrayer and the thief on the cross, and many other cases of harlots and open sinners. On the other hand He rejects the learned and those who are brilliant in good works... .[43]

Here, at last, is a positive reading of Judas' repentance, and a genuinely hopeful one, but it can hardly be taken as representative given the nature of the material discussed so far. It is puzzling to find one such reference in the midst of Luther's manifold references to Judas. So often is Judas used as an example in a negative sense, that to find him used as an illustration of sudden conversion must make the reader wonder if the passage has been understood correctly.[44] However the linking of Judas to the penitent thief on the cross seems clear enough.

In general terms, however, Luther writes in a way that makes it clear both that Judas received damnation, and that his despair was a significant factor in this event. As has been seen, the ways in which he argues this are uneven and inconsistent, and the reader might wonder why this theme should be returned to so often when it is unscriptural, and not always utilized in a coherent way. It has been argued here that Luther's reflections on Judas have a strongly pastoral function, even if this is imperfectly realized. What is particularly clear in his writing is that the way Judas is understood has implications not only for the image of God, but also for Christian discipleship and the practice of the Church. At his most strident, Luther's writings encourage intolerance of those who struggle with despair if they cannot respond as he exhorts, and vilification of the Jews. In Chapter 7 the issue of implied practice will be taken into account in the kind of Christology this book will argue for in response to its overall themes.

Finally, it should be noted that attributing despair to Judas assumes a knowledge of his mental state, but, as with the nature of his intention in handing over Christ, this cannot be known. The perspective of this book raises the suspicion that the treatment of despair, as well as in Luther's case relating to pastoral purpose, is serving some other theological function in his (and other writers') interpretation of Judas. This function is the premature resolution of a

---

43 *Luther's Works* Volume 25 'Lectures on Romans – Glosses and Scholia' (Saint Louis, Missouri: Concordia Publishing House, 1972). On Romans 8.28 see pp374-5.

44 The line taken by the anabaptist writer Balthasar Hubmaier of Friedberg might seem more characteristic of Luther, when he argues that God is omnipotent (in His secret or hidden will God can act as He chooses) but prefers to act toward human beings out of mercy (as is seen in the 'preached' will of God). Hubmaier writes that 'The omnipotent hidden God can by his secret will consign Peter to hell, and conversely raise Judas or Caiaphas to heaven. He would be doing no evil thereby; we are in his hands.' The intention is clearly to give as powerful examples as possible that God's sovereignty is unchallengeable. There is no hint that Hubmaier considers Judas to be saved; quite the contrary. 'On Free Will' (1527). *Spiritual and Anabaptist Writers*, edited by George Williams and Argel Mergal, *The Library of Christian Classics* Volume XXV (London: SCM, 1957) p133.

felt tension between repentance and damnation that occurs when Judas is considered, a tension that Calvin sensed as 'harmful', even when that consideration is of the purposive kind emphasized in this section.

5.3 Preaching the inadequacy of Judas' repentance

It has become clear that the interpretative theme most used in the tradition in relation to Judas' death is *despair.* This has been seen with reference to a variety of writers from different times and places,[45] and that this continued to be so can be adduced from a sixteenth century collection of sermons appointed by Elizabeth 1 to be 'declared and read... for the better understanding of the simple people'.[46] The sermon concerned, which deals with the subject of repentance, is worth attention not simply because of its wide dissemination, but as it offers a clear illustration of the attraction for exegetes in interpreting Judas as despairing.

The argument put forward in the sermon (and given that it is a sermon the issue of pastoral purpose is again present) is that it is no use being sorry for sins without belief in the possibility of forgiveness. What is perceived to be the scholastic teaching on repentance is criticized as inadequate, and shown to be inadequate by the case of Judas. The sermon contends that those

> ...who teach repentance without a lively faith in our Saviour Jesus Christ, do teach none other but Judas' repentance, as all the schoolmen do, which do only allow these three parts of repentance; the contrition of the heart, the confession of the mouth, and the satisfaction of the work.[47]

For, the sermon goes on, all three of these criteria are met by Judas; indeed according to them his repentance far exceeded that of Peter. Judas was so sorry that he could no longer bear to live ('contrition of the heart'), he openly confessed his fault at some danger to himself from the high priests ('confession of the mouth') and cast away the money he had received ('satisfaction of the work'). How could it be, then,

---

[45] Including Augustine and Leo. Many other examples could be given, including that of John Donne (1571-1631), who writes of the 'desperation' of Judas, and of the isolation of despair as found in figures such as Cain and Judas. The reference to 'desperation' comes in a Sermon on Psalm 109 preached in 1623. *The Sermons of John Donne* Ten Volumes, edited, with introductions and critical apparatus by George R. Potter and Evelyn M. Simpson (Berkeley and Los Angeles: University of California Press, 1953-62), Volume VI, p55 and Volume V, p86.

[46] The full title is *Certain Sermons appointed by the Queen's Majesty to be declared and read by all parsons, vicars, and curates, every Sunday and holiday in their churches; and by her grace's advice perused and overseen for the better understanding of the simple people.* It was published in 1574, and included the contents of a book of homilies from 1547 (Cambridge: Cambridge University Press, 1850).

[47] Ibid. p542.

> ...that the one was received into favour again with God, and the other cast away, but because the one did, by a lively faith in him who he had denied, take hold upon the mercy of God; and the other wanted faith, whereby he did despair of the goodness and mercy of God...?[48]

Here the sermon writer assumes that Judas cannot be saved, an assumption that raises a difficulty in relation to the account of Judas' repentance in Matthew 27.3-10. There are then two options for the preacher: to point to scriptural texts that seemingly argue that Judas is 'lost' according to God's will, or to find fault with Judas' repentance in some way. The second is clearly the more amenable option. Explaining in this way the otherwise inexplicable difference between the fate of Judas and Peter (that Judas despaired of God's goodness), does have the air of unscriptural rationalization about it. While the first option raises difficult theological questions, the second is not without its problems. Firstly, the reader might question how it could be that a close disciple of Jesus could have so little sense of the mercy of God. Secondly, the strategy is based on unscriptural inference, with the category of despair invoked in attempting to resolve the felt tension between repentance and damnation.

Since that tension cannot be resolved as it stands, the question can either be left open, or some other strategy found. One possibility would be to say that the tension has been falsely set up, and either Judas was not damned, or he did not repent. The latter is the majority view in the tradition, with despair given as the most common 'fault' in Judas' repentance. Such is the case with the sermon just discussed, and many besides. Of interest here is the publication in 1858 of a book of Lenten Sermons preached in Oxford,[49] featuring no less than three on the subject of Judas' repentance. Their concern is to explore the ways in which Judas' repentance was lacking, as they each agree it must been. Once again the tension between repentance and damnation is at issue, and as none will question the latter, it is the former that comes under scrutiny. Charles Heurtley, for example, argues in unexceptional fashion that Judas had no trust in God's mercy:

> And yet we have no reason to think, dreadful as his crime was, that it was beyond the reach of God's mercy... The blood which Judas, by his treachery, contributed to shed, cleanseth from all sin, – even, may we doubt it? – from such sin as his. But the thought of forgiveness seems never to have entered his mind. He at once gives himself over as lost... .[50]

Heurtley does not discuss how 'one of the twelve' could have so little trust in God's mercy, but asks rather why Judas' faith fails in a way that the faith of other 'failures', such as David and Peter, does not. His comments on this are interesting:

---

48 Ibid. pp542-3.

49 *Lenten Sermons preached in the evening of each Wednesday and Friday during the Season of Lent, 1858, in the Churches of St Mary the Virgin, St Giles, and St Ebbe, Oxford.* (Oxford: John Henry and James Parker, 1858).

50 Ibid. p13 (Note – the pagination begins afresh with each sermon).

> I cannot undertake to give a full and complete answer: but this much I may safely say, – that the Holy Spirit had been done despite to, and utterly driven away, in the one case; in the other, though grieved, – deeply grieved, – He still lingered, and His voice was hearkened too before it was too late.[51]

The acknowledgement that the question is a difficult one leads into comments on the Holy Spirit that may initially seem unhelpful. After all, he does not say why it should be that the Holy Spirit 'lingered' in the case of David and Peter but not Judas; indeed this could be taken to imply a failure by the Holy Spirit. This unusual linking of Judas' repentance to the Holy Spirit being 'done despite to', however, suggests a connection with the mysterious 'sin against the Holy Spirit' described at Mark 3.28-29 and parallels: 'Truly, I say to you, all sins will be forgiven the children of man, and whatever blasphemies they utter, but whoever blasphemes against the Holy Spirit never has forgiveness, but is guilty of an eternal sin.'

In his sermon, Walter Kerr, the bishop of Salisbury, argues that even the most wicked may find salvation in Christ. His intention is to use 'the sight of the terrors of [Judas'] end' to persuade his congregation 'to accept that invitation which he rejected'.[52] For Kerr, it was not that Judas was excluded, but that in despair because of his sense of sin, he refused what Christ could and would have done for him. He takes the Gospel texts such as 'one of you is a devil' (John 6.70) as neglected warnings. Kerr considers the sin that dominated Judas to be covetousness, which through its 'malignant power' worked destructively in him. However, he concludes, 'Had Judas exposed the sore and festering wounds to his Lord and Master, he would (why should we doubt it) have been saved from the betrayal of our Lord, and so from the crime of despair in which his betrayal of the Lord ended.'

In his sermon Edward Goulburn expounds at length his contention that Judas is an example of 'false repentance'.[53] Certainly it has much psychological penetration; but whether it is an adequate exegesis of Matthew 27 must remain in doubt, as will be seen. Goulburn's method is to describe four ways in which Judas' repentance appears sincere, followed by two proofs showing that it is not. The former are as follows: that Judas was restless and ill at ease in his sin, he confessed his sin before others, he made restitution of the bribe he had received, and finally confessed Christ to the chief priests, saying, 'I have sinned in *betraying* innocent blood' (Matthew 27.4). These points each directly relate to Matthew 27, something that cannot be as readily said of what follows. Goulburn goes on to argue that the basic flaw in Judas' repentance was that he had 'no regard to

---

51 Ibid. p14.

52 Ibid. p5.

53 Ibid. p4. I am grateful to Professor Frances Young for initially drawing my attention to Goulburn's sermon. Her copy of it, printed separately from the collection under discussion in which it also appears, has a quotation from Owen Chadwick written over the title, asserting that it is 'one of the great utterances of a Christian preacher in the Victorian age'. I have been unable to trace the source of this quotation.

Almighty God, whether of fear, love or trust'.[54] He asserts that no-one who commits suicide can have a grasp of another, eternal world. Judas, he argues, understood the Kingdom to belong only to this world. The former point is debatable, as is the latter. Goulburn draws not on scripture, which nowhere suggests such a view of Judas, but on reinterpretations of Judas along the lines of that found in Goethe and Klopstock.[55] This is ironic, given his earlier comments about the 'perverse ingenuity' of 'historians of the day' in 'seeking to detect virtues in a villainous character'.[56]

Goulburn's second negative point is that the repentance of Judas 'turned on the pivot of self'.[57] He was not so concerned with his sin in itself, but in the demolition of self-esteem following a realization of his own meanness. His sorrow was more related to the suffering consequent on the sin than the original action. These are certainly perceptive remarks about the human capacity for self deception, but they can only be applied to Judas in speculative fashion. The Matthean account, as was seen in Chapter 1, is in favour of genuine repentance. Goulburn, by arguing otherwise, unintentionally undercuts his powerfully expressed understanding of the incarnation. When he argues that the purpose of the incarnation 'was to pick up, and make whole, the fragments of thy poor, stumbling, bleeding, broken spirit' and that God's grace is 'omnipotent in the realm of mind no less than that of matter',[58] this only serves to emphasize that in Judas' case this purpose was not realized, nor this 'omnipotence' effective.

---

54 Ibid. p11.

55 Friedrich Gottlieb Klopstock, in his 1773 poem *Der Messias* (*The Messiah* from the German of Klopstock. The first sixteen books by Mrs Collyer, and the three last by Mrs Meeke. Two volumes, London: J. Walker, 1811), portrayed Judas as motivated by the attempt to force Jesus' hand and thereby usher in the kingdom. Johann von Goethe was influenced by this portrayal is his reworking of the legend of the wandering Jew Ahasverus. In *Poetry and Truth* (*Poetry and Truth from my own life* – a revised translation by Minna Steele Smith in two volumes, London: George Bell and Sons, 1908) Goethe writes that the thoughts of Ahasverus were directed only towards this world, and out of affection for Jesus (who he meets in his shoemaker's workshop) he sought to convert him to this way of thinking. When Jesus is seized and condemned, Goethe writes as follows: 'Judas, who apparently had betrayed his Lord, in his despair enters the workshop, and with lamentations relates how his plans had miscarried. He had been, he said, as well as the shrewdest of the other disciples, firmly convinced that Christ would declare himself regent and head of the nation. His purpose was only forcibly to compel the Lord, whose hesitation had hitherto been invincible, to hasten the declaration, and he had accordingly incited the priesthood to an act of violence, which previously they had not the courage to commit. The disciples, on their side, were not without arms, and probably all would have turned out well, if the Lord had not given himself up, and left them in the most forlorn state. Ahasverus, whom this narrative in no wise tends to pacify, only augments the agony of the poor ex-apostle, so that his only course is to hang himself with all speed' (Volume II Part III Book XV, 1775, ibid. p176).

56 Ibid. p4.

57 Ibid. p13.

58 Ibid. p19.

The difference between that 'thief Judas' and the 'penitent thief' was a 'glance of the heart towards [Christ's] compassion and power'. That 'glance' is what makes the difference between 'unlocking' the Lord's compassion and the fate of Judas, who

> ...like a falling star, dropped from the heaven of Christ's companionship into the bottomless pit of perdition. He had been with Christ in this world, but his awful lot in the future state was to be eternally severed from the light and joy of that society.[59]

The reason for this 'severance', in Goulburn's account, does not lie in any crime or wrongdoing other than failing to believe 'in the power and willingness of Christ to draw him out of the abyss of sin';[60] a failure in which Christ, whose realm extends to the 'mind' of his followers, is surely implicated. This conclusion can only be strengthened by the possibility that the memory of the 'better unborn' saying played a part in the despair attributed to Judas.[61]

Goulburn's proclamation of omnipotent grace and a healing Christ might even have been strengthened if Judas' repentance had been found acceptable to God. Whilst such an argument is rarely used, it can be found in the conclusion to a pamphlet of 1846 by W.A. Darby:

> ...the conviction must force itself inevitably on every candid mind, that Judas Iscariot was saved; that he now realizes the promised 'throne', and presents, in the heavenly world, a richer trophy of the power of CHRIST to save even 'the chief of sinners' than either the malefactor of Calvary or Saul of Tarsus: nay, that he stands in the Church triumphant as the highest monument of THE AMPLITUDE OF THE MERCY OF THE CROSS! [62]

Darby is aware that the Christian tradition almost always represents Judas as in Hell, and carefully marshals scriptural evidence to argue his case. He refers to contemporary arguments that Judas was worldly and ambitious, pointing out that there is no evidence of this in the New Testament ('Where is the record?'[63]). He writes in Origen-like fashion that Judas must have demonstrated good qualities for most of his discipleship before falling victim to the temptations of covetousness. He cites the account of Judas' repentance in Matthew, and dismisses the suggestion that Judas' sin was unpardonable, on the grounds that this would make two such sins; both the sin against the Holy Ghost and the betrayal of the Son of

---

59 Ibid. p20.

60 Ibid.

61 This possibility is mentioned in *Observations on the Conduct and Character of Judas Iscariot* by J. Bonar (Edinburgh: printed by W.Sands, A.Murray and J. Cochran; sold by W. Miller and other Booksellers, 1750) p34.

62 *Judas Iscariot – The Argument in His Case on Scripture Evidence* by W.A. Darby (Belfast: printed for the author and sold by William McComb, 1, High Street, MDCCCXLVI) p35.

63 Ibid. p4.

Man.[64] None of this, however, is as significant as his insight that the fate of Judas is bound up with the way Christ and his salvific effectiveness can be understood.

Certainly Darby's writing is worthy of greater consideration than it has hitherto received, and it is a useful counterpoint to the sermons considered in this section. His argument, however, makes the same mistake as the other writers under discussion in attempting a speedy resolution of the tension between repentance and damnation. Darby does not struggle with the tension as Barth does, and allows the matter to remain an open question. He asserts rather that Judas is indeed saved, and that therefore the paradox is dissolved. But he has at least seen that the salvation or otherwise of Judas affects one's view of the salvific 'power' of Christ. For him there is no question of Christ being defeated, and therefore Judas must be saved. Preachers such as Goulburn, Kerr and Heurtley do not agree with the latter, but are not sufficiently alert to the implications of the former.

5.4 Exploring the 'open question' of Judas' eternal destiny

The writings discussed in the last three sections have witnessed in different ways to the correctness of Barth's insight keeping the eternal fate of Judas an open question. The biggest difficulty in his account, as was argued in the introduction to this chapter, is that he does not adequately show how Judas' fate remains an 'open question', or how God's grace might prevail. One strategy that Barth does not use is that hinted at by Origen and the apocryphal Coptic text mentioned earlier; to attempt an account of what happened to Judas beyond death. Origen, for example, describes Judas as repenting falsely, as many writers in this chapter have done. His reasoning, however, is rather different from Luther and Goulburn. Laeuchli writes that, 'Origen gives an astonishing reason for this false contrition: Judas meant to anticipate Jesus in his death in order to receive *misericordia* from him.'[65] Of the outcome of this possible encounter, however, Origen is silent.

It is striking that there are writings to be found in the tradition that do explore in different ways the 'open question' of Judas, damnation and the grace of God. None of the key examples explored below are biblical exegesis or theological exposition in the ordinary sense, but can be characterized as works of the imagination. All have a seriousness of theological purpose, however, in reflecting upon the fate of Judas and how this relates to God's salvific purposes as seen in Christ. First two apocryphal texts will be examined, then a medieval legend, and finally two poems by Robert Buchanan and Ruth Etchells.

The first of the two apocryphal texts that deal with Judas' eternal destiny is the eighth/ninth century *Acts of Andrew and Paul*, which has survived in Coptic.[66]

---

64 For him there is no suggestion of a link between the two as hinted at in Heurtley's sermon earlier in the chapter.

65 Laeuchli, op cit. pp259-260.

66 *The Apocryphal New Testament – A Collection of Apocryphal Christian literature in an English translation* J.K. Elliott (Oxford: Clarendon Press, 1993) pp301-2.

It recounts that Paul has visited Amante (the underworld), seen Judas and heard his story. Judas, the reader learns, repented and gave back the money, and went to Jesus to plead forgiveness. Jesus sends Judas into the desert to repent, telling him to fear no one but God. However, the 'prince of destruction' came to Judas and threatened to swallow him up, and Judas gave in to fear and worshipped him. For a second time he went to ask for pardon, but Jesus had by this time been taken away to the praetorium. Judas therefore decided to hang himself with the intention of meeting Jesus in Amante, which he did. Jesus, however, took all the souls except that of Judas, whereupon the resident powers said to Satan that they 'are stronger than Jesus, for he has had to leave a soul with us.' Jesus then ordered Michael to take away Judas' soul also, but told Judas that he had destroyed his own hopes by worshipping Satan and killing himself. Judas was then sent back until the day of judgement.

It is commented that Amante is now desolate, but that some murderers (particularly of little children) and sorcerers are also there. The kind of company considered suitable for Judas is clear, though he is not portrayed in an entirely bad light. Twice he seeks pardon, and it is Jesus on each occasion who refuses it; the first time conditionally, the second time finally – although Judas' fate on the day of judgement itself could be said to remain open. The responsibility, however is placed clearly on Judas, for in the second rebuke Jesus tells him he has 'destroyed his own hopes.'

The *Acts of Andrew and Paul* is an important text because of its awareness of Judas' distinctive status as the only apostle to die *before* Jesus' salvific work was complete. It dramatizes the tensions so often found in relation in Judas, as the reader is torn between condemning Judas for submitting to Satan, and yet crediting him with his two pleas for forgiveness, the second of which is portrayed as the reason for his suicide. Here Judas' death is not solely the result of despair, for it takes place in desperation for a further meeting with Jesus. Judas is evidently prepared for extreme measures in pleading for pardon. The portrayal of Jesus has its tensions also, for the picture of Christ avoiding Judas' pleas for forgiveness in Amante, albeit whilst liberating *all* the other occupants, is not unequivocally positive. Nor is his dismissal of the reason for Judas' suicide, or the late demonstration that he was not *obliged* to leave Judas' soul behind – but then sends him back.

The second of the apocryphal texts referred to above, *The Book of the Resurrection of Jesus Christ by Bartholomew the Apostle*, is less important in the sense that its portrayal of Jesus and Judas is cruder and more in line with mainstream tradition. Jesus rebukes Judas with the names of thirty sins (a clear but unstated link to the 'blood money') which are the snakes that are sent to devour him in Amante. Jesus has 'wrought havoc in Hell, breaking the doors, binding the demons Beliar and Melkir and delivered Adam and the holy souls'.[67] After his rebuke to Judas, Jesus then rises from the dead. When Death and

67 Ibid. p669.

Pestilence come back to Amante to protect it, only three souls remain. According to the Paris manuscript of the book, these are Herod, Cain and Judas.

This portrayal of Judas as beyond redemption is consistent with the majority view of the tradition. His absolute condemnation is so widely assumed that the smallest qualification draws forth the comment from P.F. Baum that it is 'altogether pleasant to find... the story of Judas' weekly respite from the torments of hell.' He is referring to an episode in the legend of St Brendan set out in the *Navigatio Sancti Brendani*, a popular medieval work.[68] In it, Brendan and his companions have been voyaging southwards for a week when they see a smoking mountain which marks a way into Hell. They encounter a figure sitting on a rock, in the midst of surging waters, who turns out to be Judas. Judas tells of the torments found within the mountain, and that he has respite on Sundays and certain feast days. This respite is allowed through the mercy of Christ, because of three good deeds Judas committed during his life. One of these was placing a rock across a ditch to help pedestrians – hence the rock he is perching on now.

The narrative continues with Brendan remonstrating with the devils who come to return Judas to Hell. They question Brendan as follows: 'Why do you invoke the name of the Lord on behalf of him who handed over the Lord?'

Baum comments that many in the church were critical of the legend of St Brendan, yet it remained popular. Moreover, 'of all the miraculous adventures that befell St Brendan and his monks, it is the discovery of lonely Judas on his wave-swept rock that seems to have made the deepest impression on the mind and memory of the readers.'[69] Just why this might have been so cannot be fully known, but the legend is theologically interesting in its emphasis on mercy even for a resident of hell such as Judas. It is significant that Judas is singled out in this fashion, and not such as Herod, Pilate or Caiaphas (whom Judas tells Brendan share his torments). The legend can be placed in an Origenistic tradition in the sense that the author(s) cannot believe that one chosen by Christ could have nothing good about him (hence the invention of the good deeds), or be entirely unworthy of the Christian Spirit of mercy and forgiveness. It is also significant that Judas is not portrayed as entirely given up to Hell and Satan, for the mercy of Christ is what allows his 'Sunday rest'. The power of the resurrection therefore extends into the deepest part of hell (for Judas is the sinner of sinners) even if it does not here work to bring Judas into God's presence eternally.

The legend of St Brendan can therefore be seen as part of a minority tradition that includes such texts as the *Acts of Andrew and Paul*. From the eighteenth century there are more frequent attempts to reconsider Judas and his eternal destiny. For example, in 1772 Thomas Gent published[70] *Divine Justice and*

---

68 'Judas' Sunday Rest' by P.F. Baum (*Modern Language Review* 18, 1823, pp168-182). The narrative is based on Irish legend.

69 Ibid. p176. Baum comments that the incident is one of very few episodes to be borrowed from the *Navigatio*, being found in two medieval French Romances as well as in poems by Matthew Arnold and Rudyard Kipling.

70 York: Printed at the New Printing Office in Fosgate, price twopence (the British Library also contains an 1840 edition). Interestingly, a footnote indicates his knowledge of

Mercy displayed and Set forth in the unhappy Birth, wicked life, and miserable End of that deceitful Apostle, Judas Iscariot; who for thirty pieces of silver, betrayed and sold his Lord and Master Jesus Christ (though he indicates that he composed it much earlier). Worth mentioning here are the words Gent appends to his account of the legend, building on the fact that Christ 'in mercy, thought it humbly meet, Without Exception, kind to wash his feet', and that no Scripture explicitly says Judas is in hell. The conclusion of his account is striking, as it is one of very few texts that does leave Judas' fate as an open question. In this sense Gent is a precursor of Barth in arguing that 'none may judge his Soul, if sav'd or lost. God only knows, who was concerned most.'[71]

Robert Buchanan (1841-1901), on the other hand, is clear that the grace of God does finally prevail. He articulates this in the poem, 'The Ballad of Judas Iscariot'[72] , first published in 1874.[73] The 'ballad' describes how the soul of the 'strangled' Judas sets out, carrying his dead body, in search of a burial place. Buchanan writes that as the journey began, 'The Eye of Heaven... Open'd and shut again', and that in despair and pain the soul of Judas carries the body on and on, unable to find rest. Even a stagnant pool will not receive the body. In the course of his desperate travels, Judas' soul goes past three crosses, where three skeletons from a certain crucifixion 'swing thereon.' It may be that by not portraying the middle cross as empty, Buchanan intends an illustration of what he elsewhere proposes – a Christ shorn of 'supernatural pretensions'.[74]

The soul of Judas then wanders alone for an unspecified period, cut off from any human contact, through days like 'blinding mist' and nights like 'rushing rain'. Finally something new occurs; in the darkness a light is seen:

> For months and years, in grief and tears,
> He walked the silent night;

Islamic material about Judas: 'Mahomet wrote, that one of the Name suffered on the Cross instead of Christ. Even that Impostor honour'd the Son of God as an holy Prophet...' (pp3-4).

71 This is in contrast to works such as *The unhappy Birth, wicked life, and miserable Death of that vile Traytor and Apostle Judas Iscariot* (Durham: Printed and Sold by Isaac Lane,1750) and *A Full and true Account of the Birth, Life and Death of Judas Iscariot* (Glasgow: J.&J. Robertson, 1776) which insist on Judas' condemnation.

72 *The Complete Poetical Works of Robert Buchanan* in two volumes (London: Chatto & Windus, 1901) Volume 1, pp494-6. The first edition of Buchanan's collected works, published in 1874, included the poem which had not been included in any of his previous books. Buchanan was a playwright, novelist, journalist and humanitarian as well as a poet. He worked to counter contemporary attitudes to such issues as censorship, women's rights and socialism.

73 See *Robert W. Buchanan* by John A. Cassidy (New York: Twayne Publishers, 1973) for a brief discussion of the poem. The poem is a combination of the legend of the Wandering Jew and the motif of the 'basest man'.

74 In *Robert Buchanan: The Poet of Modern Revolt* (London: Grant Richards, 1901) Archibald Stodard-Walker refers to a series of letters written by Buchanan to the *Daily Chronicle* explaining the theme of his poem on the Wandering Jew, and containing this suggestion (p204).

Then the soul of Judas Iscariot
Perceived a far-off light.

Judas sets off like a ship towards a lighthouse, with the wind and rain against him. Now however, he is 'Push'd on by hands behind', and eventually he stands like a polar explorer in a place of snow and icicles, redolent of the frozen lake of Cocytus in Dante's *Inferno*.[75] Here the scene is reversed, however, for at the heart of this wintry place is not Satan but a place of light and feasting, with the 'Bridegroom' at the head of a table of 'wedding guests'. The final nine stanzas, which one commentator refers to as 'the glory of the ending'[76] are as follows:

The Bridegroom shaded his eyes and look'd,
And his face was bright to see–
'What dost thou here at the Lord's Supper
With thy body's sins?' said he.

'Twas the soul of Judas Iscariot
Stood black, and sad, and bare–
'I have wandered many nights and days;
There is no light elsewhere.'

'Twas the wedding guests cried out within,
And their eyes were fierce and bright–
'Scourge the soul of Judas Iscariot
Away into the night!'

The Bridegroom stood in the open door,
And he waved hands still and slow,
And the third time that he waved his hands
The air was thick with snow.

And of every flake of falling snow,
Before it touched the ground,
There came a dove, and a thousand doves
Made sweet sound.

'Twas the body of Judas Iscariot
Floated away full fleet,
And the wings of the dove that bare it off
Were like its winding-sheet.

'Twas the Bridegroom stood at the open door,
And beckon'd, smiling sweet;
'Twas the soul of Judas Iscariot
Stole in, and fell at his feet.

---

75 Dante's placing of Judas in the lowest circle of hell, trapped in Satan's mouth and surrounded by the ice of Cocytus, is discussed in the next chapter.

76 Cassidy, op cit. p105.

'The Holy Supper is spread within,
And the many candles shine,
And I have waited long for thee
Before I poured the wine!'

The supper wine is poured at last,
The lights burn bright and fair,
Iscariot washes the Bridegroom's feet,
And dries them with his hair.

In these stanzas Buchanan challenges the mainstream Christian view of Judas, represented by the fierce-eyed wedding guests who would 'Scourge the soul of Judas Iscariot Away into the night!' It is a poem that many have found moving and impressive, but as an engagement with Scriptures and the theological tensions surrounding Judas it is somewhat lacking. There is no reference to repentance, or indeed any attempt to interpret Judas' actions. It seems strange that the cross has a skeleton upon it, and yet Jesus is eschatologically present. The poem has something of a melodramatic dream-like quality about it, such that it is hard to imagine it could form the basis for substantial insight into the theology of redemption.

The one point that is intriguing is its insistence that salvation is a process that cannot be complete until Judas finds inclusion within it. Jesus will not pour the wine of the heavenly banquet until Judas, implicitly the greatest sinner of all, has been welcomed to the feast. Judas' response is described in terms drawn from Luke 7.37-48, where a sinful woman wets his feet with her tears and wipes them with her here. Jesus praises her in words here implicitly addressed to Judas, 'Your sins are forgiven'. So it is that he gives a vivid picture of salvific completeness. In order to understand this eschatological imagery it is necessary to examine Buchanan's understanding of the historical Jesus. In a note in the second edition of *The Wandering Jew* he writes that Jesus

> ...survives and will survive as a Divine Ideal, a pathetic figure, searching Heaven in vain for a sign, for a token he has not failed... He is asking himself, after eighteen hundred years of effort, the terrible question which I have put into his mouth: 'After all, are men worth saving?'[77]

For Buchanan, Jesus did fail in his earthly life, as may be guessed from the image of the skeleton on the cross. He turned away from the world as 'in its very nature, base and detestable', not realising that God's kingdom must begin on earth if it is to exist in heaven.[78] Buchanan imagines that Jesus,

> looking round on his fellows, realising the extent of human misery and perceiving the follies of human existence, ...thought, 'Surely there must be some Divine solution to the problem. Surely there must be another and fairer life to justify a life

[77] Quoted in Stodard-Walker, ibid. p202.

[78] Ibid. p204.

so ephemeral.' Therein he was right; without some such justification this life of ours is only dust and ashes.[79]

This is a strange understanding of redemption. Rather than Jesus being himself the 'Divine solution', redemption does not begin in history but in 'another life.' Buchanan, it seems, cannot accept the possibility of an incomplete redemptive process. For him, either the whole world is saved, or it is not. Since Judas is 'lost', and he does not see enough evidence of redeemed humanity around him in the late nineteenth century, he concludes that the world is tragic in its intrinsic baseness. In its baseness, he seems to be saying, it was too tough a place for Jesus and his 'beautiful dream'; Jesus, who in his 'tender and sympathizing humanity... judged men far too gently, he was far too sanguine about human perfectibility.'[80]

In a brief appearance in *The Wandering Jew*, Judas is asked why he died after the betrayal. He responds that '...I knew his promise was a lie... I knew the Man whom I had slain was not Messiah – Now, let me sleep again!'[81] This is a conclusion Buchanan is close to accepting for himself, in his extremely negative judgement of Christ's redemptive efficacy 'on earth'. Jesus is only Messiah, it seems, in the contrastingly supremely positive picture of the eschaton. However, as he sensed himself, his poem remains a 'beautiful dream'; both in its distance from the scriptural understanding of Judas, and its correlate implication of Jesus' failure to redeem the bodily Iscariot of history. In Buchanan's favour, however, is his strikingly expressed perception that without Judas the salvation of the world is incomplete. Here attention to his poem and the other texts considered here might at least work to reopen the question of Judas' salvation for those for whom the matter is closed.

After all, if Judas is condemned eternally, this affects the way Jesus is to be understood. W.A. Darby saw that the salvation of the 'chief of sinners' would be the most powerful possible witness to the power of Christ. Similarly, the author of the *Acts of Andrew and Paul* portrays the powers of Amante saying that they 'are stronger than Jesus, for he has had to leave a soul with us.' The insight of this unknown author is considerable, for the image of Christ encountering Judas in hell has greater theological credibility than Buchanan's 'beautiful dream'. If Buchanan had been aware of this earlier work, he might have written a rather different ballad about the encounter between Judas and Jesus beyond their respective deaths.

Such a poem does exist, written not by Buchanan but by Ruth Etchells. While it is not particularly well known, and indeed in poetic terms a minor work, a case can be made for its theological significance. For in Etchell's *Ballad of the Judas Tree*[82] Judas is not the last person to receive salvation, as in Buchanan's poem, but the first:

---

79 Ibid. p204.

80 Ibid. p205.

81 *The Complete Poetical Works of Robert Buchanan* Volume II, op cit. p223.

82 Quoted in *At the Cross* by Richard Bauckham and Trevor Hart (London: Darton, Longman & Todd, 1999) pp20-1.

In Hell there grew a Judas tree
Where Judas hanged and died
Because he could not bear to see
His master crucified

Our Lord descended into Hell
And found his Judas there
For ever hanging on the tree
Grown from his own despair

So Jesus cut his Judas down
And took him in his arms
'It was for this I came' he said
'And not to do you harm

My Father gave me twelve good men
And all of them I kept
Though one betrayed and one denied
Some fled and others slept

In three days' time I must return
To make the others glad
But first I had to come to Hell
And share the death you had

My tree will grow in place of yours
Its roots lie here as well
There is no final victory
Without this soul from Hell'

So when we all condemn him
As of every traitor worst
Remember that of all his men
Our Lord forgave him first

While Etchells' poem does not entirely avoid the suspicion of melodrama that attaches itself to Buchanan's work also, its scriptural allusions and coherence with mainstream, credal Christianity (the descent into hell) strengthen its theological contention: that Judas is indeed redeemed by Christ through the Son of God's descent into hell, the place of death and despair. Here is a clear answer to MacKinnon, who insists on the finality of the New Testament texts about Judas. Here is a clear answer to Barth also, who argued that it is hard to say if there is any redemptive significance for Judas in Jesus' death. In relation to the argument of this book, however, the theological weakness of Etchells' poem is that it resolves the tension between providence and tragedy rather too easily. To insist on Judas' forgiveness, as both Etchells and Buchanan do, is as mistaken as insisting on his absolute condemnation. Nevertheless, Etchells insight that the heart of the matter does not lie in the crucifixion alone, but in what Jesus did whilst being dead, is a potentially fruitful one. It qualifies the sense that Judas died 'the wrong side of the cross', for as Origen indicated, this timing enables Judas to encounter Jesus in Hell. His death, in fact, was the quickest possible route to such an encounter.

Etchells' poem might have explored the redemptive significance of that encounter at greater length, rather than declaring so quickly what she takes to be its outcome. The next chapter contains just such an exploration through an examination of the 'descent into hell' as found in the writings of Jorge Luis Borges, Dante, and Hans Urs von Balthasar. For this is the only way to explore Barth's insight that the fate of Judas should remain an 'open question.' This chapter has witnessed to the correctness of his insight, even if Barth was not himself able to convincingly demonstrate its correctness, nor how the grace of God might ultimately triumph. It is to an examination of these issues through the perhaps unexpected linking of the three writers just mentioned that this book will shortly turn.

5.5 Conclusion

A striking feature of the tradition is its witness to the validity of Barth's argument that keeping the fate of Judas an 'open question' is necessary if tragedy is to be denied. In the writing of Leo, for example, the combination of damnation and the timing of Judas' death make of him a uniquely unfortunate character. In this context, the significance of the minority view in the tradition, represented by writers such as Darby and Buchanan, is twofold:

1. Its implicit critique of the mainstream tradition that asserts Judas' damnation despite his repentance, making this either a matter of *timing* or of *incomplete repentance*, with despair identified as its main shortcoming. The former makes of Judas a tragic figure, while the latter is an illegitimate resolution of a felt tension between repentance and damnation. It also has questionable implications in relation to the providential working of God and for Christian practice.
2. It serves to reopen the question of Judas, and the polarity of wickedness and grace identified by Barth. There is the hint of a rationale for reconsidering the eternal destiny of Judas, which is not that Judas is necessarily seen as any less sinful – rather that what is at stake is the nature of the doctrine of salvation.

When despair becomes a dominant theme, as a way of resolving the felt tension between the repentance of Judas as recorded in the New Testament and the conviction that Judas was eternally damned, it implies a knowledge of Judas' state of mind. This is flawed, given that this can only be inferred from the accounts of Judas in Matthew and Acts. Here theologians fall prey to the novelistic understanding of character that this book has rejected. It is also the case that some novelistic, fictional or speculative writing can contain theological insight, as for example in the case of Robert Buchanan and Ruth Etchells. In the next chapter this will be seen also in the work of Jorge Luis Borges and Dante.

In this chapter it is writers such as Darby and the author of the *Acts of Andrew and Paul* who see clearly that the way the fate of Judas is understood affects the way Christ can be understood, particularly in relation to the efficacy and extent of his salvific power. If they, and Buchanan, reject the unequivocal damnation of Judas, it is particularly in the *Acts* and the ballad of Ruth Etchells that a theologically convincing way forward is sensed, even though the tendency to seek to resolve the difficult issue of Judas' fate one way or the other remains at work. It is to a more thorough exploration of the theme of Christ's descent into hell that this book turns in its penultimate chapter.

Chapter 6

Judas and Christ's Descent into Hell

In order to save us, [God] could have chosen any of the lives that weave the confused web of history: He could have been Alexander or Pythagoras or Jesus; he chose an abject existence: He was Judas.[1]

Jorge Luis Borges

This chapter explores the key issue identified in the latter part of the preceding one – the fate of Judas in the light of Christ's descent into hell. In my final chapter I will set out the implications of this exploration, and the analysis of the material in the preceding chapters, for Christology. The contours of a Christology shaped by the difficult questions examined in this book, and that can face the tension between providence and tragedy it identifies, will be argued.

In the previous chapter Christ's descent into hell was pointed to as the best strategy for exploring Barth's argument that the salvific status of Judas remains an 'open question'.[2] The theological significance of this is heightened when attention is drawn to an implication of the way both Barth and MacKinnon understand Judas. In different ways they make something unique of him, to the point that it almost comes to seem that Judas is (as Borges puts it in a short story discussed below) the 'secret name of God'. Barth, for example, has the perception to note that there are two deaths at the heart of the New Testament, one of which he describes as 'dark', the other 'light'. He sees Judas as the most important figure in the New Testament apart from Jesus, and suggests that with Jesus' death the Judas in Paul dies. This means that all those living subsequent to his death are no longer capable of what Judas did.

For MacKinnon, Judas is tragic in that he is an unredeemed consequence of the economy of salvation. Neither he nor Barth have seen that such 'readings' open up the possibility of a further, startling reading: that it is Judas rather than Jesus who is truly lost in order that the world may find salvation. This is because he is both necessary to the salvific death of Christ for others, and its subsequent reception, and yet finds only condemnation and rejection himself.

---

1 'Three Versions of Judas' in *Collected Fictions* translated by Andrew Hurley (London: Allen Lane, 1998) p166.

2 This view is supported by Pope John Paul II, who, writing on the subject of the possibility of universal salvation, says that, 'The silence of the Church is… the only appropriate position for Christian faith. Even when Jesus says of Judas, the traitor, "it would be better for that man if he had never been born" (Mt 26:24), his words do not allude for certain to eternal damnation.' *Crossing the Threshold of Hope* (London: Jonathan Cape, 1994) p186.

I have said this is an implication of the writing of Barth and MacKinnon, rather than something made explicit. There are at least two places in which this implication is overtly expressed – a nineteenth-century dispute between two minor American theologians, Nathanael Emmons and David Pickering, and the Borges story referred to above. Both will shortly be discussed, with particular reference to their agreement that the human race is in debt to Judas for its salvation, and yet languishes in the lowest point of hell. If this argument has any validity, it exposes a potential theological incoherence at the heart of the economy of salvation, an incoherence that Barth sensed in his declaration that the fate of Judas must remain an 'open question'. For if the salvation of humankind has in any measure a dependence on the damnation of one man, this is an injustice that radically undermines it. It gives a new slant to the famous exchange between Ivan and Alyosha in *The Brothers Karamazov*, where Ivan asks if the giving of happiness and peace to the human race could be justified if it depended on the torture and death of 'only one tiny creature'.[3] Alyosha cannot accept this, nor that the human race as a whole would accept happiness on these terms. It gives a different slant also to the statement attributed to Caiaphas at John 11.50: '...it is expedient for you that one man should die for the people, that the whole nation should not perish.'

By contrast, if the saving power of Christ can extend even to the dead Judas, the incoherence can be resolved. Therefore the second section of this chapter, following discussion of Emmons, Pickering and Borges, will focus on the contrasting treatments of Christ's descent into hell by Dante and Balthasar, with particular reference to the adequacy or otherwise of their interpretations in relation to the unique fate of Judas (to which both Dante and Balthasar witness in different ways).

6.1 Emmons, Pickering and Borges on the gratitude due to Judas

In 1827 a remarkable sermon was published, together with a contemporary review declaring that 'we have never seen a more repulsive, unjust and detestable character attributed to the Supreme Eternal, than that contained in the sermon before us').[4] In his *Sermon on the perdition of Judas*, Nathanael Emmons takes Matthew 26.24 as his text ('It had been good for that man if he had not been born') and draws a series of powerfully expressed conclusions from the role Judas plays in the Gospels. In particular he argues that Judas was an instrument in the hand of God for effecting the salvation of humankind. This unusual argument comes from a writer who cannot easily be accused of avoiding uncomfortable particularities in the narrative of the New Testament, as so many writers tend to do. His approach

---

3 *The Brothers Karamazov*, Fyodor Dostoyevsky, translated by David Magarshack (London: Penguin, 1958) p287.

4 *Sermon on the perdition of Judas*, by Nathanael Emmons D.D. with a review of the same by Rev David Pickering (Providence: Cranston and Marshall Printers, 1827).

highlights some of the theologically controversial territory opened up when these particularities are addressed.

Emmons was a Calvinist who considered that 'Calvinism has lost much of its purity and simplicity by going through so many unskilful hands of its friends.'[5] On his own account his application to the ministry almost foundered on differing interpretations of the doctrine of divine decrees, which left him with a determination to examine his religious sentiments with as much zeal as he propagated and defended them 'against all opposition'.[6] In describing his opposition to the Arminians, he emphasizes five points, amongst them absolute predestination and election, and in particular, not universal redemption.[7] It is the latter that is the subject of the sermon under discussion here.

Emmons described himself as a subject rather than text based preacher. This indicates that his approach to the New Testament makes no pretence at impartiality. He is transparently seeking to find evidence for his rigid Calvinist views. His significance for this book is that his eisegesis has alerted him to aspects of the Gospel texts unnoticed by considerably more gifted theologians. Indeed Ide suggests that Emmons was not distinguished in imagination, but rather in his ability to discern the relation of one truth to another.[8] In his sermon on Judas he illustrates that ability to make connections by alighting upon the one who 'betrayed' Jesus as a basis for his sometimes rather ponderously expressed theological views. He deserves credit for perceiving an exegetical line little explored by writers more widely known and of greater ability.

His reviewer was David Pickering, Pastor of the First Universalist Society and Church in Hudson. In an address of 1821 he had argued for universal salvation, emphasizing the impartial grace and mercy of God, and the unlimited benevolence of God.[9] He could hardly be more opposed to Emmons' views, therefore, as is evident in the tone and content of his review. While he clearly is an acute theological thinker, as will be seen, he struggles against the rather crude approach of Emmons in ways that are highly illuminating for this book.

Emmons' sermon on the perdition of Judas is in two parts. First he examines the role Judas plays in the Gospels in the light of Matthew 26.24. In the second part he draws a series of theological deductions relating to the doctrines of election and reprobation. Throughout, his logic is remorseless. He explains that Judas must be 'finally and eternally lost'[10] for nothing else explains how it would

---

5 *The Works of Nathanael Emmons, D.D. late Pastor of the Church in Franklin, Mass. with A memoir of his life.* Six volumes, edited by Jacob Ide, D.D. (Boston: Crocker & Brewster, 1842) Volume 1, which begins with a Memoir by Emmons from which the quotation is taken, pxxxiv.

6 Ibid. pxiv.

7 The other three points are original sin; the impotence of man and irresistible grace; and the perseverance of the saints.

8 Op cit. ppxli-xlii.

9 *A Calm Address to the Believers and Advocates of Endless Misery. Designed for the Benefit of the Youth* (Hudson: Ashbel Stoddard, 1821).

10 Op cit. p7.

have been better 'if he had not been born'. He must, therefore, have been a 'prodigy of wickedness',[11] betraying the one he ought to have been prepared to die for after all the privileges of discipleship.

For Emmons, what he calls the 'peculiarities' of Judas, the unique actions attributed to him in the Gospels, 'did not meet in Judas by mere chance; but were designed and effected by the supreme being'. Given that the Gospels indicate that the role of Judas was foretold in scripture, he concludes that:

> God brought Judas into being to answer wise and noble designs... He intended to save some of the human race, through the death of his Son. But if his Son, who was holy and harmless, must die, he must die by the hand of a wicked instrument. Accordingly, if the death of Christ must be fixed, so the instrument of his death must also be fixed. Hence it was as necessary that Judas should be born, as Christ should be born; that Judas should betray him, as that he should die. Therefore the life and conduct of Judas were connected with the glorious scheme of man's redemption. He was not a cypher in the world, but an important instrument in the hand of God of accomplishing the great purposes of his grace. These glorious ends were present in the mind of God, when he decreed the existence, character, conduct and state of Judas... .[12]

The first part of the sermon ends with the contention that although God knew:

> that Judas would be miserable forever... yet he did not bring him into being for the sake of his misery; but for the sake of his own glory in the salvation of myriads of the human race. And this end was a good, infinitely superior to the ruin of one person. God, therefore, had the greatest, wisest and best end, in decreeing and effecting the eternal perdition of Judas.[13]

It is this kind of passage that David Pickering, in the manner of Ivan Karamazov, describes as giving a 'repulsive' picture of God. Further, he points out, the logic of such a passage is that humankind is as 'under as great obligations of gratitude to Judas, as to Jesus Christ!'.[14] The exclamation mark indicates that Pickering considers this ridiculous, but he is correctly pointing out an implication of Emmons' argument. If it were only to do with Emmons, this would be of little significance. But Emmons has made crudely explicit the implication of much writing in the tradition about Judas, including the work of Barth and MacKinnon. Here an implication left unstated (whether consciously or unconsciously) is baldly set down to challenge the reader. Pickering points to the underlying logic that is arguably common to Barth and MacKinnon as well as Emmons, and therefore of both providential and tragic readings of Judas.

---

11 Ibid. p5.
12 Ibid. p10.
13 Ibid. p11.
14 Ibid. p29.

For if Judas is a tragic figure, as MacKinnon argues, his tragedy is indicated by the 'better unborn' text from Matthew 26.24 (and parallels). Judas is both necessary for the economy of salvation, and yet also condemned in New Testament texts of bitter finality. Indeed then, humankind has an obligation of gratitude to Judas. On the other hand, if Judas is a providential figure, as Barth argues, the most significant New Testament figure after Jesus, following whose death the Judas in Paul dies (so enabling the 'handing over' of the gospel), then humankind also has an obligation of gratitude to Judas – particularly if Judas is eternally condemned. It is Barth's unwillingness to accept the latter, and his determination to express that Judas' salvation remains an open question, that is the crucial distinction between himself and MacKinnon – and Emmons. Emmons, after all, offers as strong a providential reading of Judas as it is possible to find, ending with his conclusion that God had the wisest and best reasons for the eternal perdition of Judas. If it were not for Barth's view that the salvific status of Judas is uncertain, Emmons' conclusion would be an uncomfortably percipient summary of Barth's sophisticated analysis in C.D. II.2. Once again this emphasizes the significance of his failure to show how the 'open question' of Judas' fate might be approached.

This failure indicates something of why the writing of Dante and Balthasar on the descent into hell will be examined in the next section, as in my judgement an analysis of their divergent writing on this topic, for all the problems that will be identified with each, offers clues towards articulating a way forward that I will take up in my own treatment of the issues in the final part of the chapter. Before turning to Dante and Balthasar, however, there are aspects of the debate between Emmons and Pickering that remain to be brought out. This can be seen by relating their arguments to a theologically perceptive short story by Jorge Luis Borges; a story which explores the idea expressed by Pickering when he wrote that on Emmons' account humankind is as 'under as great obligations of gratitude to Judas, as to Jesus Christ!'

While many writers and novelists have produced work incorporating Judas, these almost invariably focus on character and motivation. Borges, however, is primarily concerned with interpretation and meaning, and this is what enables him to produce a work as theologically astute as 'Three Versions of Judas.' In 1944 Borges published *Ficciones*, which included eight stories already published as well as six new ones under the heading 'Artifices'.[15] The new works included the remarkable piece on Judas just mentioned, focusing on a fictional Swedish theologian, Nils Runeberg. Runeberg is described as a 'deeply religious man', fascinated by what he saw as 'one of theology's central mysteries'.[16] The nature

15 These stories first achieved a wide English readership with their publication in *Labyrinths* (New Directions, 1964, and Penguin, 1970). Amongst the later editions are *Fictions* (London: Calder Publications, 1991) translated by Anthony Kerrigan, and the one used here, *Collected Fictions* (London: Allen Lane, 1998) translated by Andrew Hurley.

16 'Three Versions of Judas' in *Collected Fictions* translated by Andrew Hurley (London: Allen Lane, 1998) p163.

of that mystery is indicated by the title of *Kristus och Judas*, the first edition of which is described as having been published in 1904. Borges notes that the work has as an epigraph a quotation by Thomas de Quincey: 'It is not one thing, but all the things which legend attributes to Judas Iscariot that are false.'

Borges writes that Runeberg contends the superfluity of Judas' action in pointing out Jesus, as Christ was well known and did not need identification. The meaning of his action was rather to be found on the metaphysical plane, with Judas 'in representation of all mankind' repaying the sacrifice involved in the Word becoming flesh, with his own sacrifice. As the Word 'stooped' to become mortal, so Judas stooped to commit the 'most heinous crime' of an informer and 'to dwell amid inextinguishable flames'.[17] In this Judas is 'somehow a reflection of Jesus', a conclusion which explains the kiss, the thirty pieces of silver and the voluntary death.

The story continues with Runeberg conceding some ground to his critics, who accuse him (amongst other things) of docetism and contradicting Luke 22.3 (a text Borges simply cites, leaving the reader to ascertain that it records the Satanic influence on Judas). Runeberg partially rewrites his book, conceding that Jesus 'had no need of a man to carry out His plan for the redemption of all mankind.' He then proceeds to argue that because Jesus chose Judas as one of the apostles, it is difficult to attribute his actions to something as base as greed. Rather, precisely because of Jesus' choice, Judas' actions 'merit the most sympathetic interpretation we can give them.' Runeberg therefore proposes that Judas engaged in a form of religious asceticism, mortifying not the flesh but the spirit. Believing himself unworthy of being good, he 'sought hell because joy in the Lord was enough for him. He thought that happiness, like goodness, is a divine attribute, which should not be usurped by men.'[18]

There is still, however, one more 'extravagant' version of Judas to be told, following on from these two 'justifiable' ones. Borges indicates that this is the one to be taken most seriously, describing it as Runeberg's magnum opus. After nearly two years of revision, Runeberg presents a new text to his publisher in 1909, *Den hemlige Frälsaren.* This time the epigraph is from John 1.10: 'He was in the world, and the world was made by him, and the world knew him not.' Borges writes as follows about the conclusion of this book:

> God, argues Nils Runeberg, stooped to become man for the redemption of the human race; we might well then presume that the sacrifice effected by Him was perfect, not invalidated or attenuated by omissions. To limit His suffering to the agony of one afternoon on the cross is blasphemous. To claim that He was man, and yet was incapable of sin, is to fall into contradiction; the attributes *impeccabilitas* and *humanitas* are incompatible. Kemnitz will allow that the Redeemer could feel weariness, hunger, cold, distress, hunger and thirst; one might also allow Him to be able to sin and be condemned to condemnation. For many the

[17] Ibid. p164.
[18] Ibid. p165.

> famous words in Isaiah 53... *He is despised and rejected of men; a man of sorrows, and acquainted with grief,* are a foreshadowing of the Crucified Christ at the hour of His death... for Runeberg, they are the detailed prophecy not of a moment but of the entire horrendous future, in Time and Eternity, of the Word made Flesh. God was made totally man, but man to the point of iniquity, man to the point of reprobation and the Abyss. In order to save us, He could have chosen *any* of the lives that weave the confused web of history: He could have been Alexander or Pythagoras or Jesus; he chose an abject existence: He was Judas.[19]

The indifference with which Runeberg's book was received, the story continues, came to seem to him as a confirmation of its argument. God, he thought, had ordered indifference because God 'did not want His terrible secret spread throughout the earth.' Runeberg felt that he was cursed for his discovery; even that his 'dark sin' might be 'the blasphemy against the Holy Ghost (Matthew 12:31) which shall not be forgiven.' He wandered the streets, sleepless and 'crying out for a blessing – that he be allowed to share the Inferno with the Redeemer.' To this poignant sentence Borges adds only that Runeberg died of a ruptured aneurysm less than three years after his final work, and that heresiologists will remember him for adding 'to the concept of the Son, which might have been thought long spent, the complexities of misery and evil'.[20]

Borges referred to his story as a 'Christological fantasy'.[21] To an author who preferred to indicate the whole of a subject through compact description of a particular episode, Judas was a suitable subject as being the subject of puzzling yet brief description in the Gospels. It seems that Borges has seen the potential theological incoherence at the heart of the economy of salvation identified in the introduction to this chapter, and explored it in characteristic fashion.

It can also be said that the theme of betrayal interested Borges, as can be seen in another story found in *Artifices*, 'The Shape of the Sword'. Here a cowardly Irishman who has betrayed a braver man tells the story as though he was the one betrayed.[22] At the end he tells that the betrayer 'was paid his Judas silver and ran off to Brazil', and that indeed he is the one 'who betrayed the man who saved me and gave me shelter.' The next story in *Artifices*, 'The Theme of the Traitor and the Hero', is also given an Irish setting. This time, however, the hero and the traitor are the same person: an Irish leader is shown to be traitor, and agrees to act out a drama ending in death at the hands of an unknown assassin. So doing, he can partially redeem himself and further rather than harm the cause. Here, in a related but reversed way to the final section of 'Three Versions of

---

19 Ibid. p166.

20 Ibid. p167.

21 In the foreword to *Artifices* (1944), also to be found in *Collected Fictions*, ibid. p130.

22 Ibid. pp138-142. In this guise he tells how the cowardice of the other is embarrassing, because whatever 'one man does, it is as though all men did it. That is why it is not unfair that a single act of disobedience in a garden should contaminate all humanity; that is why it is not unfair that a single Jew's crucifixion should be enough to save it' (p141).

Judas', the popular hero *is* the traitor (rather than the apparent traitor in fact being the 'hero', as in Runeberg's theology). In both stories the truth is concealed, for in 'The Theme of the Traitor and the Hero' a later researcher decides to silence his discovery, while in 'Three Versions of Judas' nobody accepts Runeberg's conclusions.

The fact that Borges was interested in pairs of opposing characters, doublings and reversals, does not necessarily mean that his 'Christological fantasy' can be dismissed as entertaining but theologically meaningless. It can be argued that Borges fastened on the role of Judas as an illustration of one of his preoccupations because he was alive to some of the nuances of the Judas texts in the Gospels and Christian tradition. Borges is indeed on familiar ground in considering Judas as a kind of polar opposite to Jesus. However, in pressing this opposition to its limit, and seeing that in his destruction Judas can look, from a certain perspective, to be the one 'lost for the sins of the world', Borges is unique, going beyond even Pickering's statement about the logic of Emmons' argument. For it is not even that equal gratitude is due to Judas and Jesus, as Judas is alone truly deserving of praise. This pushes the underlying logic of MacKinnon's position (where Judas is seen as intrinsic to salvation, yet alone receiving damnation – Christ is raised to new life) as far as it can go.

Borges wrote one further 'fantasy' involving Judas as central to the narrative of redemption. In *The Book of Sand* (1975) Borges returned to a consideration of Judas and Jesus in 'The Sect of the Thirty'.[23] The story purports to be a fourth century Latin text by an unknown author, describing a sect reminiscent of the Cainites (discussed in Chapter 4). The beliefs of the sect are summarized as follows:

> Divine mercy, to which I myself owe so many blessings, has allowed me to discover the true and secret reason for the Sect's name. In Kerioth, where it is plausibly reputed to have arisen, there has survived a conventicle known as the Thirty Pieces of Silver. That was the Sect's original name, and it provides us with the key. In the tragedy of the Cross (and I write this with all the reverence which is its due) there were those who acted knowingly and those who acted unknowingly; all were essential, all inevitable... Of knowing actors, there were but two: Judas and the Redeemer. Judas cast away the thirty coins that were the price of our souls' salvation and immediately hanged himself. At that moment he was thirty-three years old, the age of the Son of Man. The Sect venerates the two equally, and absolves the others.[24]

---

23 Ibid. pp443-445.

24 Ibid. p445. 'Kerioth' is often supposed to be the place where Judas came from, although this deduction from the name 'Iscariot' is uncertain (as was seen in Chapter 1). The Sect is described as mocking and crucifying its initiates when they reach the age of thirty three (a fate echoing that of the central character in an earlier story, 'The Gospel According to Mark' (ibid. pp397-401), who introduces an illiterate family to the gospel. The result is that they begin to revere him, and then one evening curse him and lead him outside to where they have torn down the roof beams to build a cross.

The point is, according to the manuscript, that Christ's redemptive act needed to be 'unforgettable' if it was 'to leave a wound on the imagination of mankind until the end of days.' Above all, the 'Lord disposed that the events should inspire pathos.'[25] The implication is that only Jesus and Judas were aware of this, and that the sect venerate Judas as well as Jesus for deliberately living out roles involving their own deaths. The thirty pieces are therefore 'blood money', not in the usual negative sense, but as 'the price of our soul's salvation.' Once again Borges has articulated a view of Judas as central to the narrative of redemption. Once again this truth is 'secret', known only by the members of a now presumably extinct sect described by Borges manuscript as 'never large, but now its followers are few indeed'.[26] Here, however, he does not describe Judas as God incarnate; but his final 'version' of Judas retains a force worth attending to. Borges, perhaps, is able to express some of the implications of Christian texts about Judas with unique force because he is writing fiction.

Of course the orthodox Christian account of salvation does not understand Judas as the one lost for the sins of the world. Yet if Judas has a role in the economy of salvation, and through playing that role is consigned to hell and damnation, the questions about incoherence raised in the introduction to the chapter apply. The question about Judas' fate beyond death has been identified as theologically highly significant, particularly in relation to Barth's assertion that it remains a question that is genuinely open. As has been seen, Barth does not adequately articulate how this is so. Therefore this book now turns to two key writers who have explored the nature of the (to use Borges' language) 'point of reprobation and the Abyss'. In their differing treatments can be seen the theological significance of the spectrum of approaches to Hell found in the Christian tradition. Therefore it is first to Dante and then to Balthasar that this book now turns.

6.2 Dante and Christ's limited descent into *Inferno*

With its three parts and one hundred cantos, *La Divina Commedia* shares something of the sense of order Aquinas communicates in the *Summa Theologiae.* Dante goes beyond Aquinas, however, in giving imaginative shape to the 'wickedness' of Judas that they both took for granted, and the eternal consequences of the choices he made.

His first reference to Judas is found in *Inferno*, Canto IX.27-9, where Virgil speaks of 'the circle of Judas, the deepest and darkest place, farthest from the heaven that encircles all.' In Canto XI.61-66 Virgil explains that in what is later referred to as 'Giudecca' (Canto XXXIV.117), a place 'which engulfs Lucifer with Judas' (Canto XXX.143):

---

25 Ibid. pp444-5.

26 Ibid. p443.

> ...both that love which nature makes is forgotten and that also which is added to it and which creates a special trust; therefore in the smallest circle, at the central point of the universe and seat of Dis, every traitor is consumed eternally.[27]

Judas is not mentioned in Canto XIII on suicides, presumably because this is not considered his major sin. Canto XIV tells of the Old Man of Crete (who represents human history) whose tears run into hell, appearing under different names before, says Virgil:

> ...going down by this narrow channel to where there is no more descent, they form Cocytus, and what kind of pond that is thou shalt see, so that here I do not speak of it. (116-20)

In Cantos XXXII-IV Dante indeed sees that it is a frozen lake. Those trapped within it who would weep cannot, as their tears freeze in their eyes. In this ninth circle of Hell they are placed in order of the seriousness of their treachery: to family, to country, to guests and finally to lords and benefactors. At the centre of Cocytus, Dante sees the one he names at various points as Satan, Dis, Lucifer and Beelzebub – the 'Emperor of the woeful kingdom [standing] forth at mid-breast from the ice' (XXXIV.28-29) with 'three faces on his head' (XXXIV.35). He has great bat-like wings:

> and he was beating them so that three winds went forth from him by which all Cocytus was kept frozen. With six eyes he was weeping and over three chins dripped tears and bloody foam. In each mouth he crushed a sinner with his teeth as with a heckle and thus he kept three of them in pain; to him in front the biting was nothing to the clawing, for sometimes the back was left all stripped of skin. 'That soul up there which has the greatest punishment,' said the Master, 'is Judas Iscariot, who has his head inside and plies his legs without.' (XXXIV.47-63)

The other two are named as Brutus and Cassius, who murdered the founder of the Roman Empire. Judas' treachery is against the Church, and all three have thus (as Dante sees it) refused and denied the whole divine order. Here, then, is the worst evil conceivable, and as Virgil says 'it is time to go, for we have seen all.' (XXXIV.69) Once again it seems that Judas has a unique place in the economy of salvation (and damnation), for he is the only figure directly connected to Christ in the ninth circle.

It is striking that Virgil and Dante are witnessing a scene never beheld by Christ, who in his descent into hell never ventured this 'deep'. This is clear from Canto IV of *Inferno*, where Virgil guides Dante into limbo, the first circle of hell.

---

[27] This and subsequent quotations are taken from *The Divine Comedy of Dante Alighieri, I Inferno, II Purgatorio, III Paradiso*, with translation and comment by John D. Sinclair (New York: Oxford University Press, 1939). Dis is the name of the city whose wall marks the boundary between sins of weakness and sins of the will, and for Dante the most serious of the latter are 'fraud', particularly 'treachery'.

Here are to be found virtuous pagans and unbaptized infants. Dante is troubled by this, as he knows people of 'much worth' are suspended in limbo, and so he asks Virgil if anyone has ever gone out from the first circle into paradise. He expresses his question in veiled language, as Christ is unknown and cannot be named in hell, and Virgil answers in similar fashion:

> I was new in this condition when I saw a mighty one come here, crowned with a sign of victory. He took from among us the shade of our first parent, of Abel his son, and of Noah, of Moses, law-giver and obedient, of the patriarch Abraham, and of King David... and many others, and he made them blest. And I would have thee know that before these no human souls were saved. (IV.52-62).

The significance of Christ's descent into hell is explained by Beatrice in Canto VII of *Paradiso,* where she outlines the entire history of salvation. She begins with 'our first parent' of whom she comments:

> By not enduring for his good a rein on his will, the man that was never born, condemning himself, condemned all his progeny; therefore mankind lay sick below in great error for many ages, till it pleased the Word of God to descend where the nature that was separated from its Maker He united with Himself in His own person by sole act of His Eternal Love. (VII.25-33)

Here it is clear that separation from God can only be overcome by the descent of the Son. This 'act of Eternal Love', however, only extends as far as Limbo and therefore leaves eight circles of hell under condemnation. Such an understanding is problematic even within Dante's schema. If, for example, Adam has responsibility for the condemnation of the entire human race, why is he placed in Limbo? He is not one of the virtuous pagans whose fate so concerned Dante. Further, if 'all' Adam's progeny can only be united with God through Christ's descent, the limited extent of this descent seems to require an explanation Dante never explicitly gives. This is so despite the fact that for him hell is part of God's creation, rather than (say) made by Satan. In this sense it can be seen that while Christ has endured the dereliction and abandonment of the cross, he has not experienced the distance from God represented by the ninth circle.

Christ may have led the 'man that was never born' to blessedness, but the one for whom 'it would have been better if he had not been born', having arrived in the ninth circle only just prior to Christ's descent, continues to remain in that region unseen even by the very 'Word of God'. An implication of this, it could be argued, is that Christ's redemptive powers are limited, for if Christ has not penetrated to the centre of hell, indeed those resident there must 'Abandon every hope' (III.9). Dante would not have seen the matter thus, however, for reasons expressed by Aquinas as follows:

> That some were not delivered from every part of hell, as from every situation in the world, is not to be ascribed to a want of power on Christ's part, but to their different conditions. As long as men draw breath they can be converted to faith and charity,

> for in this life men are not confirmed in either good or evil; after their departure from this world, however, they are so fixed.[28]

Aquinas distinguishes between those who have committed sins in their own right, and those who are in hell solely because of original sin. The latter are for him the 'holy patriarchs', also described as 'the just' whom Christ has 'inwardly visited by grace'.[29] If Christ only descends to the place of the patriarchs, for Aquinas 'the effects of his presence were felt in a way in all parts of hell'.[30] These effects are threefold; the holy patriarchs are brought to eternal glory, those in purgatory are given the hope of this glory, and those who are damned are confounded 'for their unbelief and malice'.[31] As Christopher Ryan has pointed out, the very choice of Virgil as guide indicates the importance Dante ascribes to the 'living out of the moral virtues',[32] but for all his sympathy with virtuous pagans, it is clear that they will remain in Hell. The reason for this, as pithily expressed by Charles Singleton, is that 'the pagans did not have sanctifying grace or the three theological virtues that attend such grace.'[33]

Ryan aptly describes the eternal fate of Virgil and other virtuous pagans as 'tragedy in the strictest sense'[34] because nothing they were able to do, however fine, is sufficient to avert that fate. Though he does not spell this out, this is presumably because they were outside the covenant people of Israel. For Aquinas, it can be said of the patriarchs that, by the grace of God, they had faith in Christ 'even during their lifetime'.[35] Dante surely assents to this, for there is no other way of comprehending why Adam, Abel, Noah, King David and others are liberated from hell whilst Virgil and other virtuous occupants of limbo remain.

This is a difficult conclusion for most modern readers of Dante, for it seems unjust. Most of the occupants of hell are there because of their folly and malice which has caused suffering to others, but this is not so for those of whom Dante writes at *Purgatorio* VII. 35-7 that they 'were not clothed with the three holy virtues but without sin knew the others and followed them every one.' They made no decision for or against Christ, because they never encountered him either in the flesh or through grace as the patriarchs did.

---

28 *Summa Theologiae* 3a.52 (Volume 54 *The Passion of Christ* 3a.46-52, Blackfriars: Eyre & Spottiswoode, 1965). Question 52: Christ's descent into hell, Article 6: 'did Christ set some of the damned free from hell?' p173.

29 Ibid. p159, Article 2: 'did Christ descend into the hell of the damned?'

30 Ibid.

31 Ibid.

32 Christopher Ryan, 'The theology of Dante', Chapter 9 in *The Cambridge Companion to Dante* edited by Rachel Jacoff (Cambridge University Press, 1993) p142.

33 *The Divine Comedy* translated, with a commentary, by Charles S. Singleton. *Inferno* Volume 2. Commentary (Bollingen Series LXXX, Princeton, New Jersey: Princeton University Press, 1970) p60.

34 Op cit. p142.

35 Op cit. p171.

From the perspective of this book it is not simply the fate of the virtuous pagans (also explored in *Paradiso* XIX) that is problematic in Dante, it is also the fate of sinners. Ryan comments that the torments of the latter are 'the result not of tragedy, but of folly'.[36] In this sense their actions and resultant fate were avoidable and unnecessary. This kind of view has a Pelagian ring to it, for it arguably does not take sufficiently seriously the moral vulnerability of the human race because of original sin. In the case of Judas, it is difficult to characterize his actions simply as 'folly' because they are characterized in the New Testament as having a close affinity with the salvific purposes of God, and arise out of the intersection of Judas' life with that of the Saviour who called him.

For Dante, however, his view of Judas is made clear by his position in Satan's mouth in the lowest depths of hell. The portrayal is reminiscent of the simonists 'who, rapacious, prostitute for gold and silver the things of God' (Canto XIX.2-3). This recalls the link between Judas and simony made by writers such as Peter Damian, Rupert of Deutz, and Peter Abelard.[37] In the simonists' part of the seventh circle of hell are holes in 'livid stone'. Out of 'the mouth of each projected the feet of a sinner and the legs as far as the calf' (XIX.22-24). Here Dante addresses Boniface:[38] 'Surely [our Lord] asked nothing but "Follow me", nor did Peter or the others take gold or silver from Matthias when he was chosen for the place lost by the guilty soul.' (XIX.93-6) Moreover as Dante leaves Giudecca he notices that Lucifer has his 'legs held upward' and wonders 'how he is thus fixed upside down.' Virgil explains that this is because Lucifer 'fell down from heaven' (XIX.121). Marc Cogan argues that:

> Dante's punishments externalize the intentions, motives and choices that inform the various sins... making manifest what may have been obscured in the original act... the traitors, so coldly calculating as to betray family, country, sovereign for gain, are set in ice.[39]

In similar vein, Dino Cervigni points out Judas is both unidentifiable (except by God and Lucifer) and unable to communicate. Judas' posture parodies Lucifer's and

> ...his own betrayal of the Word through words, whose use he is now denied forever. Ultimately, both Lucifer, the rebel against the eternal Word, and Judas, the betrayer of the Word made flesh, share the same torment: the denial of the word... Lucifer

36 Op cit. p142.

37 As discussed in the fourth section of Chapter 3 of this book.

38 This is Pope Boniface VIII, a powerful figure responsible for Dante's exile from Florence.

39 'Delight, Punishment and the Justice of God in the Divine Commedia' *Dante Studies CXI* (New York, 1993) p41.

> and Judas, the archrebel and the archtraitor, ironically deprive each other of the word.[40]

Dante's treatment of Judas, then, has most affinities with John's Gospel and the 'Augustinian' view - that Satan and Judas are bound together in opposition to God's purposes (and yet ultimately serve those purposes). Lucifer executes God's judgement on Judas, who in his turn silences Lucifer.[41] Christ, however, is literally out of the picture altogether.

The affinity with John in Dante's writing, noted above, is seen also in *Purgatorio*, where Judas is related first to avarice and then the Jews. In Canto XX Dante and Virgil meet Hugh Capet (king of France, 987-996 B.C.) who denounces the subsequent Capetian kings for their avarice, and gives examples of the downfall of the avaricious. In language picking up on the description of the death of Judas at Acts 1.18 ('he burst open in the middle and all his bowels gushed out'), Dante sees a time '...which brings another Charles out of France... he comes forth unarmed and only with the lance with which Judas jousted, and so couches it that he bursts the paunch of Florence...' (XX.71, 73-5). This refers to Charles of Valois and his treacherous dealings with Florence, from which he gains only 'sin and shame'. Canto XXI.82-84 makes reference to Titus (Emperor of Rome from 79-81 A.D., and responsible for the capture of Jerusalem in 70 A.D.) as follows: 'In the time when the good Titus, by help of the King Most High, avenged the wounds from which poured the blood sold by Judas...'. In *Paradiso* Judas' actions are implicated in the sin of Adam through a speech by the Emperor Justinian which tells how Titus won 'Vengeance upon vengeance for the ancient sin' (VI.93).

It can be seen that in the space of few words Dante paints a picture of Judas that is both graphic in its depiction of his punishment and distance from God, and thorough in associating him with Satan, the sin of Adam, avarice, treachery and the Jewish people. Canto XIX of *Inferno* also alludes to his place amongst the twelve, which was 'lost'. Through all this Dante's poetic imagination is at the service of Christian 'orthodoxy' and an understanding of Judas that Aquinas and Augustine would have recognized. The weakness of this portrayal is its avoidance of the problematic questions surrounding Judas from the New Testament onwards.

---

40 'The Muted Self-Referentiality of Dante's Lucifer' *Dante Studies CVII* (New York, 1989) p56.

41 That the inhabitants of hell 'suffer well-defined torture appropriate to their sins' indicates that Dante's theological purposes were more important to him than following current artistic and literary trends. Medieval art and drama usually portray demons as inflicting pain with implements of torment, whilst in *Inferno* the punishment of sinners usually takes place without visible demons. The portrayal of Satan is perhaps more conventional; for example Jeffrey Russell points out that bat wings were the norm from the twelfth century onwards. In fact only from the ninth century were representations of the Devil common, probably because of the increasing popularity of stories of the saints in conflict with evil. See Jeffrey Burton Russell, *Lucifer – The Devil in the Middle Ages* (London: Cornell University Press, 1984) p227.

There is no sense of Judas as chosen by Christ, one of the twelve, and playing a crucial part in the economy of salvation. There is nothing about his repentance, or any sense of difficulty in placing Judas beyond the reach of Christ. That Christ descended only as 'deep' as the first circle of hell is unproblematic for Dante for the reasons discussed above. His theological viewpoint is able to accept, albeit with difficulty, the justice of virtuous pagans residing eternally in Hell because the grace of God never came their way, and they never truly loved God. This viewpoint accepts, with rather greater ease, that if the effect of Christ was felt thoughout Hell this was for the confounding rather than the salvation of the damned. Balthasar's treatment of Christ's descent into Hell simply does not operate on this kind of basis, as will be seen. That this is so perhaps explains what might at first sight seem rather surprising: that Balthasar never refers to Dante in his own account of the descent into hell, nor the aspects of Aquinas' discussion highlighted above.

6.3 Hans Urs von Balthasar and Christ in the 'Lowest Hell'

Balthasar is rare amongst theologians in showing an awareness of the work of W. Popkes on the language of 'handing over' in the New Testament. This becomes apparent in *Mysterium Paschale*, where he discusses the significance of the 'principal concept' represented by the use of *tradere* in the passion of Christ.[42] He writes that the incarnational character of the New Testament implies a 'co-humanity' that includes others in the drama[43] of redemption. Even if the primary drama of the passion is played out between the Father and the Son, there are many others involved and active in what unfolds. It conforms to this 'co-humanity' that (as Augustine, Aquinas and Donne saw in Chapter 4):

> ...besides the Father who hands over, and the Son who is handed over, there appear as a third actor the traitor who is hander-over also. Judas, one of the Twelve, is 'he who hands over', the *traditor*.[44]

Balthasar's comments on this in *Mysterium Paschale* are brief but full of insight. He reflects that there is an 'extremely paradoxical character' to the inter-play

---

42 pp107f in *Mysterium Paschale*, translated by Aidan Nichols, (Edinburgh: T.&T. Clark, 1990).

43 The use of the word 'drama' has a particular significance in Balthasar's theology. Building on Hegel's distinction between epic, lyric and dramatic, Balthasar argues that the first two are capable of articulating something of God's relationship to the world, but are incomplete without their joint presence within the perspective of the dramatic. See, for example, pp53-62 of the second volume of *Theo-Drama* (Ignatius Press, San Francisco 1990). The significance of Balthasar's understanding of the dramatic will receive further discussion later in this section.

44 Ibid. pp109-110.

between the handing over of God and sinners. Two pages earlier he has characterized the handing over by God as an 'abandonment', now the handing over by sinners is described as 'betrayal'. The reader is left to infer a positive reading of the former (as illustrative of the depth of divine love) and a negative reading of the latter (some form of opposition to Christ), and the paradoxical character of this interrelationship is not lessened by Balthasar's general comment that in the Old Testament God has human 'executors' of his will who nevertheless have to accept responsibility and judgement for the sinfulness of their actions.

Balthasar then attempts to offer a way of exploring the paradox he has identified. Drawing on the work of Luthi, he rejects as faulty any interpretation that in 'polemical fashion' attempts to identify 'a personal or national "black sheep".'[45] He acknowledges that there is a sense in the Gospels in which Judas and Israel are cast in the role of reprobation, but argues that 'from the perspective of the universalist affirmations of the New Testament, [Judas] is the visible agent of all that sinners – Christians, Jews, pagans – do in common.'[46] Here is a good example of an aspect of Balthasar's work identified by MacKinnon: that he constantly writes with an awareness of the Holocaust although rarely referring directly to it.[47]

Now follows a crucial section in Balthasar's argument. He states that, 'The handing over of Jesus in the Passion remains a mystery; for this reason, the concurrently operative elements cannot be strait-jacketed into any comprehensible system.'[48] Here there is both agreement and disagreement with Barth: agreement that the action of Judas must be interpreted in the light of the whole economy of salvation, but disagreement about doing this within the kind of providential meta-narrative Barth constructs. Balthasar is aware of the different levels at which this interpretation can take place, but argues that no one approach should be allowed to predominate. It is theologically important that there is 'slow integration' of the different aspects.[49]

Balthasar's resistance to 'strait-jacketing' must be understood in relation to the approach explored in the five volumes of *Theo-Drama*, where he describes the weaknesses of the epic and lyrical perspectives unless they are integrated within

---

[45] Ibid. p110. The work of K. Luthi's referred to is his Dissertation 'Judas Iskarioth in der Geschichte der Auslegung von der Reformation bis zur Gegenwart' (Zurich: Zwingli Verlag, 1953).

[46] Ibid.

[47] See 'Some reflections on Hans Urs von Balthasar's Christology with special reference to Theodramatik II/2 and III' in *The Analogy of Beauty – The Theology of Hans Urs von Balthasar* (edited by John Riches, Edinburgh: T. & T. Clark, 1986) pp164-179. MacKinnon writes that 'In the pages of his work... there is comparatively little that treats directly of these horrors; but the nervous tension of the whole argument bears witness to the author's passionate concern to present the engagement of God with his world in a way that refuses to turn aside from the overwhelming, pervasive reality of evil... he insists on a vision that can only be won through the most strenuous acknowledgement of the cost of human redemption' p165.

[48] Ibid. p110.

[49] Ibid.

the dramatic. Taking up Hegel's distinction between the epic, lyric and dramatic, he relates the first to theology, and the second to spirituality. What he means is that the epic perspective assumes an impartial standpoint and completed action. Epic is about universal significance, and tends to 'smooth out the folds'[50] by offering an account of history with a strong element of necessity in which the actions of individuals are an expression of a broader teleology. Lyric, on the other hand, is the expression of the inner, subjective voice of faith. Balthasar gives the example of Ignatian spirituality, where imagination and creativity have a role in bringing past events to 'life'.

The tension between the 'epic' search for objective distance and 'lyric' dependence on the human subject can only be resolved, argues Balthasar, within 'the dramatic dimension of revelation, in which alone they can discover their unity'.[51] The theologian writes as one *within* this revelation (and so committed to a form of apophaticism, in that one cannot objectify that which one is caught up in), taken over by it and witnessing to it. The responsibility of all witness is to pass on the good news that 'God has made his own the tragic situation of human existence, right down to its ultimate abysses; thus, without drawing its teeth or imposing an extrinsic solution on it, he overcomes it.'[52]

It can be seen that Balthasar wants to respect the particularity of history, and make it clear that the engagement of God with that history is total. The action of God involves no avoidance of difficulty, no 'smoothing out', no 'drawing of teeth'. It is the responsibility of witnesses to be truthful to such a revelation of God in Christ. The charge against Barth is that his systematizing approach 'strait-jackets' the dramatic revelation of God. It tends to pattern and organize the complexity of human experience in a way that does not do full justice to the engagement of God with that experience.

Balthasar's argument that the epic and lyric perspectives need to be united with the dramatic, and his notion of 'slow integration', are akin to my argument about attending to the tension between tragic and providential readings of Judas. The crucial question, however, is whether or not Balthasar can avoid the temptations and difficulties he has outlined in his own theology. He is after all a theologian, and therefore the immediate suspicion is that the tendency towards the 'epic' mode may prove hard to avoid. He does, moreover, write about the *resolution* of the epic and lyric within the dramatic. In this book, I have preferred to write about *attending* to the tension between the providential and the tragic, aware that this is uncomfortable theological territory. It is usually easier to avoid such tension, or to ignore it, and certainly easier to seek to resolve it rather than confront it. This is not to say that resolution is impossible, but to acknowledge that it is difficult. The argument here is that the kind of resolution that works

---

50 p54 *Theo-Drama: Theological Dramatic Theory II: Dramatis Personae: Man in God* (San Franciso: Ignatius Press, 1990) Translated by Graham Harrison.

51 Ibid. p57.

52 Ibid. p54.

through seeking epic 'objectivity' is likely to be illusory in its dependence on 'drawing the teeth' of the surd elements in human experience.

Balthasar does show awareness of the tension between providential and tragic readings of Judas, when he insists that the only way to engage with the 'mystery' of the handing over is via a trinitarian approach. In this he accords with one of the conclusions of Chapter 3 after examination of Augustine, Aquinas and Donne. Such an approach, he argues, reveals the different aspects of what is taking place when Jesus is delivered to his enemies in the Passion. Firstly, God the Father is handing over his Son out of love for His creation (Roman 8.32, John 3.16). Secondly, this is a self-gift of Christ out of love for humanity (John 10.18). Thirdly, Jesus' self-gift, revealing as it does the love of the Father, 'becomes the model for our imitation… it is Paul who is selected to reproduce in himself Christ's suffering...'. This all takes place under the judgement of God, involving as it does the 'bitter obedience' of Gethsemane and the evil done to Christ by his enemies.

The obedience of Christ is crucial to Balthasar's argument, as it emphasizes the trinitarian nature of what is happening. This is an aspect neglected in a quote by Popkes that he otherwise offers approvingly, in which the statement that God hands over his Son is seen to be one of

> ...the most unheard of affirmations of the New Testament. We must understand the expression to 'hand over' in its proper meaning, without diluting it to a mere 'mission' or 'gift'. Here was done what Abraham was spared from doing in Isaac. The Christ was deliberately given over by the Father to a deadly destiny. God rejected him to the death-dealing powers.... Here the *theologia crucis* comes to expression in a way than which none more radical can be conceived.[53]

This quote has something of the flavour of MacKinnon about it, and Balthasar's response is to concur as long as the insight it offers is seen within a trinitarian perspective. It is not that Christ is a martyr; he is rather the Son of God. Balthasar articulates his understanding, as follows:

> Christ must be God if he is to place himself at the disposal of the event of love which flows from the Father and would reconcile the world with itself that in him the entire darkness of all that is counter to God can be judged and overcome. In this happening, the active handing over by men can only play a subordinate role, and the very contradiction between human treason and the love of God in giving his Son must be bonded together with the 'contradiction of the Cross' and there find its resolution. But for that to happen, the handing over, the arrest, the placing in chains, and the leading away by myrmidons must be taken with historical seriousness of an absolute kind.[54]

---

[53] Quoted Ibid. pp111-12. The quotation comes from W. Popkes, *Christus traditus. Eine Untersuchung zum Begriff der Dahingabe im Neuen Testament* (Zurich: Zwingli Verlag, 1967).

[54] Ibid. p112.

Here Balthasar comes close to breaking his own stricture about not allowing any one aspect of the handing over to predominate in interpreting it. The generalised language of 'event of love', 'world' and 'darkness' comes close to subsuming the bitter particularity of the passion within a trinitarian rhetoric. Given that the passage quoted follows closely on that of Popkes, however, and ends with an insistence on 'historical seriousness', Balthasar does avoid the temptation he himself identifies – of strait-jacketing the handing over into a readily comprehensible system. Questions remain about the 'subordinate role' of the human agents involved in the Passion, the way in which they are 'judged and overcome', and the kind of 'resolution' offered by the Cross.

Balthasar therefore goes on to develop the theme of 'handing over', and elects to do this within 'the ampler context of the theological structure of humankind'.[55] In the second volume of *Theodramatik*, he refers to the 'dramatic character of existence as a whole, as judged by the light of revelation'.[56] There Balthasar prefers to avoid examining individual figures, although in a footnote he does describe Judas as 'between the Old and New Covenants'.[57] His motivation for this is that he is concerned with 'the dramatic character of existence as a whole'. In view of the suspicion articulated earlier in this section, that a theology may find the temptation of the 'epic' hard to resist, this seems an inauspicious move. In Balthasar's own terms, can the lyric perspective be respected if individual figures are not to be discussed? When a general structure for comprehending the 'various conditions and situations *(status)* of mankind' is to be proposed, is this not likely to 'smooth out the folds' made by the dense New Testament texts witnessing to the awkward figure of Judas?

Balthasar's approach can be seen in *Mysterium Paschale*, where he elucidates this 'theological structure' of human existence in terms of the non-elect (the pagans), the chosen people (the Jews) and the disciples. The latter are a new choice out of the Jewish people, the Christians. Judas is in one sense a Christian, as 'one of the twelve', but according to Balthasar is 'interiorly attached to the profane ideal of the Messiah shared by the leading Jews; he denies his New Testament faith in favour of an alleged Old Testament alternative.'[58]

Judas, it seems, occupies a peculiar, even unique place in Balthasar's account (as he does in the writing of Leo discussed in Chapter 4, where Judas is the only disciple to die before the resurrection). His theological structure of humankind is threefold: pagan, Jew and Christian. Judas lies 'between' the second and third of these, and this sets up a tension in the argument. Balthasar wants to focus on an overall structure, or 'existence as a whole'. For example, he writes of the theological significance of the threefold 'handing over' – from Christians to Jews, Jews to pagans, and then pagans to death. The place of the

---

55 Ibid. pp112-113.

56 *Theo-Drama: Theological Dramatic Theory II: Dramatis Personae: Man in God*, op cit. p10.

57 Ibid. p10 (footnote).

58 Op cit. p113.

Christian in this schema is taken by Judas, who apparently is 'interiorly' still a Jew (it should be noted that this interpretation has no explicit basis in scripture). This is significant given the crux of Balthasar's argument, which is that 'all of humanity's representatives are integrated from the outset into guilty responsibility for Jesus' death.'[59] Therefore, despite his view of Judas' understanding of the Messiah, he needs to emphasize also that Judas belongs to Christianity.

So it is that when he offers a theological ascription of responsibility he begins with Judas, bringing together some of the most powerful Judas texts from the New Testament:

> 'Satan entered' into Judas (John 13.27); he is 'lost', the 'son of perdition' (John 17.12), whose frightful end (Matthew 27.3-10) corresponds to the prophetic word and becomes a ghastly public warning (Acts 1.18ff). Only when Christendom has acknowledged this shameful stain on its escutcheon can it look around for another scape-goat and come to underline the guilt of the Jews... .[60]

This is as close as Balthasar comes to explicit reference to the Holocaust. He refuses to assign principal responsibility to any one group, quoting Romans 11.32: 'For God has consigned all men to disobedience, that he may have mercy on all.' For Balthasar the 'three-fold chain' of handing over he has identified 'convicts all human beings in their guiltiness'.[61] He then tries to show that all attempt to offload their responsibility. He refers, for example, to Judas' attempt to bring back the money, and Pilate's refusal to accept moral responsibility. His conclusion is as follows: 'No-one wishes to be responsible. That is why they are all guilty.'[62]

Here can be seen once more the difficulty of shoehorning Judas into a theological schema; a case of epic 'smoothing out the folds' contrary to Balthasar's stated intention. The awkwardness of one who is 'between Old and New Covenants' for a threefold structure has already been identified, and now Balthasar's verdict about responsibility just does not work in relation to Judas. It is evident from Matthew 27 that Judas *does* accept responsibility; he speaks of 'betraying innocent blood' prior to hanging himself. Here the criticism that Ford (echoing the approach of MacKinnon) makes of Barth, that he does not take seriously enough the nature of Judas' death, can be justly applied to Balthasar also. It must also place a question mark over Balthasar's stated intent in *Theodramatik* to avoid examining individual figures in favour of the 'dramatic character of existence as a whole'. This has a methodological similarity to Barth's providential narrative in CD II/2, despite the opposing nature of their approach in other ways, most strikingly in Barth's intense focus on the individual character of Judas. By this I mean that both focus on the language of 'handing over' as a way of integrating Judas into the wider drama of salvation history, in Barth's case through

---

[59] Ibid. p114.

[60] Ibid.

[61] Ibid. p115.

[62] Ibid.

reference to Israel and Paul. Both seek to 'place' Judas within an overarching account of the ways of God with His creation.

One of the criticisms of Barth made in Chapter 2 was that he failed to give adequate content to his insistence that Judas' fate remained an open question. Balthasar has suggested that God finds all people guilty in relation to the death of Christ, in order that there may be mercy for all. The similarity with Barth might raise questions about Balthasar's ability to sustain such a suggestion, particularly as the way he has described the 'theological structure of humankind' is not entirely coherent in relation to the particularity of Judas. Might this incoherence mean that Balthasar's account of the salvific process through Good Friday, Holy Saturday and Easter Sunday will be unable to take full account of Judas' apparently unique placing 'between the Old and New Covenants'? Does his assertion that Christ's 'redeeming act consists in a wholly unique bearing of the total sin of the world by the Father's wholly unique Son'[63] really imply the possibility of redemption for Judas?

These questions will be born in mind as we turn to examine Balthasar's treatment of Holy Saturday. He introduces this by saying that as in Jesus' earthly ministry 'he was in solidarity with the living, so, in the tomb, he is in solidarity with the dead.'[64] In pursuing what this means, Balthasar elucidates the phrase from the Apostles Creed, 'He descended into hell', at some length. He considers that the word 'descended' gives the unintended impression that the dead Jesus performed an action only possible for someone living, and prefers the language of 1 Peter 3.19 – that Christ 'went and preached to the spirits in prison'. What was preached was the Gospel, the good news (1 Peter 4.6). Balthasar's chosen phrase is in fact 'being with the dead', with the 'preaching' understood in the non-verbal sense of bearing the sin of others through active suffering, as on the cross. This 'solidarity with the condition of the dead,' he argues, is 'the prior condition for the work of redemption'.[65]

Here Balthasar is writing against the traditional interpretation of the harrowing of hell, with its imagery of struggle and battle, and as such implicitly against Dante. He sees such a portrayal as overly (and unnecessarily) mythological, as the key theological points are straightforward and twofold: first, Jesus' experience of death; second, God's raising of Jesus from death. In considering the Scriptural justification for these points, Balthasar points out that the phrase 'from the dead' occurs many times in the New Testament. He does not specify texts, but examples are Luke 24.46 ('Thus it is written that the Christ should suffer and on the third day rise from the dead') and Acts 13.34 ('And as for the fact that [God] raised him from the dead...'). These imply for him 'a point of departure – namely, being with the dead.'[66] Amongst the many other texts he does consider are those such as Romans 14.9 ('For to this end Christ died and lived again, that he might be Lord both of the dead and of the living') and those that

63 Ibid. pp137-8.
64 Ibid. p149.
65 Ibid. p150.
66 Ibid. p153.

speak of 'binding the strong man' (Mark 3.24-27 and parallels) and entering his house to plunder his goods.[67]

For Balthasar such texts speak primarily of the power of God, but power of a very particular kind, derived from 'the fact that the Lord was dead (he has experienced death interiorly) and now lives eternally, having vanquished death in itself and for all, making it something "past".'[68] Given the approach taken in this book, the question arises as to whether or not the clause 'for all' is inclusive of Judas. While not explicitly referring to Judas, Balthasar makes himself clear:

> ...the doctrine of Christ's preaching in Hades gives expression to the fact that the Righteous One died for the unrighteous (1 Peter 3.18); even for those who were lost and without hope, his atoning death has brought salvation.[69]

Here Balthasar is as inclusive as he can be. In this supreme act of obedience, Christ enters into solidarity with 'everything that is sheerly contrary to God'.[70] For Balthasar this only makes sense if it is understood in trinitarian fashion. The logic of his argument runs as follows: if God is the creator of all that is, including human freedom and its consequences, then ultimately Hell, and the power of judgement over it, belongs to God. In Christ, however, God sends his Son to *save* Hell instead of judging it (as contrasted with Dante, where Christ liberates the patriarchs, but confounds everyone else in their sin). This can only be achieved by the Son being introduced to Hell as a dead man, so that He can enter into all that is most imperfect and indeed evil in creation. In *Inferno*, Christ enters Hell, as a 'mighty one... crowned with a sign of victory'. There is no question either of 'solidarity' with sinners or of salvation for them.

For Balthasar, Dante's careful schema, and the theology of which it is expressive as found pre-eminently in Aquinas, is simply inadequate with respect to the devastating 'obedience of a corpse' demonstrated by Christ. Crucial to this is not simply that Christ enters Hell, but that he experiences every aspect of it, even its 'lowest' point – the point that is spiritually furthest from God. Balthasar emphasizes this with a quotation from Gregory the Great, who affirms that 'Christ went down into the deepest abysses of the sea, when he went into the Lowest Hell....'[71] Christ is able to cross this 'deepest Hell' because he is not bound by any sin, thereby opening a way to Heaven. Here is seen something crucial about the nature of God: the God who creates a world containing the possibility of the radical misuse of free will (including the Holocaust) is prepared to experience this

---

[67] See section 2 ('The New Testament') of Chapter 4 ('Going to the Dead: Holy Saturday') Ibid. pp152-60. Although brief, the section does illustrate that there is more scriptural background to von Balthasar's account than 1 Peter 3.19. Take, for example, Romans 10.6ff: 'But the righteousness based on faith says, "Do not say in your heart, 'Who will ascend into heaven?' " (that is, to bring Christ down) or " 'Who will descend into the abyss?' " (that is, to bring Christ up from the dead).'

[68] Ibid. p156.

[69] Ibid. p160.

[70] Ibid. p174.

[71] Ibid. p175.

radical misuse and its consequences in the person of God the Son. Here is seen both the costliness and extent of redemption, and its essentially trinitarian structure. It is only if the Holy Spirit is able to unite the Father and the Son at their point of deepest estrangement that salvation can occur.

On the question as to what work Christ actually does in Hell, Balthasar is insistent that he can only be introduced there as 'a dead man'. And yet, he writes, Christ must take in 'with his own eyes' the 'vision of chaos' that is Hell.[72] It is such language that leads Ben Quash to argue that Balthasar 'ought to allow [Christ] really to be *dead*'.[73] Quash considers Balthasar's account of the descent to be both too lyric (in talking of Christ's subjective experience) and too epic (in placing Hell outside human history, remote from social and structural evil). His point is that the truth of human beings is found less in their subjectivity than in terms of their presence to others and the Other. Quash may be unfair to Balthasar here, and certainly the notion of 'seeing' can be read in the sense articulated by Augustine in *De Trinitate.* There he writes that 'the way in which the Son sees the Father is simply by being the Son.'[74] In a similar way, Christ can be described as 'seeing Hell' simply by *being* the dead Son in that place.

What this book can take from Quash's criticism is that Balthasar writes of the social element of Christ's descent only in the most generalized way. Dante has his own 'theological structure' of humanity, as represented by the categorizing of the nine circles, but this structure is filled out by reference to particular, named individuals. So if Dante could learn from Balthasar about the theological importance of Christ descending below limbo, Balthasar might have learnt from Dante about the importance of the particular – especially for a theology seeking to integrate the epic and lyric within the dramatic dimension of revelation.

Balthasar never does discuss *Inferno*, but he does refer to an aspect of Patristic writing (taken up the Scholastics) that puts some parts of Hell beyond the reach of the salvific powers of Christ. The earlier analysis of Dante will indicate my agreement with his verdict that this is 'poor theology'.[75] The Scholastics agreed that Hell had four areas: pre-Hell, Purgatory, the Hell of unbaptized infants and the true Hell of fire. For most the area of pre-Hell 'remained the proper field of play of the redemptive action'.[76] Balthasar expresses his view plainly: 'this whole construction must be laid to one side.'[77]

His justification for this laying aside is expressed in terms of the difference between 'Hades' and 'Hell'. He argues that Hell cannot exist outside of Christ, for the word carries the implication of judgement. Hades, on the other hand,

---

[72] Ibid. p174.

[73] 'Drama and the Ends of Modernity', being Chapter 4 in *Balthasar at the End of Modernity* by Lucy Gardner, David Moss, Ben Quash and Graham Ward (Edinburgh: T&T. Clark, 1999) p168.

[74] *The Trinity* introduction, translation and notes by Edmund Hill O.P. (New York: New City Press, 1991) p99.

[75] *Mysterium Paschale*, op cit. p176.

[76] Ibid. p177.

[77] Ibid.

expresses the absence of any access to God, as in the Old Testament Sheol. In affirming the theological mistakenness of envisaging areas of Hell beyond Christ's salvific scope, however, Balthasar does not want to go to what he describes as the 'opposite extreme' of universalism in which all human beings, whether before or after Christ, are saved:

> In rising from the dead, Christ leaves behind him Hades, that is, the state in which humanity is cut off from access to God. But by virtue of his deepest trinitarian experience, he takes 'Hell' with him, as the expression of his power to dispose, as judge, the everlasting salvation or the everlasting loss of man.[78]

Here can be seen the way in which the writings of Balthasar on Holy Saturday can fill out Barth's argument about the salvation of Judas remaining an 'open question.' For what Christ does in Hell is a saving event that shows the extent of the salvific effects of the cross. Unlike in Dante, the power of the cross is shown to reach right into 'the abyss of deadly perdition'[79] and so by clear implication the 'son of perdition' (or 'son of destruction', John 17.12) is included within its scope. It is not that Judas is clearly saved, as envisaged in the poems by Buchanan and Etchells discussed in the last chapter. Rather it is that the offer of salvation is made even to the dead, which I take to include the newly dead Judas, and 'the dead will decide on their response to that offer.'[80] In this way human freedom continues to be respected, unlike in Aquinas and Dante where one's eternal destiny is fixed at death, and the decision will be influenced by the orientation of an individual's earthly life.

Balthasar is careful to make no claims about the *number* of persons so redeemed. In a footnote he refers to patristic speculation on this subject, ranging from an emptying of Hades in the sense of universal redemption (Cyril of Alexandria) to a highly selective vision based on faith and good works (Gregory the Great).[81] He offers a nuanced rejection of dramatic portrayals of the harrowing of hell involving images such as the breaking down of gates or a joyful encounter between Christ and Adam – these may have a role in 'pious contemplation', he argues, but they 'go beyond what theology can affirm'.[82] The Church can only follow Christ 'at a distance', and what is required theologically is a 'being dead with the dead God'.[83]

It is hard to envisage a starker injunction than this against speculative system building in theology. This is in accordance with his argument, discussed earlier, that no comprehensible system can account for the handing over of Christ. It is in accordance with his insistence on the 'slow integration' of different aspects to the material under discussion. Through all this the reader gains a sense of why

---

78 Ibid.
79 Ibid.
80 Ibid. p178.
81 Ibid. p187 (footnote 115).
82 Ibid. p181.
83 Ibid.

Balthasar has resisted any temptation to portray Christ as 'active' in Hell. If a 'manifesto of life' is planted 'within eternal death'[84] there are no dramatic actions or specific exhortations involved. In *Pneuma und Institution* he expresses the matter as follows:

> Into this finality (of death) the dead Son descends, no longer acting in any way, but stripped by the cross of every power and initiative of his own, as one purely to be used, debased to mere matter, with a fully indifferent (corpse) obedience, incapable of any active act of solidarity.... He is (out of an ultimate love however) dead together with them. And exactly in that way he disturbs the absolute loneliness striven for by the sinner: the sinner, who wants to be 'damned' apart from God, finds God again in his loneliness, but God in the absolute weakness of love who unfathomably in the period of nontime enters into solidarity with those damning themselves.[85]

Nowhere does Balthasar relate this solidarity to any individual, whether Adam, Judas or any other. As indicated earlier, he has set out to articulate a 'theological structure' of humankind in which the place of Judas was uneasily expressed as between the Old and New Covenants. In this he unwittingly adds to that sense of the uniqueness and difference of Judas found in all of the writers considered in this chapter, and in many others throughout this book, from Origen to Leo to Barth. This illustrates that his strategy of attempting a description of the dramatic character of the whole of human existence is undermined by his decision not to relate this to individuals.

The overwhelming strength of his account of Holy Saturday, nevertheless, is that it can show that there is a genuine possibility of redemption for Judas. Because Jesus leaves no region of Hell unvisited, the love of God is extended in a very particular way even to what Dante portrayed as the ninth circle, the lowest point of the abyss. In this way the redemption of Judas does remain a possibility. It cannot be said that he is finally damned, and so MacKinnon's tragic reading is undermined. Not that Barth's providential narrative is entirely affirmed, but his insight about the 'open question' of Judas' salvific status is given credence and a way of giving it theological content explored.

6.4 Conclusion

This chapter has ranged across a wide spectrum of theological approach, from the Calvinist predestinarian views of Emmons to references to what Origen called *apocatastasis* – that is an universal redemption in which all people are saved. In terms of Judas' eternal fate, this indicates that the spectrum of possibilities run

84 Ibid. p180.

85 *Pneuma und Institution*, 1974, p409. Quoted in *The von Balthasar Reader* Edited by Medard Kehl and Werner Löser, Translated by Robert J. Daly and Fred Lawrence (Edinburgh: T&T. Clark 1982) p153.

from his being predestined to Hell by God, with no hope of salvation, to his salvation being eschatologically guaranteed. In his account of Christ's descent into hell, Balthasar's position seems to be rather that the final salvation of Judas may be *hoped for*, rather than either denied (as in Emmons or Dante) or assumed. For all the criticisms made of Balthasar in the preceding section, this view accords with the emphasis throughout this book on attending to the theological tension between polar opposites. In my final chapter I will draw out the contours of what might be the subject of another book – the Christological implications (including the implications for exploration of the 'problem of evil') of all that has been explored up to this point. What I am seeking is a Christology facing, rather than attempting to deny or resolve, the tension between providence and tragedy that has emerged through this study of Judas Iscariot.

Chapter 7

A Christology Facing the Tension between Providence and Tragedy

An omniscience or even an infallible foreknowledge is not at all necessarily connected with Jesus' dedication to his mission and to the one who sent him... .[1]

Wolfhart Pannenberg

The previous chapter should not give the impression that Balthasar has articulated a Christology entirely adequate to the reading of Judas argued for in this book. Throughout the preceding chapters, both explicitly and implicitly, it has been argued that any account of the economy of salvation must take full account of the totality and particularity of the Gospel accounts of the incarnate Christ. This is because Christian orthodoxy witnesses to the faith that the historical mission of the incarnate Son expresses the eternal nature of the triune God. The Son expresses that nature not simply in his relation to God the Father and Holy Spirit, but also in the manner of his engagement with the temporal realities of people and place. This is part of what Balthasar means by his insistence on a *dramatic* Christology, even though he falls prey to the kind of schematization identified in the previous chapter.

The argument of this book is that a theologically crucial aspect of Jesus' engagement with temporality, as the eternal Word now made flesh, is his relation to Judas Iscariot. What sense can be made, for example, of the one through whom the created order came to be and is sustained, saying as the incarnate Word that it would have been better if Judas had never come to be? What sense can be made of the incarnate Son's choice of Judas as 'one of the twelve', and the consequences of this choice? In responding to such questions, the momentum of the argument throughout this book suggests some invalid responses to such questions, as well as indicating a way forward.

In relation to what may not be said, any view of Judas as simply a necessary pawn in a celestial game must be ruled out of court. Such a doctrine of providential ordering was argued for by Emmons early in Chapter 6, and criticized as 'repulsive' by Pickering. The reason for the reaction of the latter was that Emmons imputed a massive injustice to God, in which the means (the instrumental use and damnation of an individual) is taken to justify the end (salvation).

---

1 Pannenberg, Wolfhart *Jesus – God and Man* translated by Lewis L. Wilkins and Duane A. Priebe (London: SCM, 1968) p333.

Pickering might have pointed out that Emmons hardly refers to the role of Christ, picturing both Christ and Judas as living out a fixed and determinate destiny. Not only does the idea of God deliberately damning Judas for the sake of a salvific scheme fall foul of the kind of objection Dostoyevsky places in the mouth of Ivan Karamazov, and validate the position of Borges' fictional theologian, it implies both an inadequate Christology and doctrine of providence.

Emmons does not discuss Jesus' relation to Judas in temporal terms, but entirely in relation to an irresistible providence. But if the incarnate Son is expressive of the eternal nature of God, this means that providence must be understood in trinitarian fashion also. If the providence of God is as controlling and manipulative as Emmons argues, it begins to be hard to see why there was any need for the incarnation at all. If God can marshal human lives in such fashion, why not simply offer salvation directly, rather than through the Son? Yet the incarnation reveals that God takes human history seriously, and engages with its temporality and limitation rather than simply overruling it by divine *fiat.*

Another reading of Judas that may be discounted is to see him as simply a tragic mistake – a victim of Jesus' initial misjudgement, continued inability to influence him, and historical circumstances. The problem with such a reading is that it evacuates the Gospel drama of its divinity, for if Jesus' relations with others were not characterized and shaped by his relation to the Father and the Spirit, what is the point of the incarnation? Human history is shot through with tragedy and suffering, and simply to point to another example at the heart of the New Testament does not get us very far theologically.

7.1 Incarnation and limitation

The nub of the issue is the *way* in which the incarnate Son's relations with others, and indeed his whole engagement with the temporality of human history, is to be characterized. Clearly it cannot be known from a human perspective what it feels like to be God incarnate, or exactly what was going on from Jesus' perspective in relation to any aspect of the Gospel narratives. Reflection on scripture and aspects of the tradition as explored in this book, however, do enable some points to be made. Ascribing omniscience to Jesus, for example, in the sense of an exact knowledge of personality and future events, is problematic. It is true that the Chalcedonian definition of Christ as both fully human and fully divine has not prevented many interpreting the incarnation in this way. Indeed a writer such as E.L. Mascall sees himself as defending Chalcedonian orthodoxy when he claims 'to have shown the possibility of the reconciliation of a real omniscience in our Lord's human nature with an equally real growth and development'.[2]

In his discussion of this issue, Mascall never focuses on Jesus in relation to Judas, or indeed on any of the particulars of the Gospel narratives. Such a

---

2 Mascall, E.L. *Christ, the Christian and the Church – A Study of the Incarnation and its Consequences* (London: Longmans, Green and Co Ltd, 1946) p65.

focus, as has been seen in this book, undermines any understanding of Jesus Christ, the incarnate Word, as omniscient. If Jesus can perceive what to humanity in general are the mysteries of other people's hearts and the future, then Judas becomes a cipher chosen for a particular purpose, with his participation in the ministry of Jesus, culminating in the footwashing and last supper, a chimera awaiting its real purpose of 'handing over'. The alternative is that an omniscient Jesus, who can see exactly what is to come, is simultaneously unable or unwilling to save one of his disciples from falling into evil and the hands of the devil.

But if Jesus' engagement with Judas and the whole of human temporality is seen in trinitarian fashion, with that engagement shaped by his relation to the Father and the Spirit, how are his temporal relations to be characterized if not by omniscience? To argue that in Christ we see the self-limitation of the Word is true enough, but more needs to be said if this characterization is to be more than an abstraction vulnerable to the weaknesses of 'epic' theology as articulated by Balthasar. Saying, more, however, is hardly a simple task as it involves approaching the heart of the mystery of the incarnation.

Clearly it is only through the resources of scripture and tradition that anything can be said at all. Scripture, Chalcedon, and the doctrine of the Trinity provide a framework for at least approaching a way of interpreting Jesus and Judas that does some kind of justice to the tension between providence and tragedy identified in this book. It can be said that the ministry of Jesus, the 'Word made flesh' (John 1.14) takes place within a world created and sustained through the Word. This can only be stated because the incarnate life of the Son reveals that Jesus is the revealer, the one through whom God engages with human temporality. What is revealed is the relation of the Son to the Father and the Spirit within human history. MacKinnon describes this as a 'transcription into the conditions of our existence'[3] of the receptivity and responsiveness of trinitarian relations.

Human existence, it hardly need be said, is characterized by limitation, failure and suffering as much as by creativity and compassion. To do one thing is to leave another undone. The consequences of actions cannot be fully known. Human beings cannot fully understand one another, let alone the purposes of God, and misuse the free will and autonomy God has given. In the previous chapter, a key aspect of the significance of the descent into hell was seen to be that God in Christ experienced the consequences of the radical misuse of free will. By this argument Balthasar indicates his view that the abuse of free will is the central aspect of the human condition.

The contention of this book is that human *limitation* is at least as central, for God has created a world in which human beings live finite, contingent lives where perceptions of others and their creator are bounded by biology and culture. This human limitation causes more difficulty in characterizing the incarnation than the misuse of free will, for it can relatively easily be stated that the incarnate Son had free will but never misused it ('one who in every respect has been tempted as

---

3 'The Relation of the Doctrines of the Incarnation and Trinity' in *Themes in Theology – the threefold cord. Essays in Philosophy, Politics and Theology.* (Edinburgh: T & T. Clark, 1987) p163.

we are, yet without sin' – Hebrews 4.15). It is not so straightforward in relation to limitation, for this is an inescapable aspect of what it is to be human (cf. Genesis 2.17, 'but of the tree of the knowledge of good and evil you shall not eat...'). A virtuous human life can be pictured or imagined, even if attaining such a life in practice is extremely difficult. But to speak of a human life with unlimited perception and understanding of past, present and future is problematic, because such a manner of existence does not seem recognizably human at all.

The incarnate Son can be characterized as sinless, therefore, but not as without limitation, for incarnation necessitates limitation. Limitation in itself may be one of the causes of human destructiveness, but it is hard to see how it can be characterized as sinful in itself.[4] Part of the mission of the Son, therefore, was to live a life in which, when compared with the eternal *perichoresis* of the Trinity, everything is seen 'in a mirror dimly' (1 Corinthians 13.12). This is not to deny the uniqueness of Jesus' vision of God; the uniqueness of his relation to his Father and the Spirit. But it is to say that his was an immediacy to God, a transparency to God, that was now qualified by his participation in human history.[5] And if the immediacy to God that is evident throughout the Gospels, giving rise to Jesus' proclamation of the Kingdom and all that follows, is an immediacy qualified by its historical context; then the perception of the incarnate Son in relation to those amongst whom he lived and worked must have been subject to history to at least the same extent. Jesus could not see into the hearts of those around him with the omniscience of the Father.

Jesus' perspective on the call of Judas to be 'one of the twelve' and all that subsequently happened up to the last supper and Gethsemane, cannot be entirely known. But if it can be said that Jesus did *not* include Judas in the twelve because he could foresee the need for a human agent to hand him over, what can be said in relation to the texts in which Jesus speaks negatively of Judas, perhaps in particular the 'better unborn' texts of Mark 14.21 and parallels? Leaving aside critical discussion of which words may be attributed to Jesus himself, and the possibility that the Gospels are written in a fashion that tends to emphasize Jesus' foreknowledge (particularly in John), it seems that what is being expressed is a sense of disturbance and incomprehensibility in relation to Judas. But Mark 14.21, with its affirmation that 'the Son of Man goes as it is written of him', indicates the conviction of the Gospel writers that nevertheless all was somehow within the providence of God the Father. The vocabulary of παραδίδωμι indicates this also, although focusing too much on this could lead to an understanding of providence

4 Pannenberg comments, however, that 'in Augustine's sphere of influence a limitation on his knowledge was felt unworthy of Jesus because such a limitation was understood as a lack conditioned by sin… .' Op cit. p333.

5 Here I have been helped by Raymond Moloney's use of the phrase 'immediacy to God in history', which is his translation of H. Riedlinger's German: 'geschichtliche Gottesschau'. See Chapter 10 of Moloney's book *The Knowledge of Christ* (London and New York: Continuum 1999), in particular pp137-8.

along the lines of manipulating chess pieces on a board (with God co-ordinating the different 'handings over' in a way the individuals involved are unaware).

The fact of Jesus' limitation, his immediacy to God bounded by immersion in human history, was itself within the providence of God. The universal mission represented by Jesus' proclamation of the Kingdom was always in tension with what the incarnate Son could historically achieve, and the fact that Jesus' life included failure and suffering was also within this providence. In this sense one of the questions running through the book, whether or not Judas represents a defeat for Jesus, can be answered in the affirmative. But within this kind of understanding, even that human limitation sometimes results in events that can be characterized as tragic, such as Judas' death the 'wrong side' of the crucifixion, can be seen as within the providence of God. This providence, however, is triune and must be understood through the prism of Christ's immediacy to God in history. The providence of God the eternal Trinity is not evidenced in acts of divine *fiat*, but in the willingness of Christ not only to die on the cross but to descend into Hell, from where he was raised by the Spirit to resurrection life. It is theologically crucial that he descends not as a victor but in deathly solidarity with all that is in opposition to God.

Paradoxically, the descent of Christ in power as seen in Dante offers limited salvation to the occupants of Inferno. On the other hand, the descent of the dead Christ, limited by all that binds human beings and keeps them from God, makes possible the offer of salvation for all. Only in the descent of the dead Christ can there be hope for Judas, and indeed hope for all people – as long as it is recalled that this aspect of the economy of salvation should be characterized not in respect of categorizing humanity (as in Balthasar), but in terms of human particularity (as in Dante).

A properly trinitarian view of the incarnation, therefore, allows the limitation of the Son to be seen in its proper context as self-limitation; as willed by God and within the providence of God. Jesus not only lived through the consequences of limitation in others (failure to understand his person and mission, culturally conditioned hostility, etc) but himself affected others in a variety of ways he could not foresee. It is common in Christological discourse to speak of Jesus bearing the consequences of sin on the cross, but here it can be seen that the consequences of creation and incarnation are not borne by the Son alone. Particularly in relation to Judas, it is seen that Jesus' facing of the consequences of human limitation to the point of death, includes facing the consequences of his own actions. These consequences are seen in their darkest aspect in relation both to Judas and the Jewish people (of whom Steiner wrote that they had been 'betrayed' by Jesus).

From this perspective the 'co-humanity' of which Balthasar writes, the involvement of others in the drama of redemption, needs deepening and extending. Yes, others besides the Father and the Son are involved in the 'handing over' of the Son, but not simply in the sense of contributing to all that leads to the crucifixion. Such is a staple of Christian preaching, but this 'co-humanity' must be understood in a wider sense as taking in not only all that precedes the crucifixion, but all that flows from it is as well. Christ, a transcription of the trinitarian relations in human history, characterized by limitation as well as sinlessness, cannot achieve salvation for the world without involving others in the suffering and cost of that salvation. It seems, therefore, that there are *two* deaths for our salvation, with that of Judas just preceding the crucifixion, even though the death of Christ is the primary revelation of God.

The economy of salvation, therefore, cannot be properly understood by focusing solely on the incarnate Word. It is not that Judas is the 'secret name of God' as in Borges' story, but that he is nevertheless part of what God is revealing through the totality and particularity of the events narrated in the Gospels. If this revelation 'stops' at the death of Judas, then there is a finality about his tragedy and a rupture in what God reveals. But if Judas' fate is not entirely determined by his final actions and manner of death, but through the descent into hell remains 'open', then the revelation and providence of God are seen in their true light. To say that this providence is costly, and reaches to depths of human suffering and alienation from God, is another way of saying that it is trinitarian.

Judas, therefore, should be understood as caught up in the suffering and cost of salvation, not as one to be vilified and scapegoated. This applies to the Jewish people also. Such a judgement makes it plain that the Christology outlined here has implications for Christian practice, and that a failure to understand Judas in the manner outlined in this book has had terrible consequences in the past, particularly in the Holocaust. A more recent example, albeit of an entirely different magnitude to the horror of Auschwitz, will serve to illustrate the point.

A few month's after the publication of Klassen's *Judas – Betrayer or Friend of Jesus?* in Britain (June 1996), the press was full of coverage of 'runaway' Scottish Bishop Roderick Wright. Following reports of his relationship with a divorced woman, Bishop Wright was described as a 'lying Judas' guilty of betrayal, treachery, and of taking the press 'silver' (Report, *The Times*, 23 September 1996). The point in relation to this book is not the status of his wrongdoing but how the community of faith reacted to it. Here is an illustration of the validity of Kierkegaard's assertion, quoted at the beginning of this book, that 'One will get a deep insight into the state of Christianity in every age by seeing how it interprets Judas.'[6]

The Times for September 23 1996 records a spokesman for Cardinal Winning arguing that Wright has effectively excommunicated himself: '...the reality is that he has cut himself off from the church.' This is akin to those in the tradition who argue that by his actions Judas has cut himself off from God and any hope of restoration. The nub of the matter from the perspective of this book is not that individuals or their behaviour should be justified or their intentions speculated upon, but that the basic narrative of Christianity evidences that the encounter of human beings with Christ involves suffering, sinfulness and tragedy. That this is so does not place individuals who fall short beyond the reach of Christ, who enters

---

6 Søren Kierkegaard, *Journals and Papers* Volume 2, F-K. Edited and translated by Howard V. Hong and Edna H. Hong (Bloomington: Indiana University Press, 1970) p512. See also my article 'Judas Iscariot, Bishop Roderick Wright and the Testing of Eucharistic Boundaries' *Theology* (March/April 1998).

even the lowest reaches of hell. Even in hell there is the possibility of recognition, response and forgiveness.

In this sense the language of 'cutting off' is a refusal to engage with the tension between divine judgement and mercy, and a refusal to recognize that human difference and sin, however threatening, is never beyond the providential economy of God. If Jesus was able to recognize in Judas one whom was not to be excluded from the footwashing and last supper, it seems precipitous of contemporary Christian communities to refuse to recognize in errant members (whatever their actions) at least the possibility of continued membership of the body of Christ. When the revelation and providence of God are understood in the sense argued for in this book, it is seen that Judas (and so any other individual, group or nation) is not unredeemably *different* or beyond the trinitarian God's salvific scope.

The kind of understanding of incarnation and limitation described above, therefore, is able to offer some illumination in relation to the tension between providence and tragedy identified in this book as descriptive of the place of Judas Iscariot in Christology. This tension cannot be resolved from within human history, and the outline of a trinitarian understanding of providence indicated above should not be taken to imply otherwise. There is no way of offering any final answer or resolution to many hard questions, such as those that relate to Judas, the Holocaust, or of any of the other examples of evil or suffering that all too regularly afflict God's creation. What is required is attending to such questions rather than closure, and in relation to the particular issues discussed here, attending to (rather than avoiding or dismissing) the tension between providence and tragedy they evidence. For the Christian theologian, this requires above all a participation in Christ's descent, and a pointing to what is so apprehended: 'being dead with the dead God'.[7]

---

7 Hans Urs von Balthasar, *Mysterium Paschale* translated with an introduction by Aidan Nichols O.P. (Edinburgh: T&T Clark, 1990) p181.

Appendix

'Evil' – extracts from an unpublished lecture series delivered in the Divinity School, University of Cambridge, during the Lent terms of 1962 and 1963 by Donald M. MacKinnon, Norris-Hulse Professor of Divinity.

Lecture 1

Professor Raphael of Glasgow, a practising Jew, argues that Christianity and Judaism alike have no place for the tragic. MacKinnon considers this to be wrong so far as Christianity is concerned. To argue that the two are incompatible implies that the Christian view of human existence has no place for the sheerly intractable – for that which in the end defeated moral effort, making of the story of such effort a 'sound and fury signifying nothing.'

Allow one serious exception – Racine's *Phaidre.* But the spiritual tradition in which Racine was nourished has vanished. Jansen exceptional. Only in Racine do we get the complete pessimism of Sophocles, as in *Oedipus Tyrannus, Electra, Trachiniae* and *Antigone.*

The Biblical theologians are freaks, speaking of self mastery, mastery of the environment, etc. But cf. *Oedipus Tyrannus*:

- man's determined effort to find out the truth; truth that concerns himself.
- only Sophocles refers to a plague in Thebes: cf. contemporary situation – early years of the Pelopponesian war, plagues, etc.

Oedipus is involved in guilt simply because he seeks to avoid it. If he had remained in Corinth he would not have precipitated the events that led to tragedy.

We are told that this is far from Christianity, which has no ultimate dualism. Its view of the world is optimistic, not pessimistic. But MacKinnon is concerned with the sheerly intractable, which as man tries to avoid it is thrown into guilt. The mistake is to suppose that precisely this problem is not raised at a new level in Christianity.

Cf. St Mark's Gospel, Chapter 14.17ff (the last supper and Gethsemane). Vincent Taylor argues that here is not blind fate but the destiny of God. Judas is playing a role in the destiny of God, so is not responsible. The way that Jesus is going is one which God had willed, and freely accepted by Jesus himself, as in Gethsemane.

For MacKinnon, what the Father wills and what Jesus accepts is that he should be betrayed by one of the twelve. 'For whom it was better if he had not been born'. He agrees with Taylor that the passion narrative makes it clear that:

a. The way is willed for Christ by God.
b. Jesus freely accepts this journey but whatever the precise service given by Judas was, it was Judas' act that made the way possible.

Judas was morally responsible (Taylor). We can only speculate about his motives. Judas' action was that of a morally responsible agent, and yet that makes it in no way less indispensable to the divine purpose than if God had been activating an automaton.

'In the lost boyhood of Judas, Jesus was betrayed.' We cannot escape the admission that where the traitor was concerned Jesus was defeated. He was not *Christus Victor* for him. This defeat was something which Jesus freely accepted, but if Taylor is right, what Jesus freely accepted was willed by God – 'good it were for that man' – but Judas' birth was willed by God – if God exists. Yet if he had not been born, how would the Scriptures have been fulfilled - how would Jesus' free acceptance have been carried out – here, are we so far from an ultimate dualism, an element of sheer intractability? Or must we, if we deny the element of intractability that limits divine power, be compelled to lay the damnation of Judas at the door of the omnipotent Himself?

Was Judas' act in the providence of God? If it were, what are we to say? Better it were that that man had not been born.

Lecture 2

Whitehead – Christianity is a religion perennially in search of a metaphysic.
MacKinnon – Christianity is a religion perennially compelled by its nature to come to terms with philosophy both critical and speculative.

In Judas we see the problem/mystery of moral evil. The Christian tradition availed itself of the resources of philosophy in order to deal with the most unmanageable of problems.

Distinction (1.) Moral vs physical evil. 'Evil' refers to both. German – *das Böse* – moral evil; *übel* – physical evil. Kant tackled both moral and physical evil in his Inaugural Dissertation. The Lisbon earthquake had occurred fifteen years earlier, and compelled Kant to reckon with *übel* as much as *Böse*, although ethics were separate from nature for Kant. Yet his fundamental 'ought = can' demands that man's natural environment does not render altogether futile the effort to fulfil the moral law.

Distinction (2.) Theodicy vs Status of evil.
Theodicy: a justification of the presence in the world of those elements signified by the above – justification of the ways of God to man. Much of what we know as attempts to solve the problem of evil are attempts at theodicy. Dibelius writes that a very great deal of the theology of St Paul is elaborate theodicy, i.e. justification to man/Israel/Paul himself.

Can we justify evil, whether we think of moral or physical evil, by reference to the good that comes out of it? For example, if Adam was never buried, there would have been no work of redemption. Praise given to Adam's sin, is thereby given to the crimes of Hitler!! Theodicy says that out of the unquestionably evil, good comes whose attainment is inconceivable without evil, but of such magnitude as to justify evil. We may be able to justify in our own life the idea that out of evil, good has come, but are we justified in making this a law of the universe? This formal similarity in all attempts at theodicy is the outcome of an underlying monistic bias.

But those who argue always in terms of particulars are naturally pluralistic in impulse. What are the unacknowledged assumptions that underlie attempts at theodicy? They must be monistic assumptions. Although no doubt themselves confident that they are on the side of the angels, they are also determinists: for whatever is, must be, in order that the whole being self-justifyingly good shall be articulated. That goes not only for the sins of the saints but also for the less edifying activities of serial killers. Underlying the impulse of attempts to justify the ways of God to man is the conviction that a monistic point of view can be attained, for which the contribution of evil to the articulation of good can be discerned as a fundamental law. But are we as sure that such a point of view exists and can be attained, as we are sure that what Eichmann did was evil? Are we as confident about the former as we are confident that the latter things are evil?

Does the enterprise work? Aren't its assumptions hazardous? Commonsense pluralism puts a question mark against speculative monism. There is no way of redemption but defeat, in that therefore the traitor is unredeemed.

Lecture 8 (final section)

According to New Testament criticism, the saying of Mark 14.21 that the 'Son of man goeth indeed as it is written, but woe to that man by whom he is betrayed' could not have come from the lips of Jesus, but the status of the tradition is very early. The problem it concerns is near the centre of the record – that the coming of Jesus was appalling ill-fortune for some of those who came into contact with him. 'In the lost boyhood of Judas, Jesus was betrayed': had Judas never met Jesus, the bitter experience of boyhood would not have borne such terrible fruit. It is arguable that in the ministry of Jesus we meet the ministry of one who bore in Himself the full weight of one of the most fundamental contradictions of human life – i.e. between the duty of justice (to see things as they are, unmask pretence, to refuse the comfort of deceit about the very stuff of which human beings are made) and the claim of pity, mercy.

In the portrayal of the fourth gospel, Jesus knew what was in man. This is the judgement of this world – the light has come but men loved darkness. In the synoptic Gospels, when He beheld the city He wept.

For MacKinnon personally the conflict between claims of truth and justice (Butler) and those of mercy and pity, are the most fundamental and searching conflict. In Christian revelation, where moral evil is concerned there can be no greater burden laid upon any than the burden of this conflict in its extremity – this conflict which Jesus endured.

The portrayal of Jesus as *Christus Victor* fails to bring out that Jesus was actually defeated – what is significant is his endurance. The ultimate contradiction of the moral life is that evil is not resolved by achieving it.

There is that lacking in Jesus' experience of suffering which must be acknowledged – cf. Paul on making up what is lacking in the suffering of Christ. Also to admit that judgement is involved. 'Attend and consider whether there be any sorrow like unto his sorrow'.

Bibliography

Abbott-Smith, G. *A Manual Greek Lexicon of the New Testament* (Edinburgh: T.&T. Clark, 1986).

Abelard, Peter *Ethics* (or *Scito te ipsum* – 'Know thyself'), An edition with introduction, English translation and notes by D.E. Luscombe (Oxford: Clarendon Press, 1971).

Abraham a Santa Clara *Judas der Ertz-Schelm* herausgegeben von Felix Bobertag (Damstadt: Wissenschaftliche Buchgesellschaft, 1968).

Aland, Kurt (editor) *Synopsis of the Four Gospels – Greek-English Edition of the Synopsis Quattuor Evangeliorum.* On the basis of the Greek Text of Nestle Aland 26th Edition and Greek New Testament 3rd Edition (Stuttgart: German Bible Society, seventh edition,1984).

Albright, W.F. and Mann, C.S. *Matthew – Introduction, translation and notes* The Anchor Bible (New York: Doubleday, 1984).

Aldiss, Brian 'Judas Danced' in *The Canopy of Time* (London: Faber & Faber, 1961) pp63-80.

Al-Khoury, Touma *The Contemplations of Judas Iscariot* Edited by Archpriest Michel Najim (California: Oakwood Publications, 1995).

Alter, Robert and Kermode, Frank (editors) *The Literary Guide to the Bible* (London: Fontana, 1989).

Ambrose *Letters 1-91, Fathers of the Church*, Volume 26 (Washington: Catholic University of America, 1954).

Ambrose *Cain and Abel, Fathers of the Church*, Volume 42 (1961).

Anderson, David *The Gospel of Mark* The New Century Bible Commentary (Grand Rapids, Michigan: Eerdmans, 1976).

Anderson, Ray S. *The Gospel According to Judas – Is There a Limit to God's Forgiveness?* (Colorado Springs: NavPress, 1991).

Andrewes, Lancelot *The Liturgical Sermons of Lancelot Andrewes* Volume I Nativity, Lenten and Passion (Durham: Pentland Press, 1992).

Andreyev, Leonid *Judas Iscariot and other stories* translated by Walter Morison (London: John Westhouse, 1947).

Anonymous *Certain Sermons appointed by the Queen's Majesty to be declared and read by all parsons, vicars, and curates, every Sunday and holiday in their churches; and by her grace's advice perused and overseen for the better understanding of the simple people.* Published 1574, including the contents of a book of homilies from 1547 (Cambridge: Cambridge University Press, 1850).

Anonymous *The unhappy Birth, wicked life, and miserable Death of that vile Traytor and Apostle Judas Iscariot* (Durham: Printed and Sold by Isaac Lane, 1750). [Preceded by an address 'to the Reader', inverse, signed T.G.].

Anonymous *A Full and true Account of the Birth, Life and Death of Judas Iscariot* (Glasgow: J.&J. Robertson, 1776).

Anonymous *A Plain Commentary on the first Gospel by an Agnostic* (London: Williams and Norgate, 1891).

Arndt, William F. and Gingrich, R. Wilbur *A Greek-English Lexicon of the New Testament and other early Christian literature* (Chicago: University of Chicago Press, 1957/1979).

Asch, Sholem *The Nazarene* translated from the Yiddish by Maurice Samuel (London: George Routledge & Sons, 1939).

Auden, W.H. *The Dyer's Hand* (London: Faber and Faber, 1948).

Augustine of Hippo *Sermons on the Liturgical Seasons, Fathers of the Church*, Volume 38 (Washington: Catholic University of America, 1959).

Augustine of Hippo *The Free Choice of the Will, Fathers of the Church*, Volume 59 (1968).

Augustine of Hippo *Expositions on the Book of Psalms* (392-420) The Nicene and Post-Nicene Fathers Volume VIII (Edinburgh: T. &T. Clark/Grand Rapids, Michigan: Eerdmans, reprinted 1989).

Augustine of Hippo *The Trinity* introduction, translation and notes by Edmund Hill O.P. (New York: New City Press, 1991).

Augustine of Hippo *Tractates on the Gospel of John 55-111, Fathers of the Church*, Volume 90 (1994).

Augustine of Hippo *Tractates on the First Epistle of John, Fathers of the Church,* Volume 92 (1995).

Bacon, B.W. 'What did Judas betray?' *Hibbert Journal* (volume XIX for 1920-1) pp476-493.

Bacon, B.W. *The Gospel of the Hellenists* (New York: Henry Holt & Co, 1933).

Baldwin, Aaron Dwight *The Gospel of Judas Iscariot* (Chicago: Jamiesin-Higgins, 1902).

Balthasar, Hans Urs von *The von Balthasar Reader* Edited by Medard Kehl and Werner Löser, Translated by Robert J. Daly and Fred Lawrence (Edinburgh: T.&T. Clark, 1982).

Balthasar, Hans Urs von *Theo-drama – Theological Dramatic Theory* Translated by Graham Harrison.
Volume 1: *Prologomena* (San Francisco: Ignatius Press, 1988).
Volume II: *The Dramatis Personae: Man in God* (1990).
Volume III: *The Dramatis Personae: The Person in Christ* (1992).
Volume IV: *The Performance* (1994).

Balthasar, Hans Urs von *Mysterium Paschale* translated with an introduction by Aidan Nichols O.P. (Edinburgh: T&T Clark, 1990).

Balthasar, Hans Urs von *The Theology of Karl Barth* (San Francisco: Ignatius Press, 1992).

Barbour, R.S. 'Gethsemane in the Tradition of the Passion' *New Testament Studies* 16 (1969-70) pp231-251.

Barrett, C.K. *A Commentary on the First Epistle to the Corinthians* (London: A.& C. Black, 1971).

Barth, Karl *Church Dogmatics* II. The Doctrine of God Part 2 (Edinburgh: T.& T. Clark, 1942).

Barth, Karl *Dogmatics in Outline* (London: SCM Press, 1949).

Barton, John (editor) *The Cambridge Companion to Biblical Interpretation* (Cambridge: Cambridge University Press, 1998).

Bartnik, C. 'Judas l'Iscariote, histoire et théologie.' *Collectanea Theoligica* 58 (1988) pp57-69.

Bauckham, Richard and Hart, Trevor *At the Cross* (London: Darton, Longman & Todd, 1999).

Baum, P.F. 'The English Ballad of Judas Iscariot' *Publications of the Modern Language Association*, 31 (1916) pp181-189.

Baum, P.F. 'The Mediaeval Legend of Judas Iscariot' *Publications of the Modern Language Association*, 31 (1916) pp481-632.

Baum, P.F. 'Judas's Red Hair' *Journal of English and Germanic Philology* (1922) pp520-529.

Baum, P.F. 'Judas's Sunday Rest' *Modern Language Review* (1923) pp168-182.

Beadle, Richard (editor) *The York Plays* (London: Edward Arnold, 1982).

Belcher, F.W. 'A Comment on Mark xiv. 45' *The Expository Times* (May 1953) p240.

Bernard, J.H. 'The Death of Judas' *Expositor*, Sixth Series (Volume IX, 1904).

Bernard, J.H. *A critical and exegetical Commentary on the Gospel according to St John* (Edinburgh: T.& T. Clark, 1928).

Betz, O. 'The Dichotomized Servant and the End of Judas Iscariot (Light on the dark passages: Matthew 24.51 and parallels; Acts 1.18)' *Revue de Qmran* 5 (1964-66) pp 43-58.

Biblia Sacra Latina - Ex Biblia Sacra Vulgatæ Editiones (London: Samuel Bagster & Sons, 1977).

Biblia Sacra Polyglotta (Londini: Sumptibus Samuelis Bagster M.DCCC.XXXI).

Billings, J.S. 'Judas Iscariot in the Fourth Gospel' *The Expository Times* 51(1939-40) pp156-7.

Black, Matthew (general editor) *Peake's Commentary on the Bible* (Middlesex: Nelson, 1962).

Bloom, Harold *Shakespeare – The Invention of the Human* (London: Fourth Estate, 1999).

Bonar, J. *Observations on the Conduct and Character of Judas Iscariot* (Edinburgh: printed by W. Sands, A. Murray and J. Cochran; sold by W. Miller and other Booksellers,1750).

Borges, Jorge Luis *Collected Fictions* translated by Andrew Hurley (London: Allen Lane, 1998).

Bouchard, Larry *Tragic Method and Tragic Theology – Evil in Contemporary Drama and Religious Thought* (University Park and London: The Pennsylvania State University Press, 1989).

Bowden, John *Karl Barth – Theologian* (London: SCM Press, 1983).

Bowden, John *Who's Who in Theology* (London: SCM Press, 1990).

Brodie, Thomas L. *The Gospel According to John – A Literary and Theological Commentary* (New York: Oxford University Press, 1993).

Bromiley, Geoffrey W. *Introduction to the Theology of Karl Barth* (Edinburgh: T.& T. Clark, 1979).

Brown, Raymond E. *The Death of the Messiah – From Gethsemane to the Grave. A Commentary on the Passion Narratives in the Four Gospels.* Two volumes, part of the Anchor Bible Reference Library (London: Geoffrey Chapman, 1994).

Brownson, J. 'Neutralizing the Intimate Enemy: The Portrayal of Judas in the Fourth Gospel' *Society of Biblical Literature Seminar Papers* 1992, pp 49-60.

Bruce, F.F. *Commentary on The Book of the Acts – the English text with introduction, exposition and notes* New London commentary on the New Testament (London: Marshall, Morgan & Scott, 1954).

Buchanan, Robert *The Complete Poetical Works of Robert Buchanan* in two volumes (London: Chatto & Windus, 1901).

Bultmann, Rudolf *The Gospel of John – A Commentary* (Oxford: Basil Blackwell, 1971).

Busch, Eberhard *Karl Barth. His life from letters and autobiographical texts,* (London: SCM, 1976).

Cadman, W. *The Last Journey of Jesus to Jerusalem – its purpose in the light of the Synoptic Gospels* (London, Humphrey Milford: Oxford University Press, 1923).

Calvin, John *The Gospel according to St John 1-10* translated by T.H.L. Parker. One of a series of Calvin's Commentaries issued under the general editorship of David W. Torrance and Thomas F. Torrance (Edinburgh: Oliver & Boyd Ltd, 1959).

Calvin, John *The Gospel according to St John 11-21* (Edinburgh: Oliver & Boyd Ltd, 1961).

Cane, Anthony 'Ontology, Theodicy and Idiom: The Challenge of Nietzschean Tragedy to Christian Writing on Evil' *New Blackfriars* (Volume 77 No. 900, February 1996).

Cane, Anthony 'Judas Iscariot, Bishop Roderick Wright and the Testing of Eucharistic Boundaries' *Theology* (March/April 1998).

Cane, Anthony 'Contested Meanings of the Name "Judas Iscariot" ' *The Expository Times* (Volume 112 Number 2, November 2000).

Carey, S.P. *Jesus and Judas* (London: Hodder & Stoughton, 1931).

Cargas, H.J. (editor) *Holocaust Scholars Write to the Vatican* (Westport, Connecticut: Greenwood Press, 1998).

Carrington, Philip *According to Mark – A running commentary on the oldest gospel* (Cambridge: Cambridge University Press, 1960).

Carson, D.A. *Divine Sovereignty and Human Responsibility – Biblical perspectives in tension* (London: Marshall Pickering, 1994).

Cassidy, John A. *Robert W. Buchanan* (New York: Twayne Publishers, 1973).

Cervigni, Dino 'The Muted Self-Referentiality of Dante's Lucifer' *Dante Studies CVII* (New York, 1989).

CETEDOC CD Rom *Library of Christian Latin texts* (Brepols-Turnhout: Universitas Catholica Lovaniensis, 1994).

Chase, F.H. 'On ΠΡΗΝΗΣ ΓΕΝΟΜΕΝΟΣ in Acts 1.18' *Journal of Theological Studies* (January 1912) pp278-285.

Chase, F.H. 'Note on ΠΡΗΝΗΣ ΓΕΝΟΜΕΝΟΣ in Acts 1.18' *Journal of Theological Studies* (1912) p415.

Chrysostom, John *Commentary on Saint John the Apostle and Evangelist* Homilies 48-88 *Fathers of the Church*, Volume 41 (Washington: The Catholic University of America Press, 1960).

Claudel, Paul *Un poete regarde la croix* (Paris: Gallimard, 1935).

Claudel, Paul *Mort de Judas* (Paris: Gallimard, 1988).

Cogan, Mark 'Delight, Punishment and the Justice of God in the Divine Commedia' *Dante Studies CXI* (New York, 1993).

Coggins, R.J. & Houlden, J.L. (editors) *A Dictionary of Biblical Interpretation* (London/Philadelphia: SCM/Trinity Press International, 1990).

Cowper, B. Harris (translator) *The Arabic Gospel of the Infancy,* in *The Apocryphal Gospels* (London: Williams & Norgate, 1874).

Cranfield, C.E.B. *The Gospel according to St Mark – An introduction and commentary* (Cambridge: Cambridge University Press, 1966).

Creed, John Martin *The Gospel according to St Luke* (London: MacMillan, 1965).

Crouzel, Henri *Origen* translated from the 1985 French edition by A.S. Worrall (Edinburgh: T.& T. Clark, 1989).

Cyril of Jerusalem *The Works of St Cyril of Jerusalem, Volume 2*, Fathers of the Church, Volume 64 (Washington: The Catholic University of America Press, 1970).

Dalman, Gustaf *The Words of Jesus – considered in the light of post-biblical Jewish writings and the Aramaic language* (Edinburgh: T.& T. Clark, 1902).

Damian, Peter *Letters 31-60* translated by Owen J. Blum, *The Fathers of the Church – mediaeval continuation* (Washington: The Catholic University of America Press, 1990).

Daniell, David (editor) *Tyndale's New Testament* translated from the Greek by William Tyndale in 1534 (New Haven: Yale University Press, 1989).

Danker, F.W. *A Greek-English lexicon of the New Testament and other early Christian literature* [based on Arndt and Gingrich, revised and edited by Danker] (Chicago, London: University of Chicago Press, 2000).

Dante Alighieri *The Divine Comedy* Italian text with translation and comment by John D. Sinclair, in three volumes: I Inferno, II Purgatorio, III Paradiso (New York: Oxford University Press, 1939).

Darby, W.A. *Judas Iscariot – The Argument in His Case on Scripture Evidence* (Belfast: printed for the author and sold by William McComb, 1, High Street, 1846).

Deissmann, Adolf ' "Friend, wherefore art thou come?" ' *The Expository Times* 33 (1921-1922) pp491-3.

de Quincey, Thomas 'Judas Iscariot', from de Quincey's *Collected Writings* (edited by David Masson), Volume VIII *Speculative and Theological Essays* (Edinburgh: Adam and Charles Black, 1890) pp177-206.

Derrett, J. Duncan M. 'The Iscariot, M^{e}sira, and the Redemption' *Journal for the Study of the New Testament* 8 (1980) pp2-23.

D'Evelyn, Charlotte *Meditations on the Life and Passion of Christ (from British Museum Addit. Ms. 11307)* (London: published for the Early English Text Society by Humphrey Milford, Oxford University Press, 1921).

de Voragine, Jacobus *The Golden Legend – Readings on the Saints* translated by William Granger Ryan, in two volumes (Princeton, New Jersey: Princeton University Press,1993).

Dieckmann, B *Judas als Sündenbock: Eine Verhängnisvolle Geschichte von Angst und Vergeltung* (Munich: Kösel, 1991).

Donne, John *The Sermons of John Donne* Ten Volumes, edited, with introductions and critical apparatus by George R. Potter and Evelyn M. Simpson (Berkeley and Los Angeles: University of California Press, 1953-62).

Dostoyevsky, Fyodor *The Brothers Karamazov*, translated by David Magarshack (London: Penguin, 1958).

Dickinson, Michael *The Lost Testament of Judas Iscariot* (Dingle, Co. Kerry: Brandon, 1994)

Dronke, P. *The Medieval Lyric* (London: Hutchinson, 1968).

Drury, John *Luke* (London: Fontana, 1973).

Dunn Wilson, D. *The portrayal of Judas Iscariot in Christianity* (unpublished M.Phil thesis, University of Sussex, 1982).

Edersheim, Alfred *The Life and Times of Jesus the Messiah* in two volumes (London: Longmans, Green & Co, 1890).

Edwards, Jonathan *The Works of Jonathan Edwards*, Volume 12 (New Haven: Yale University Press, 1994) Harry S. Stout, General Editor. 'An Humble Inquiry into the rules of God concerning the qualifications requisite to compleat standing and full communion in the visible Christian Church' (pp165-348). 'Misrepresentations Corrected, and Truth Vindicated' (pp349-503).

Elliott, J.K. (editor) *The Apocryphal New Testament – A Collection of Apocryphal Christian literature in an English Translation* (Oxford: Clarendon Press, 1993).

Emmons, Nathanael *Sermon on the perdition of Judas,* with a review of the same by Rev David Pickering (Providence: Cranston and Marshall Printers, 1827).

Emmons, Nathanael *The Works of Nathanael Emmons, D.D. late Pastor of the Church in Franklin, Mass. with a memoir of his life.* Six volumes, edited by Jacob Ide, D.D. (Boston: Crocker & Brewster, 1842).

Emmons, Nathanael *A Discourse [on Matthew xxv.31-46] concerning the process of General Judgement in which the modern notions of Universal Salvation are particularly considered* (Philadelphia: MDCCXCI).

Endo, Shusako *Silence* (London: Penguin, 1980).

Enslin, M.S. 'How the story grew: Judas in Fact and Fiction' *Festschrift to honor F. Wilbur Gingrich* (Leiden: E.J. Brill, 1972) pp123-141.

Epiphanius, Bishop of Salamis – selected passages from the *Panarion* translated by Philip R. Amidon, S.J. (New York, Oxford: Oxford University Press, 1990).

Ephrem Syrus *Fragments of the Commentary of Ephrem Syrus upon the Diatessaron,* translated by J. Rendel Harris (London: C.J. Clay & Sons, 1895).

Erasmus, Desiderius *Paraphrase on John* translated and annotated by Jane E. Phillips (Toronto: University of Toronto Press, 1991).

Erasmus, Desiderius *The Correspondence of Erasmus - letters 1356 to 1534 (1523-4)* translated by R.A.B. Mynors and Alexander Dalzell, annotated by James M. Estes (Toronto: University of Toronto Press, 1992).

Evans, C.F. *Saint Luke* (London/Philadelphia: SCM/Trinity Press International, 1990).

Fairburn, A.M. 'Studies in the Life of Christ. XV – The Betrayer' *Expositor*, (Volume XII, 1880) pp47-70.

Filson, Floyd V. *A Commentary on the Gospel according to St Matthew* (London: Adam and Charles Black, 1960).

Ford, David *Barth and God's Story – Biblical Narrative and the Theological Method of Karl Barth in the Church Dogmatics* (Frankfurt am Main: Verlag Peter Lang, 1981).

Forshall, Josiah and Madden, Frederic (editors) *The New Testament in English* according to the version by John Wycliffe about A.D. 1380 and revised by John Purvey about A.D. 1388. (Oxford, Clarendon Press, 1879).

Frei, Hans *The Eclipse of Biblical Narrative – a study in eighteenth and nineteenth century hermeneutics* (New Haven and London: Yale University Press, 1974).

Furnivall, Frederick J. (editor) *Early English Poems and Lives of Saints (with those of the wicked birds Pilate and Judas)* (Berlin: Asher & Co, 1862; reprinted New York: Amy Press, 1974).

Gardner, Lucy; Moss, David; Quash, Ben; Ward, Graham *Balthasar at the End of Modernity* (Edinburgh: T&T Clark, 1999).

Gärtner, Bertil *Iscariot* (Philadelphia: Facet Books, Fortress Press, 1971) translated by Victor I. Gruhn from the German of Gärtner's 'Judas Iscariot', an essay which appeared in *Die rätselhaften Termini Nazoräer und Iskariot* (Horae Soederblomianae [Travauz publies par la Société Nathan Söderblom], 4; Uppsala, 1957) pp37-68.

Gent, Thomas *Divine Justice and Mercy Displayed – Set forth in the unhappy Birth, wicked life, and miserable End of that deceitful Apostle, JUDAS ISCARIOT* (York: Printed at the New Printing Office, in Fosgate, 1772).

Gingrich, F.W. 'Judas', entry in Volume 2, E-J, of *The Interpreter's Dictionary of the Bible* (New York: Abingdon Press, 1962) pp1006-8.

Glare, P.G.W. (editor) *Oxford Latin Dictionary* (Oxford: Clarendon Press, 1982).

Glasson, T.E. 'Davidic links with the betrayal of Jesus' *The Expository Times* 85 (1973-4) pp118-119.

Goethe, J.W. von *Poetry and Truth from my own life* A revised translation by Minna Steele Smith in two volumes (London: George Bell and Sons, 1908).

Goulburn, Edward Meyrick 'The Repentance of Judas', A Sermon preached in the Church of St Giles, Oxford, on Wednesday, Feb. 24, 1858, being the festival of St Matthias. *Lenten Sermons* No. 8 (Oxford and 377, Strand, London: John Henry and James Parker,1858).

Graves, Robert *King Jesus* (London: Cassell, 1946).

Green, F.W. *The Gospel according to St Matthew* (Oxford: Clarendon Press, 1936).

Green, H. Benedict *The Gospel according to Matthew*, New Clarendon Bible (London: Oxford University Press, 1975)

Halas, Roman *Judas Iscariot – a scriptural and theological study of his person, his deeds and his eternal lot* (Washington: Catholic University of America Press, 1946).

Hand, W.D. 'A Dictionary of Words and Idioms Associated with Judas Iscariot. A Compilation based mainly on material found in the Germanic languages' *Publications in Modern Philology* 24/3 (Berkeley and Los Angeles: University of California Press, 1942) pp 289-356.

Harris, J.R. 'Did Judas Really Commit Suicide?' *American Journal of Theology*, IV (July, 1900) pp490-513.

Haugg, Donatus *Judas Iskarioth in den neutestamentlichen Berichten* (Freiburg im Breisgau: Herder, 1930).

Hein, K. 'Judas Iscariot: Key to the Last-Supper Narratives?' *New Testament Studies* 17 (1970-1) pp227-232.

Heming, Joseph *Judas Excommunicated, or a Vindication of the Communion of Saints being A brief examination and clear Refutation of Mr Peter Lightfoots Arguments for proof of Judas his receiving the Sacrament of the Lords Supper (which, could he prove, makes nothing at all for a mixt Communion).* (London: Printed for Giles Calvert at the black Spread-Eagle near the West end of Pauls, 1649).

Heym, Stefan *The Wandering Jew* (London: Picador, 1985).

Hick, John *Evil and the God of Love* (London: MacMillan, 1985).

Hilary of Poitiers *The Trinity, Fathers of the Church*, Volume 25 (Washington: Catholic University of America, 1954).

Hill, David *The Gospel of Matthew* The New Century Bible Commentary (Grand Rapids, Michigan: Eerdmans, 1972).

Holleran, J. Warren *The Synoptic Gethsemane – A Critical Study* (Roma: Universita Gregoriana Editrice, 1973).

Hoskyns, Edwyn *The Fourth Gospel* edited by Francis Noel Davey (London: Faber & Faber, 1940/ second edition, revised, 1947).

Hueter, J.E. *Matthew, Mark, Luke, John... Now Judas and His Redemption (In Search of the Real Judas)* (Brookline Village, MA: Branden, 1983).

Hughes, Kirk T. 'Framing Judas' *Semeia* 54 (1991) pp223-238.

Ingholt, Harald 'The Surname of Judas Iscariot' in *Studia Orientalia Ioanni Pedersen... dicata*, (Copenhagen: Munksgaard, 1953) pp152-162.

Irenaeus of Lyons *Against the Heresies, Ancient Christian Writers – the works of the Fathers in translation* No.55 (New York: Paulist Press, 1992).

Jacoff, Rachel (editor) *The Cambridge Companion to Dante* (Cambridge: Cambridge University Press, 1993).

Jeffrey, David Lyle (general editor) *A Dictionary of Biblical Tradition in English Literature* (Grand Rapids, Michigan: Eerdmans, 1992).

Jerome *The Homilies of Saint Jerome*, volume 1, 1-59, *Fathers of the Church*, Volume 48 (Washington: Catholic University of America, 1964).

Jerome *The Homilies of Saint Jerome*, volume 2, 60-96, *Fathers of the Church*, Volume 57 (1966).

John Paul II *Crossing the Threshold of Hope* (London: Jonathan Cape, 1994).

Johnson, Sherman *The Gospel according to Mark* (London: A.& C. Black, 1960).

Kahn, J. 'Judas Iscariot: A Vehicle of Medieval Didacticism' *Dissertation Abstracts International* 37 (1976).

Kazantzakis, Nikos *Christ Recrucified* (London: Faber and Faber, 1962).

Keener, Craig S. *A Commentary on the Gospel of Matthew* (Grand Rapids, Michigan: Eerdmans, 1999).

Kermode, Frank *The Genesis of Secrecy - On the Interpretation of Narrative* The Charles Eliot Norton Lectures 1977-1978 (Cambridge, Massachusetts: Harvard University Press, 1979).

Kierkegaard, Søren. *Journals and Papers* Volume 2, F-K. Edited and translated by Howard V. Hong and Edna H. Hong (Bloomington: Indiana University Press, 1970).

Kipling, Rudyard 'On the Gate – A Tale of "16" ' from *Debits and Credits* (London: MacMillan, 1926) pp331-56.

Kittel, Gerhard (editor) *Theological Dictionary of the New Testament* (Grand Rapids, Michigan: Eerdmans, 1964).

Klassen, William 'Judas Iscariot' *Anchor Bible Dictionary* Volume 3 (1992) pp1091-6.

Klassen, William *Judas – Betrayer or Friend of Jesus?* (London: SCM, 1996).

Klopstock, Friedrich Gottlieb *The Messiah* From the German of Klopstock. The first sixteen books by Mrs Collyer, and the Three last by Mrs Meeke. Two volumes (London: J. Walker, 1811).

Knox, A.D. 'The Death of Judas' *Journal of Theological Studies* (Volume 25,1924) pp289-90.

Kuryluk, Ewa *Salome and Judas in the Cave of Sex – The Grotesque: Origins, Iconography, Techniques* (Evanston, Illinois: Northwestern University Press, 1987).

Lake, K. 'The Death of Judas' in *The Beginnings of Christianity* edited by F.J. Foakes-Jackson and K. Lake, Part I (London: MacMillan, 1933).

Laeuchli, Samuel 'Origen's Interpretation of Judas Iscariot' *Church History* Volume XXII, No. 4 (December 1953) pp253-268.

Langford, Michael J. *Providence* (London: SCM, 1981).

Lash, Nicholas *Believing Three Ways in One God* (London: SCM, 1992).

Lash, Nicholas 'The stuff of legend' (obituary of Donald MacKenzie MacKinnon) *The Guardian,* Saturday March 5 1994.

Layton, Bentley (editor) *The Gnostic Scriptures* (London: SCM, 1987).

Leaney, A.R.C. *A Commentary on the Gospel according to St Luke* (London: A.& C. Black, 1958).

Lenten Sermons preached in the evening of each Wednesday and Friday during the Season of Lent, 1858, in the Churches of St Mary the Virgin, St Giles, and St Ebbe, Oxford. (Oxford: John Henry and James Parker, 1858).

Liddell, Henry George and Scott, Robert *A Greek-English Lexicon* (Oxford: Clarendon Press ninth edition,1940, 1977). With a 1968 supplement.

Lightfoot, R.H. *St John's Gospel – A Commentary*, edited by C.F. Evans (Oxford: Clarendon Press, 1956).

Lindars, Barnabas *New Testament Apologetic* (London: SCM 1961).

Linklater, Eric *Judas – a novel* (London: Jonathan Cape, 1939).

Loades, Ann & McLain, Michael (editors) *Hermeneutics, the Bible and Literary Criticism* (London: MacMillan, 1992).

Lohse, Bernhard *Martin Luther – An Introduction to his life and work* (Edinburgh: T.& T. Clark, 1987).

Longenecker, Richard *Biblical Exegesis in the Apostolic Period* (Grand Rapids, Michigan: Eerdmans, 1975).

Lüdemann, Gerd *Early Christianity according to the Traditions in Acts – a commentary* (London: SCM, 1987).

Luther, Martin *Luther's Works* edited by Jaroslav Pelikan, (Saint Louis, Missouri: Concordia Publishing House).
Volume 6 'Lectures on Genesis' Chapters 31-37 (1970).

Volume 7 'Lectures on Genesis' Chapters 38-44 (1965).
Volume 8 'Lectures on Genesis' Chapters 45-50 (1966).
Volume 11 'First lectures on the Psalms' *Psalms 76-126* (1976).
Volume 14 'Selected Psalms III' (1958).
Volume 18 'Minor Prophets I' (1975).
Volume 22 'Sermons on the Gospel of John' Chapters 1-4 (1957).
Volume 24 'Sermons on the Gospel of John' Chapters 14-16 (1961).
Volume 25 'Lectures on Romans – Glosses and Scholia' (1972).
Volume 29 'Lectures on Titus, Philemon and Hebrews (1968).
Volume 30 'The Catholic Epistles' (1967).
Volume 32 'Career of the Reformer II' (1958).
Volume 38 'Word and Sacrament IV' (1971).
Volume 41 'Church and Ministry III' (1966).

Luthi, K. *Judas Iskarioth in der Geschichte der Auslegung von der Reformation bis zur Gegenwart* (Zurich: Zwingli Verlag, 1955).

Lutyens, D.B. *Judas Iscariot: a play* (London: Eyre & Spottiswoode, 1951).

MacKinnon, Donald *A Study in Ethical Theory* (London: Adam & Charles Black, 1957).

MacKinnon, Donald *Borderlands of Theology and other essays* Edited and introduced by George W. Roberts and Donovan E. Smucker (London: Lutterworth Press, 1968).

MacKinnon, Donald *The Stripping of the Altars* (London: Fontana, 1969).

MacKinnon, Donald *The Problem of Metaphysics* (London: Cambridge University Press,1974).

MacKinnon, Donald *Explorations in Theology 5* (London: SCM, 1979).

MacKinnon, Donald 'Some reflections on Hans Urs von Balthasar's Christology with special reference to Theodramatik II/2 and III' in *The Analogy of Beauty – The Theology of Hans Urs von Balthasar* Edited by John Riches (Edinburgh: T.& T.Clark, 1986) pp164-179.

MacKinnon, Donald *Themes in Theology – the threefold cord* (Edinburgh: T.& T. Clark, 1987).

Maccoby, Hyam *Judas Iscariot and the Myth of Jewish Evil* (New York: The Free Press, 1992).

Macquarrie, John *Jesus Christ in Modern Thought* (London: SCM, 1990).

Malina, B.J. and Rohrbaugh, R.L. *Social Scientific Commentary on the Synoptic Gospels* (Minneapolis: Fortress Press, 1992).

Marin, Louis *The Semiotics of the Passion Narrative – Topics and Figures* translated by Alfred M. Johnson (Pittsburgh, Pennsylvania: The Pickwick Press, 1980).

Marsh, John *The Gospel of Saint John* (Middlesex: Penguin, 1968).

Marshall, Howard *The Gospel of Luke – A commentary on the Greek text* (Exeter: The Paternoster Press, 1978).

Mascall, E.L. *Christ, the Christian and the Church – A Study of the Incarnation and its Consequences* (London: Longmans, Green and Co Ltd, 1946).

Maximus of Turin *The Sermons of St Maximus of Turin, Ancient Christian Writers series* (Westminster, Maryland: Newman Press, 1989).

May, Herbert G. and Metzger, Bruce M. (editors) *The New Oxford Annotated Bible with Apocrypha, Revised Standard Version, Containing the Second Edition of the New Testament And an Expanded Edition of the Apocrypha* (New York: Oxford University Press, 1977).

McAlpine, Campbell *Loyalty, Betrayal and Offence* (Tonbridge: Sovereign World, 1994).

McFadyen, Alastair *Bound to Sin – Abuse, Holocaust and the Christian Doctrine of Sin* (Cambridge: Cambridge University Press, 2000).

McGlasson, Paul *Jesus and Judas – Biblical Exegesis in Barth* American Academy of Religion Academy Series, Number 72 (Atlanta, Georgia: Scholars Press, 1991).
Meier, John P. *A Marginal Jew – Rethinking the Historical Jesus* Volume Three, 'Companions and Competitors' (New York: Doubleday, 2001).
Mellinkoff, R. 'Judas's Red Hair and the Jews' *Journal of Jewish Art* 9 (1982).
Micklem, Philip A. *St Matthew* Westminster Commentary (London: Methuen,1917).
Millor, W.J. and Brooke, C.N.L. (editors) *The Letters of John of Salisbury* Volume Two – The Later Letters (1163-1180) (Oxford: Clarendon Press, 1979).
Moloney, Raymond *The Knowledge of Christ,* (London and New York: Continuum, 1999).
Moltmann, Jurgen *The Crucified God* (London: SCM, 1974).
Moltmann, Jurgen 'Theodicy', entry in *A New Dictionary of Christian Theology* (London: SCM, 1983) pp564-6.
Moore, George *The Brook Kerith – a Syrian story* (London: Heinemann, 1927).
More, Thomas *A Treatise upon the Passion,* in *The Complete Works of St. Thomas More* (Volume 13) edited by Gary E. Haupt (London: Yale University Press, 1976).
Morin, J.A. 'Les deux derniers des Douze: Simon le Zelote et Judas Iskarioth', in *Revue Biblique* 80 (1973) pp332-358.
Morris, Leon *The Gospel according to John, revised edition* (Grand Rapids, Michigan: Eerdmans, 1995).
Moule, C.F.D. *The Gospel according to Mark* (Cambridge: Cambridge University Press, 1965).
Munck, Johannes *The Acts of the Apostles – introduction, translation and notes* The Anchor Bible (New York: Doubleday, 1967).
Munro, J.J. 'The Death of Judas (Matt. xxvii. 3-8; Actsi.18-19)' *Expository Times* (Volume 24, 1913) pp235-6.
Nestle, E. 'Another peculiarity of Codex Bezae' (p140) and 'The Name of Judas Iscariot in the Fourth Gospel' (p240) *The Expository Times* (volume 9, 1897-8).
Nestle, E. 'The Fate of the Traitor' *Expository Times* (volume 23,1912) pp331-2.
Nichols, Wallace *The Saga of Judas* (London: Newman Wolsey, 1949).
Nietzsche, Friedrich *The Birth of Tragedy* translated by Francis Golffing (New York: Doubleday, 1956).
Nineham, D.E. *The Gospel of St Mark* (London: Adam and Charles Black, 1968).
O'Donnell, John *Hans Urs von Balthasar* (London: Chapman, 1992).
Origen *Origen Contra Celsum* translated by Frederick Crombie Volume II of *The Writings of Origen,* Volume XXIII of the Ante-Nicene Christian Library (Edinburgh: T.&T. Clark, 1872).
Origen *Homilies on Genesis and Exodus, Fathers of the Church,* Volume 71 (Washington: Catholic University of America Press, 1982).
Origen *Commentary on the Gospel according to John,* Books 1-12. *Fathers of the Church,* Volume 80 (1989).
Origen *Commentary on the Gospel according to John,* Books 13-32. *Fathers of the Church,* Volume 89 (1993).
Origen *Homilies on Luke, Fragments on Luke; The Fathers of the Church,* Volume 94 (1996).
Origen *Commentary on the Epistle to the Romans,* Books 6-10, *Fathers of the Church,* Volume 104 (2002).
Paffenroth, Kim *Judas – Images of the Lost Disciple* (Louisville: Westminster John Knox Press, 2001).
Panas, Henryk *The Gospel according to Judas* (London: Hutchinson, 1977).
Pannenberg, Wolfhart *Jesus – God and Man* translated by Lewis L. Wilkins and Duane A. Priebe (London: SCM, 1968).

Papias 'Fragments of Papias' in *Fathers of the Church*, Volume 1, *The Apostolic Fathers* (Washington: Catholic University of America, 1947).

Paulinus of Nola *Letters of St Paulinus of Nola* (*Ancient Christian Writers*, Volume 1, letters 1-22 (Westminster, Maryland: Newman Press, 1967).

Pepler, H.D.C. *Judas, or The Betrayal – a play in one act with prologue and epilogue* (Ditchling: St Dominic's Press, 1926).

Pickering, David *A Calm Address to the Believers and Advocates of Endless Misery. Designed for the Benefit of the Youth* (Hudson: Ashbel Stoddard,1821)

Pickering, David *Sermon on the perdition of Judas*, by Nathaniel Emmons D.D. with a review of the same by Rev David Pickering (Providence: Cranston and Marshall Printers, 1827).

Plummer, Alfred *The Gospel According to S. Luke* (Edinburgh: T.& T. Clark, 1901).

Popkes, W. *Christus Traditus: Eine Untersuchung zum Begriff der Hingabe im NT*, Abhandlungen zur Theologie des Alten und Neuen Testaments no. 49 (Zurich: Zwingli Verlag 1967).

Prosser, Eleanor *Drama and Religion in the English Mystery Plays – a re-evaluation* (Stanford, California: Stanford University Press, 1961).

Purvis, J.S. *The York Cycle of Mystery Plays – A Complete Version* (London: SPCK, 1962).

Pyper, H.S. 'Judas', entry in *The Oxford Companion to Christian Thought* edited by Adrian Hastings (Oxford: Oxford University Press, 2000) pp355-6.

Pyper, H.S. *Modern gospels of Judas: canon and betrayal* Literature and Theology; 15 (2) June 2001, p111-22.

Rand, E.K. 'Mediaeval lives of Judas Iscariot' in *Anniversary Papers by Colleagues and Pupils of George Lyman Kittredge* (Boston: Ginn & Co: 1913) pp305-316.

Raphael, D.D. *The Paradox of Tragedy* The 1959 Mahlon Powell lectures (London: George Allen & Unwin Ltd, 1960).

Rawlinson, A.E.J. *St Mark* Westminster Commentary (London: Methuen, fourth edition, 1936).

Redlich, E. Basil *St Mark's Gospel – A Modern Commentary* (London: Duckworth, 1948).

Reeves, Troy D. *Index to the Sermons of John Donne* Volume 2, Index to Proper Names (Salzburg, Austria: Institut für Anglistik und Amerikanistik, Universität Salzburg, 1980).

Reider, N 'Mediaeval Oedipal legends about Judas' *Psychoanalytic Quarterly* 29 (1960) pp515-527.

Richards, R. *The Character and End of Judas* A Sermon Preached August the 20th, 1823 in Queen-Street Chapel, Sheffield, before the Associate Independent Congregations of Sheffield, and Attercliffe (Sheffield: J. Blackwell, 1823).

Richardson, Alan and Bowden, John (editors) *A New Dictionary of Christian Theology* (London: SCM, 1983).

Riches, John (editor) *The Analogy of Beauty – The Theology of Hans Urs von Balthasar* (Edinburgh: T.& T. Clark, 1986).

Rowlands, Samuel 'The betraying of Christ. Iudas in despaire.' (London: Printed by Adam Islip, 1598) in *The Complete Works of Samuel Rowlands 1598-1628* Now First Collected. Volume First, Printed for the Hunterian Club, MDCCCLXXX.

Rubinstein, Richard L. & Roth, John K. (editors) *Approaches to Auschwitz – The Legacy of the Holocaust* (London: SCM, 1987).

Russell, Jeffrey Burton *Lucifer – The Devil in the Middle Ages* (London: Cornell University Press, 1984).

Ryle, John Charles *Expository Thoughts on the Gospels* volumes 1 and 2 (Cambridge: James Clarke, 1969).

Salmond, S.D.F. *The Gospel of St Mark* (Edinburgh: T.C. & E.C. Jack, date unknown).

Sanders, J.N *A Commentary on the Gospel according to St John*, edited and completed by B.A. Mastin (London: A.& C. Black, 1968).

Saperstein, Marc *Moments of Crisis in Jewish-Christian Relations* (London/Philadelphia: SCM/Trinity Press International, 1989).

Saramago, Jose *The Gospel According to Jesus Christ* (London: Harvill, 1993).

Saward, John *The Mysteries of March – Hans Urs von Balthasar on the Incarnation and Easter* (London: Collins, 1990).

Sayers, Dorothy L. *The Man Born to be King – A Play-Cycle on the Life of our Lord and Saviour Jesus Christ* (London: Gollancz, 1947).

Schnackenburg, Rudolf *The Gospel According to St John* Volume Two, on chapters 5-12 (London: Burns & Oates, 1980).

Schneemelcher, W. (editor) *The New Testament Apocrypha* Volume Two – 'Writings relating to the Apostles and Apocalypses and Related Subjects' (London: Lutterworth Press, 1965).

Schueler, D.G. 'The Middle English Judas: An Interpretation' *Publications of the Modern Language Association,* 91 (1976) pp840-857.

Schweitzer, Albert *The Quest of the Historical Jesus – a critical study of its progress from Reimarus to Wrede* translated by W. Montgomery (London: A.& C. Black, 1910/1926).

Schwenchfeld, Caspar 'An Answer to Luther's Malediction' (1544), in *Spiritual and Anabaptist Writers, The Library of Christian Classics*, Volume XXV, edited by George Williams and Angel Mergal (London: SCM, 1957).

Sherlock, W. 'The Potter's Field' *Expositor*, Seventh Series,Volume VI (1908).

Singleton, Charles S. *The Divine Comedy* translated, with a commentary. *Inferno* Volume 2. Commentary, Bollingen Series LXXX (Princeton, New Jersey: Princeton University Press, 1970).

Sisam, Kenneth (editor) *Fourteenth Century Verse and Prose* (London: Clarendon Press, 1921).

Springer, Carl P.E. *The Gospel as Epic in Late Antiquity – the* Paschale carmen *of Sedulius* (Leiden: E.J. Brill, 1988).

Starkey, Digby P. *Judas, A Tragic Mystery* (Dublin: William Curry, 1843).

Steiner, George *The Death of Tragedy* (London: Faber, 1961).

Steiner, George 'A Note on Absolute Tragedy' in *Literature and Theology* (Volume 4.2, July 1990) pp147-156.

Steiner, George 'Tribute to Donald MacKinnon', *Theology* (January/February 1995) pp2-9.

Steiner, George *No Passion Spent – Essays 1978-1996* (London: Faber, 1996).

Stevens, Martin and Cawley, A.C. (editors) *The Towneley Plays* Volume One – Introduction and Text (Oxford: Oxford University Press, 1994) p432.

Stevens, Martin and Cawley, A.C. (editors) *The Towneley Plays* Volume Two – Notes and Glossary (Oxford: Oxford University Press, 1994).

Sticca, Sandro *The Latin Passion Play: Its Origins and Development* (Albany: State University of New York Press, 1970).

Stodard-Walker, Archibald *Robert Buchanan: The Poet of Modern Revolt* (London: Grant Richards, 1901).

Strauss, D.F. *The Life of Jesus Critically Examined* translated by George Eliot, 1840 (Philadelphia: Fortress Press, 1972).

Sturrock, John *Paper Tigers – The Ideal Fictions of Jorge Luis Borges* (Oxford: Clarendon Press, 1977).

Surin, Kenneth *Theology and the Problem of Evil* (Oxford: Blackwell, 1986).

Surin, Kenneth (editor) *Christ, Ethics and Tragedy – essays in honour of Donald MacKinnon* (Cambridge: Cambridge University Press, 1989).

Sykes, S.W. (editor) *Karl Barth: Studies of His Theological Method* (Oxford: Clarendon Press, 1979).

Tarachow, Sidney 'Judas, the Beloved Executioner' *Psychoanalytic Quarterly* 29 (1960) pp528-554.

Tasker, J.G. 'Judas Iscariot', entry in *A Dictionary of Christ and the Gospels* edited by James Hastings, Volume 1 (Edinburgh: T.& T. Clark, 1906) pp907-913.

Taylor, Archer 'O du armer Judas' *The Journal of English and Germanic Philology* Volume XIX (1920) pp318-339.

Taylor, Vincent *The Life and Ministry of Jesus* (London: MacMillan, 1954).

Taylor, Vincent *The Gospel according to St Mark* (New York: St Martin's Press, 1966).

Thomas Aquinas *Summa Theologiae* (Blackfriars: Eyre & Spottiswoode, 1965).
Volume 54 *The Passion of Christ* 3a.46-52.
Volume 59 *Holy Communion* 3a.79-83.

Thomas Aquinas *Commentary on the Gospel of St John* Part I translated by James A. Weisheipl (New York: Magi Books, 1980).

Thomas, R.S. *Selected Poems 1946-1968* (Newcastle: Bloodaxe Books, 1986).

Thompson, John *The Lost and Undone Son of Perdition: or the birth, life and character of Judas Iscariot. Faithfully translated, from several ancient authors, of undoubted credit* (Catskill: Printed for Samuel Peck, 1808).

Tödt, H.E. *The Son of Man in the Synoptic Tradition* (London: SCM, 1965).

Torrey, C.C. 'The Name "Iscariot" ' in *Harvard Theological Review* 36, (1943).

Upton, J.A. 'The Potter's Field and the Death of Judas (Matt 27.3-10; Acts 1:15-20).' *Concordia Journal* 8 (1982) pp. 213-219.

Van Engen, John H. *Rupert of Deutz* (Berkeley: University of California Press, 1983).

Vanstone, W.H. *The Stature of Waiting* (London: Darton, Longman and Todd, 1982).

Weatherhead, Leslie *Personalities of the Passion* (London: Hodder and Stoughton, 1942).

Weitz, Morris 'Tragedy' in *The Encyclopaedia of Philosophy* Volume 8 (New York: MacMillan, 1967).

Westcott, B.F. *The Gospel According to St John – The authorized version, with introduction and notes* (London: John Murray, 1903).

Wiersbe, Warren W. (compiler) *Classic Sermons on Judas Iscariot* (Grand Rapids, Michigan: Kregel Publications, 1995).

Wilcox, Max 'The Judas Tradition in Acts 1.15-26' *New Testament Studies* 19 (1972/3), pp438-452.

Williams, Charles 'Terror of Light' in *Collected Plays* (London: Oxford University Press, 1963) pp325-374.

Whittaker, F.H. 'The Fate of the Traitor' *Expository Times* (Volume 23, 1912) p478.

Williams, Bernard *Shame and Necessity* (Berkeley: University of California Press, 1993).

Williams, H.A. *Tensions – Necessary Conflicts in Life and Love* (Glasgow: Collins, 1976).

Williams, Raymond *Modern Tragedy* (London: Verso, 1966/1979).

Williams, Rowan *The Wound of Knowledge – Christian Spirituality from the New Testament to St John of the Cross* (London: Darton, Longman and Todd; second, revised edition, 1990).

Williams, Rowan *Arius – Heresy and Tradition* (London: SCM, second edition, 2001).

Wollaston, Isabel *A War Against Memory? – the future of Holocaust Remembrance* (London: SPCK, 1996).

Wright, Arthur *A Synopsis of the Gospels in Greek – after the Westcott and Hort text* (MacMillan, 1903).

Wright, Arthur 'Was Judas Iscariot "The First of the Twelve"?' *The Interpreter* 13 (April 1917) pp18-25.

Wycliffe, John *The New Testament in English* according to the version by John Wycliffe about A.D. 1380 and revised by John Purvey about A.D. 1388. Edited by Josiah Forshall and Frederic Madden (Oxford: Clarendon Press, 1879).

Yerby, Frank *Judas, My Brother – The Story of the Thirteenth Disciple. An Historical Novel* (London: Heinemann, 1969).

Young, Frances, 'Origen', *A Dictionary of Biblical Interpretation* edited by R.J. Coggins & J.L. Houlden (London/Philadelphia: SCM/Trinity Press International, 1990) p501.

Young, Robert *Analytical Concordance to the Holy Bible* (Guildford and London: Lutterworth Press, eighth edition, 1939).

Index

Abbott-Smith, G. 48
Abelard, Peter 90, 102, 103, 110, 123, 167
Acts of Andrew and Paul (Coptic text) 145-6, 147, 151, 154
Albright, W. F. 51
Alger of Liège 90, 101-104
Ambrose, St 106, 132
anointing of Jesus 27-8, 29, 30, 39, 63
anti-Semitism 4, 59, 78, 80, 81, 82, 85
apostles, the twelve 15-16, 24, 26, 29, 32, 37, 106, 184; *see also* Judas Iscariot: one of the twelve
Aquinas, Thomas 90, 105, 106, 114, 122-4, 126, 163, 166, 176, 178
Arndt, William F. 48
Augustine, St, of Hippo 89-90, 102, 104, 105, 114, 121, 124, 125, 126, 177
  Judas as 'not chosen' 99-101, 103, 106, 110, 120; *see also* Judas Iscariot: one of the twelve
  Judas, repentance, death, eschatological salvation/damnation 129-131, 137
  linguistic parallelism of 'handing over' 117-120, 123

Ballad of Judas Iscariot, The (Robert Buchanan) 148-150
Ballad of the Judas Tree (Ruth Etchells) 151-3, 154
Balthasar, Hans Urs von 57, 65, 159, 169-179, 181, 183, 185
Barrett, C. K. 26, 28, 36, 37, 38
Barth, Karl 59, 86-8, 89, 127-8, 130, 131, 133, 145, 155, 158, 159, 170
  Judas, eschatological salvation/damnation 64, 67, 88, 127-8, 131, 152, 153
  Judas, excursus on 5, 60-70, 76, 113
Bartholomew the Apostle 146
Baum, P. F. 147
Belcher, F. W. 44
blood money 50, 146; *see also* silver, thirty pieces; Field of Blood
Book of the resurrection of Jesus Christ, The (Bartholomew the Apostle) 146-7
Borges, Jorge Luis 155, 159-163, 182, 186
Brendan, St 147
Brodie, Thomas L. 37
Brothers Karamazov, The (Fyodor Dostoyevsky) 156, 158, 182
Brown, Raymond 13, 18, 41, 49
  on linguistic issues 19-21, 40, 44, 45-6, 48
Buchanan, Robert 129, 148-151, 152, 153, 178
Büchsel, Friedrich 21, 116

Caiaphas 26, 35, 156
Cainites 68, 120-121, 125, 162
Calvin, John 135, 140
Carson, D. A. 31
chief priests 28, 29, 30, 42, 48, 49, 50, 62, 116, 124, 140; *see also* Caiaphas
Chrysostom, St, John 105, 106, 110
  on Judas' participation in footwashing 89, 96-8
Church Dogmatics (Karl Barth) 60
Commentary on John (Rupert of Deutz) 101
Commentary on Matthew (Hilary of Poitiers) 104
Commentary on St John (John Chrysostom) 96
Commentary on the Gospel according to John (Origen) 91, 92-3, 96, 116
Commentary on the Gospel of St John (Thomas Aquinas) 105
Contra Celsum (Origen) 91
Cuno, Abbot 104
Cyril of Alexandria 178

Dalman, Gustaf 18
Damian, Peter 102, 103, 167
Danker, Frederick William 48

Dante Alighieri 159, 163-9, 176, 177, 178, 185
Darby, W. A. 144-5, 151, 153, 154
Daub, Carl 68
Daube, David 22, 23
De servo arbitrio (Martin Luther) 133, 138
De Trinitate (Augustine) 177
Decretum (Ivo) 103
Deissmann, Adolf 45, 46
Derrett, J. Duncan 21, 22, 23, 33
Divina Commedia, La (Dante Alighieri) 149, 163-9, 177
Divine Justice and Mercy displayed and Set forth in the unhappy Birth, wicked life, and miserable End of that deceitful Apostle, Judas Iscariot (Thomas Gent) 147-8
Donne, John 124-6
Dostoyevsky, Fyodor 182; *see also Brothers Karamazov, The*
Drury, John 33

economy of salvation 33, 47, 48, 76, 82, 88, 93, 95, 114, 116, 117, 121, 125, 126, 142, 145, 155-169, 181, 185-6, 170
Edwards, Jonathan 90, 107-110
Ehrman, Albert 17
Emmons, Nathaneal 156-8, 159, 162, 181-2
Epiphanius, St, Bishop of Salamis 121
Etchells, Ruth 129, 151-3, 178; *see also Ballad of the Judas Tree*
Ethics (Peter Abelard) 103, 123

Field of Blood 50, 51, 52
Foerster, Werner 25
footwashing, participation of Judas 36-7, 56, 87, 88, 89, 91, 93, 96-9
Ford, David 60, 69, 70, 174
fulfilment of scripture 30, 31, 34-5, 36, 37, 40, 47, 50, 51, 54, 55, 56-7, 119

Gent, Thomas 129, 147-8
Germinal (George Moore) 73
Gethsemane 39, 43, 48, 67, 78, 172, 184
Gingrich, R. Wilbur 48
Goethe, Johann von 143
Golgotha 67
Gospel of Judas (Cainite text) 120-121
Goulburn, Edward 142-4, 145
Greek, translation issues; *see also* παραδίδωμι
  'change of mind/repentance' 48
  'friend' 75-6
  'it is enough' 40
  'kiss' 44
Green, H. Benedict 35
Gregory the Great 176, 178

handing over *see* παραδίδωμι
Haugg, Donatus 12
Hebblethwaite, Brian 85-6
Hell, descent into 67, 131, 159, 185
  Balthasar, Hans Urs von 175-9
  Dante Alighieri 163-9
Herod 21
Heurtley, Charles 141, 145
high priests, *see* chief priests
Hilary, St, of Poitiers 104, 105, 121-2
Holleran, J. Walter 40
Holocaust 4, 7, 59-60, 75, 77, 78, 80, 81, 170, 174, 176, 186
Holy Spirit and repentance of Judas 142, 177
Hoskyns, Edwyn 39
Humble Inquiry into the rules of God concerning the qualifications requisite to compleat standing and full communion in the visible Christian Church, An (Jonathan Edwards) 108

Incarnation 182-7
Ingholt, Harald 18
Irenaeus, St, of Lyons 121
Ivo, St 103

James, brother of John 52
Jerome 114, 130-131, 137
Jesus
  anointing 27-8, 29, 30, 39, 63
  betrayal 24-6, 29, 31, 32, 33, 35, 36, 38-47, 55, 116
  'bread of life'/ 'living bread' 24, 35
  death and descent into Hell 29, 67, 131, 159, 175-9, 185-6
  foreknowledge and fulfilment 25, 29, 30, 33-9, 89, 91-2, 184
  Passion 22, 50, 101, 102, 107, 102-3, 170
Judaites *see* Cainites

Judas – Betrayer or Friend of Jesus? (William Klassen) 186
Judas Iscariot
  betrayal / delivering up 27, 28, 29, 30, 32, 36, 37-8, 39, 41, 42-7, 52, 54, 74, 116, 122
  'better unborn' 31, 32, 33, 34, 35, 57, 73, 74, 78, 156, 158, 184
  calls Jesus 'Rabbi' 35, 42-4, 55
  death 30, 47-54, 55, 63, 74, 95, 127-132, 138, 174, 186
  as defeat for Jesus 37, 73-4, 76, 88, 90, 97, 113, 185
  despair 48, 133-140
  eschatological salvation/damnation 34, 36, 37, 55, 85-6, 127-154, 179-80
    Augustine, St, of Hippo 99-100, 129-131, 133, 137
    Balthasar, Hans Urs von 169-179
    Barth, Karl 64, 67, 88, 127-8, 131, 152, 153
    Jerome 130-131
    Leo the Great 128, 131-3
    Luther, Martin 133-140
    MacKinnon, Donald M. 74-7, 85-6, 127-8, 133
    Origen 131, 134, 145
  'Iscariot' name 16-18, 27, 54, 80-81
  'Judas' name 18, 63
  kiss 39, 42-5, 47, 63, 130
  money box, keeper of 28, 29, 39, 55, 81
  one of the twelve 15-16, 25, 26, 27, 28, 32, 34, 37, 48, 52, 54, 61, 89, 90, 94, 98, 99-101, 102, 103, 106, 110, 120, 169, 184
  participation at footwashing 36-7, 56, 87, 88, 89, 91, 93, 95, 96-8, 99, 110
  participation in Last Supper 36, 41, 56, 87, 88, 89, 101-110
  salvific status 63, 145, 155-6, 159, 175, 178-9
  satanic influence 25-6, 28, 30 36, 38, 39, 41, 46, 55, 64, 80, 92-5, 98, 99, 100, 105, 108, 119, 124, 132
  'son of destruction' 34-5, 46, 55, 64

Keener, Craig S. 49-50
Kerr, Walter 142, 145
Kidron Valley 39, 42
Klassen, William 18, 19, 20, 23, 62, 186
Klopstock, Friedrich Gottlieb 143
Knowledge of Christ, The (Raymond Moloney) 12

Lash, Nicholas 77, 78
Last Supper 31, 32, 35, 36, 50, 72, 89, 109, 122, 184
  participation of Judas 41, 56, 87, 88, 89, 101-110
Laeuchli, Samuel 90, 95, 96, 116, 145
Lectures on Genesis (Martin Luther) 133, 134
Leo the Great 128, 131-3, 153, 173
limit(ation), in relation to Christ 25, 93-5, 98, 100, 101, 106, 110, 183-7
Lindars, Barnabas 34, 50, 52, 53-4
Lombard, Peter 101
Luther, Martin 104, 115, 128, 133-140, 145
Luthi, K. 28, 170

Maccoby, Hyam 18
McGlasson, Paul 60, 61, 66
MacKinnon, Donald M. 59, 70, 86, 90, 98, 113, 126, 127-8, 133, 152, 155, 158, 159, 170, 183
  Atonement and Tragedy (essay, 1967) 79
  lectures on 'Evil' 71-7, 189-192
  Order and Evil in the Gospels (broadcast talk, 1963) 6, 78
  Study in Ethical Theory, A (1957) 77-8
  'tragic' reading of Gospels 6-7, 77-86
Malina, B.J. 49
Mann, C. S. 51
Mary, sister of Martha 27, 28, 39, 63
Mascall, E. L. 182
Mastin, B. A. 27
Matthias 51, 52, 64, 106, 138
Meier, John P. 116
Misrepresentations Corrected and Truth Vindicated (Jonathan Edwards) 109
Moloney, Raymond 12
Moore, George 73
Morin, J. 19
morsel of bread 38, 39, 80, 92-5, 98, 100, 102, 105

Mount of Olives 39, 50
Mysterium Paschale (Hans Urs von Balthasar) 9, 169, 173

Navigatio Sancti Brendani 147

Oedipus Rex 72
Origen 48, 89-90, 103, 110, 114, 121, 123, 129, 131, 153
  on Judas 91-2, 94-6, 99, 134, 145
    participation in footwashing 93, 95, 97, 98, 110
  on linguistic implications of παραδίδωμι 116-117, 118, 120
Otbert, bishop of Alger of Liège 101

παραδίδωμι 100, 113, 115, 116, 117, 184-5
  Hebrew equivalents compared, 'natan'/'masar' 21, 22, 49
  Latin equivalents compared, 'trado'/'prodo' 114-115, 118, 169
  linguistic parallelism/translation (handing over) 14, 19-24, 41, 43, 55, 66, 115-116, 122, 126
    Abelard, Peter 123
    Aquinas, Thomas 122-4
    Augustine, St, of Hippo 120-121, 123
    Balthasar, Hans Urs von 169-74
    Barth, Karl 61-2, 65, 66, 68, 69, 87, 113
    Brown, Raymond 19-21
    Büchsel, Friedrich 21
    Cainites' text 120-121
    Chrysostom, St, John 97
    Donne, John 125
    Klassen, William 19, 20, 23-4
    Origen 116-117, 118, 120, 123
    Westcott, B. F. 21
  passive, significance of use 40, 42, 56, 116
  providence, used to express workings of 113, 116-119, 125
Passion of Jesus 22, 50, 101, 102, 107, 122-3, 170
Passover 27, 31, 36, 38, 107
Paul 64, 65, 66-7, 69-70, 100, 116, 123
Paulinus, St, of Nola 93-4
Peter 15, 21, 24, 34, 47, 51, 62, 64, 93, 105, 140, 141
Pickering, David 156, 157-8, 159, 162, 181-2
Pilate 21, 26, 35, 62, 123, 136
Plato 78, 79
Pneuma und Institution (Hans Urs von Balthasar) 179
Popkes, Wiard 20- 21, 116, 169, 172, 173
potter's field 48, 50, 51
privatio boni 75, 77, 86
Problem of Metaphysics, The (Donald M. MacKinnon) 82
providence of God 30, 31, 33, 50-51, 52, 54, 61, 67, 69, 73-4, 88, 98, 99, 106, 110, 117, 181-2, 185-7

Quash, Ben 177

Rabbi (addressed to Jesus) 35, 42-4, 55
Raphael, D.D. 71
Rawlinson, A.E.J. 32
Rettig, John 118-119
Rohrbaugh, R. L. 49
Rupert of Deutz 90, 99, 101-104, 110, 167
Ryan, Christopher 166, 167

Sancta Clara, Abraham 68
Sanders, J. N. 27
Satan and Judas 25-6, 27, 28, 36, 38, 39, 41, 46, 55, 64, 80, 92-5, 98, 100, 105, 108, 116, 119, 124
Schnackenburg, Rudolf 25
Schweizer, Eduard 31
Schwenckfeld, Caspar 104-105
Sect of the Thirty, The (Jorge Luis Borges) 162-3
self-limitation (God) 56, 57, 88, 90, 183; *see also* limit(ation), in relation to Christ
Sententiae (Peter Lombard) 101
Septuagint 25, 38, 52
Sermon on the perdition of Judas (Nathanael Emmons) 156-8
Sermons on the Gospel of St John (Martin Luther) 134
Shape of the Sword, The (Jorge Luis Borges) 161

silver, thirty pieces 30, 41, 47-8, 50, 81
Simeon, brother of Joseph 136
Singleton, Charles S. 166
Steiner, George 80-81, 185
Stoddard, Solomon 107
Study in Ethical Theory, A (Donald M. MacKinnon) 77-8
Summa Theologiae (Thomas Aquinas) 104, 105, 106, 122, 163
Surin, Kenneth 84

Taylor, Vincent 15, 72-3
Theme of the Traitor and the Hero (Jorge Luis Borges) 161-2
Theodramatik (Hans Urs von Balthasar) 7-8, 170-173, 174
Thomas, one of the twelve 24
Three Versions of Judas (Jorge Luis Borges) 159-161, 162
Tödt, H. E. 40
Torrey, William 17-18
Tractates on the Gospel of John (Augustine) 99, 101
Trinity, The (Hilary of Poitiers) 122
Tyndale, William 115

Van Engen, John H. 101
Vulgate New Testament 114, 126

Wandering Jew, The (Robert Buchanan) 150-151
Westcott, B. F. 22, 26, 27, 55-6
Wilcox, Max 52
Williams, Rowan 3-4, 14
Williams, Solomon 109
Wycliffe, John 115, 116